D0918539

Fallen freedom

Fallen freedom

Kant on radical evil and moral regeneration

GORDON E. MICHALSON, Jr.

Oberlin College, Ohio

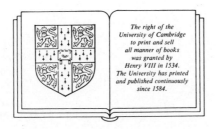

The right of the
University of Cambridge
to print and sell
all manner of books
was granted by
Henry VIII in 1534.
The University has printed
and published continuously
since 1584.

Cambridge University Press

Cambridge

New York   Port Chester   Melbourne   Sydney

Published by the Press Syndicate of the University of Cambridge
The Pitt Building, Trumpington Street, Cambridge CB2 1RP
40 West 20th Street, New York, NY 10011, USA
10 Stamford Road, Oakleigh, Melbourne 3166, Australia

© Cambridge University Press 1990

First published 1990

Printed in Great Britain at the University Press, Cambridge

British Library cataloguing in publication data

Michalson, Gordon E. (Gordon Elliott)
Fallen freedom: Kant on radical evil and moral
regeneration.
1. Christian doctrine. Freedom. Theories of Kant,
Immanuel, 1724–1804
I. Title
233'.7'0924

Library of Congress cataloguing in publication data

Michalson, Gordon E., 1948–
Fallen freedom: Kant on radical evil and moral regeneration /
Gordon E. Michalson
p. cm.
ISBN 0–521–38397–8
1. Kant, Immanuel, 1724–1804. Religion innerhalb der Grenzen der
blossen Vernunft. 2. Ethics. 3. Religion. 4. Kant, Immanuel,
1724–1804 – Views on good and evil. 5. Good and evil. 6. Kant,
Immanuel, 1724–1804 – Views on free will and determinism. 7. Free
will and determinism. 8. Regeneration (Theology) I. Title.
B2792.R453   1990
210–dc20 89–48586
CIP

ISBN 0 521 38397 8 hardback

GG

To the memory of Hans W. Frei
1922–1988

Contents

Contents

Preface

This book has its origins in embarrassment. The embarrassment was my own and would occur every year with uncanny regularity, as I taught the first semester of a year-long survey course in modern religious thought in the West. Invariably, as we worked through Kant's *Religion within the Limits of Reason Alone*, astute class members would ask questions such as the following: "What exactly is the difference between an 'original predisposition' to good and a 'natural propensity' to evil?" "If moral evil is produced by human freedom, why does Kant say it is 'innate'?" "If moral evil is 'radical' in the way Kant says it is, how can human freedom get rid of it?" "If Kant is a Newtonian, why does he talk about 'supernatural cooperation' when he discusses moral regeneration?" "What exactly is the relationship between human freedom and divine grace in Kant's view of salvation?"

In response to such questions, I became very adept over the years at mumbling vague replies that skillfully alluded to the "profundity" of the Kantian teaching while also having the effect of redirecting my students' attention toward other parts of Kant's book, with which I was more comfortable and about which I had already written. As much at home as I was with certain of Kant's views, I frankly had no idea how to answer many of the questions that arose in connection with his theories of radical evil and moral regeneration. As I reflected on these matters, I developed a more complex attitude toward Kant and toward the eighteenth century in general, and I began to regard in a new light Richard Rorty's comment that the "Enlightenment has been a favorite target ever since Adorno blamed it for Los Angeles."

Moreover, as I surveyed the secondary literature for help, I gradually realized that discussions of these matters – when they occurred at all – were either subsidiary to larger-scale accounts of Kant's moral and religious views (and thus given very short shrift) or else the sorts of summaries that have the effect of laying out one's puzzlements in neat narrative order, rather than solving them. Furthermore, it seemed very peculiar to me that, though there is one book-length study of Kant's view of moral evil in French, there are no others. Although I am keenly aware of the implications of what, in a different

context, Jonathan Bennett once referred to as a "welcome gap in the literature," I eventually decided to try to produce a book-length study of the issues
that had so puzzled my students, and me as well.

The result is what I would characterize as a piece of textual analysis set in
an interpretive framework that indicates why we should be interested in
Kant's views on radical evil and moral regeneration, even if he turns out to
be wrong on every point he takes up. We should be interested, not because
of anything Kant finally claims about evil or salvation, but because the sheer
instability of his position is a telling indicator of difficulties facing religious
thought in our own day as well as his. This wider interpretive aspect came
to me only slowly, as I worked on the text of the *Religion* and struggled with
Kant's shifting of idioms as he developed what frankly seemed like a thinly
disguised recasting of the Christian doctrine of original sin, framed for the
most part in the language of his ethical rationalism. To a great extent, the
most severe challenge in dealing with Kant's account of radical evil and moral
regeneration is figuring out how to integrate, or otherwise reconcile, his
Christian language and his rationalist-Enlightenment language. The
approach that other theories in the book invite (such as his view of the
institutional church) – an approach that understands his rationalist idiom as
exercising a progressive moral reductionism on traditional Christian teach-
ings – is useful to an extent and is of course in keeping with the overall
intentions that Kant announces in his two Prefaces. But that approach foun-
ders, finally, on the fact that moral evil is for Kant lodged mysteriously in
the human will in ways that make it impossible to expel through human
effort alone: in this case, the translation of an orthodox Christian claim into
an ethical-rationalist substitute will solve no problems, since the will is the
source of its own difficulty. Kant would have saved both himself, and his
interpreters, a great deal of trouble if he had only joined the bulk of his
enlightened peers and claimed that moral evil has its source in ignorance,
not the will. As it is, moral evil is for him no mere epistemological failing,
but something much deeper and more mysterious.

Ibsen once said that "we are sailing with a corpse in the cargo." Similarly,
Kant's disturbing account of the way the free will turns against its own best
interests suggests that each of us carries a malevolent stowaway that could
come to life at any moment, without cause or explanation. More puzzling
still is the unsettling fact that, though the moral crippling thus produced
apparently renders us incapable of saving ourselves, we remain under the
obligation to do so. There is thus something profoundly equivocal about
Kant's position, as he weaves his way between idioms and attempts to balance out the proper proportions of innateness and free election in the emerg-

ence of moral evil, and of human effort and divine assistance in the recovery from it. Rather than simply accusing Kant of holding contradictory views – as though he could have seen and solved his problem if he had only looked harder – I am suggesting that the instability in his thinking is the inevitable result of a divided cultural inheritance – something which even a brilliant thinker such as Kant could not clearly see, no matter how hard he looked. His difficulties are the difficulties of his historical setting rather than of philosophical argumentation. The awkwardness of his position is thus symptomatic of the fate of every religious liberal, whose lot it apparently is to live in a zone of discomfort, somewhere between modernity and tradition. Kant is not closing off an era with his equivocal and unstable account of the relation between human capacities and divine aid, but inaugurating one.

Portions of this work have previously appeared in somewhat different form in the following articles: "The Non-Moral Element in Kant's Moral Proof of the Existence of God," *Scottish Journal of Theology* 39 (1986); "The Inscrutability of Moral Evil in Kant," *The Thomist* 51 (1987); and "Moral Regeneration and Divine Aid in Kant," *Religious Studies* 25 (1989). My thanks to the editors of these journals for permission to use material from those articles in this book.

As in the past, I have been greatly aided in the work on this book by the National Endowment for the Humanities and by Oberlin College. An N.E.H. Summer Stipend helped to get the project off the ground, while an N.E.H. Fellowship for College Teachers made possible its completion. My colleagues in Oberlin's Religion Department have shown not only gratifying and ongoing support for my research interests, but uncommon tolerance toward my leave patterns as well, while Dean Al MacKay took welcome initiatives that generously supplemented my N.E.H. funding. Kenneth Surin of Duke University was good enough to bring this project to the attention of Cambridge University Press, where I have had the good fortune to have the well informed and efficient assistance of editor Alex Wright. I am grateful to all of these parties for their help and for their implicit confidence in my efforts.

For almost two decades now, virtually everything I have thought and written about has been filtered through my ongoing contact with Malcolm Diamond, Henry Levinson, and Jeff Stout. Their importance to me as conversation partners is surpassed only by their value to me as friends. In the Preface to one of her books, Judith Shklar has said that there "is, of course, something silly about thanking one's friends for being one's friends" – but I am happy to follow her example and do so anyway. I look forward to the next twenty years.

I completed this work while enjoying several months as a Visiting Senior

Member of Linacre College, Oxford, during Trinity Term, 1989. My thanks to the Principal and permanent Members of Linacre for their kind hospitality during that period, and especially to Robert Morgan, who was good enough to nominate me for membership.

Finally, my earliest research for this project got under way while I was a Visiting Fellow in the Religious Studies Department at Yale University. My host on that occasion was the late Hans Frei, who was then the Department Chairman. All those who came under his extraordinary influence as a mentor and friend – and I realize there are many – will appreciate at least some of the feeling that lies behind the dedication of this volume, while sharing in the sadness that he is not here to witness its completion.

Introduction

If there are Gods they will reward your goodness. If there are none, what does anything matter?

Clytemnestra to Achilles, *Iphigenia at Aulis*

I do not understand my own actions. For I do not do what I want, but I do the very thing I hate.

Romans 7:15

Think of the history of religious thought in the West since about 1750 as an ongoing referendum on the idea of "otherworldliness." From Enlightenment attacks on priestcraft and supernaturalism to the liberation theologies of our own day, key issues in religious thought often turn on the question of whether humanity's proper understanding of itself and its hopes for fulfillment should be couched in "this-worldly" or "otherworldly" terms. Likewise, questions regarding God's activity and sheer reality always occur against the background of the deeply problematic nature of all appeals in the modern world to anything that, in principle, eludes observation, measurement, and verification. A vote in the referendum over other-worldliness is ultimately a vote concerning the relevance or importance to human life of a transcendent power or a hidden, saving action.

A complex web of forces helped to bring about this referendum, but the most powerful of these was no doubt the new idea of nature that emerged in the seventeenth century and was eventually codified by Newton. For this new mechanistic view – "cleaner" and less "Gothic" than the heavily Aristotelian medieval view – eliminates the notion of a multi-tiered universe (including a "place" where God dwells and the "saved" go) while simultaneously discrediting the idea that the natural world is either subject to capricious divine intervention or pervaded with latent meanings and providential purposes. The new arena of meaning and purposiveness is neither a hidden, supernatural zone nor the world of nature taken by itself, but rather the world of human thought, intention, and control. God's central position and commanding role are gradually displaced by an increasing preoccupation with human subjectivity, crystallized in the Cartesian *cogito* in ways that we now associate with an emergent modernity. Biblical patterning of human experience gives way to disenchantment, and the divine will is set in competition with – if not eclipsed altogether by – an autonomous human subject. A "disenchanted world is correlative to a self-defining subject," Charles Taylor reminds us, for our modern "categories of meaning and purpose apply exclusively to the thought and actions of subjects, and cannot find a purchase in the world they think about and act on."[1]

As we now know, this set of developments presented enormous difficulties for the thinker who wanted to embrace the new, scientifically based outlook while remaining, in some sense at least, "religious." In particular, there seemed to be no obvious way in this new situation to articulate a concept of transcendence that would do justice to the powerful new sense of human subjectivity and control while still retaining meaningful continuity with traditional language about God and divine action. Consequently, intellectually sophisticated religious thought during the last two hundred years or so – what we might broadly term "liberal" religious thought – has become the sustained search for a substitute for supernaturalism in the account of faith and transcendence. As such, this liberal tradition has been remarkably inventive in its efforts to transpose the "real" point of the religious message out of traditional terms defined by supernatural intervention and into terms that find a secure fit in human consciousness and history. The external, visible miracle that involves a disruption of natural law and holds irresistable appeal for Cecil B. DeMille is gradually displaced by the internal, hidden miracle of subjective change or personal transformation, leading eventually to the peculiar marriage of Christianity and existentialism.

Immanuel Kant occupies a special place in relation to this referendum over otherworldliness, for he helped to insure that it would occur and defined more than a few of its key terms. It was Kant's genius to show how – that is, to show how to have both science and religion without obvious intellectual sacrifice. Moreover, it was a telling indicator of how things would go among his successors that he achieved this result by greatly enhancing the role of private, individual consciousness or subjectivity in his account of the religious life. Kant could afford to have both science and religion precisely because he located the assurance of the latter, not in the outer, observable world of either natural or supernatural occurrences, but in the inner, hidden world of rational beings always apprehending the pull of an invisible moral law. "Once we give up, as Kant did, on the idea that scientific knowledge of hard facts is our point of contact with a power not ourselves, it is natural to do what Kant did: to turn inward, to find that point of contact in our moral consciousness – in our search for righteousness rather than for truth."[2] As a good Newtonian, Kant could not conceive of divine action involving an intrusion into the visible natural order, and as an ethical rationalist with a strong pietistic background he was temperamentally disposed to view something like personal character formation as the heart of the religious life. His strategy of separating science and religion thus went hand in hand with his strategy of moving to the interior recesses of subjectivity when depicting what was most important in human life. In the course of his pursuit of this twofold strategy, Kant made the individual's consciousness of autonomy the very essence of religious faith.

Consequently, Kant's position in the referendum over appeals to other-worldliness in religious matters would seem to be squarely on the side of those voting for a purely "this-worldly" account of religion. More specifically, his accent on the ethical dimensions of authentic religion – his insistence that faith is primarily a matter of practical doing rather than of theoretical believing – would appear to transform traditional beliefs about divine activity into an emphasis on a strictly human moral capacity in the account of salvation. On this reading of Kant, the result of his position would be the reconfiguration of the dichotomy between the otherworldly and worldly, or between the supernatural and natural, into a dichotomy between divine transcendence and human autonomy, with humanity's hopes for fulfillment clearly packed into the latter. Presumably, "salvation history" becomes naturalized in terms of the domain of autonomous human effort, and the functions of the divine will are transferred to a moral law that rivets our attention to the world that is immanent.

The matter is not so simple, however, and Kant in fact relates to the referendum in an utterly complex way. For despite what we might automatically think about him, certain features of Kant's moral and religious stance leave him not quite knowing how to vote, and his indecisiveness is a telling indicator of a certain ambivalence running through subsequent religious thought. More than most, Marx would accurately grasp this feature of Kant's position, perceptively linking it with the insight that, unlike the French and the English, the Germans were not very good at having political revolutions. The "impotent German burghers did not get any further than 'good will,' " claims Marx, and Kant himself "was satisfied with 'good will' alone, even if it remained entirely without result, and he transferred the *realization* of this good will, the harmony between it and the needs and impulses of individuals, to *the world beyond*."[3] Despite the element of caricature, Marx's comment is not bad as a description of Kant's second postulate of practical reason – the postulate of the immortality of the soul – which, in a certain light, appears to be a crude grafting of an outmoded idea, borrowed from the repudiated religion of otherworldliness, to his own ethically based and presumably immanent rational religion. The difficulties that commentators traditionally have in making sense of this postulate in the context of Kant's moral theory in general (especially the role played by the idea of "happiness") are both well known and a symptom of the instability in his thinking – or of an enfeebling half-heartedness, as Marx himself would no doubt suggest. The half-heartedness lies in Kant's unwillingness to transform the positive result and content of the good will into purely historical and social terms, rather than project human perfection into an infinitely distant noumenal realm, with no practical bearing on our present circumstance. Marx thus appreciates that Kant's vote in the referendum is not so obvious after all, for Kant has not totally left heaven for earth.

Without question, the most significant signal that Kant's profile on these matters is not as clear-cut as we might have supposed is the way he handles the problem of moral evil. In his late (1793) work, *Religion within the Limits of Reason Alone*, Kant develops a theory of what he calls "radical evil" that is sufficiently problematic in itself that Karl Barth once called it absolutely "the last thing one would expect" to find Kant writing about, following his earlier ethical writings.[4] The theory looks suspiciously like the Christian doctrine of original sin, just the sort of thing the thinkers of the Enlightenment normally prided themselves on eliminating from the roster of traditional ideas worthy of serious consideration. To make matters worse, Kant so defines radical evil that it appears to confront humanity with a problem that it cannot solve through its own worldly autonomous powers, making this the key point where the tension between the this-worldly and the otherworldly enters in, in the form of a tension between human autonomy and transcendent assistance. What gives the expression "radical" evil its point is what Kant calls the corruption of the underlying ground of all our maxims, and our dilemma becomes clear once we realize that the only way out of radical evil is through the production of good maxims. In other words, in order to save ourselves we have to call on precisely the resource that we ourselves have spoiled.

This evil is *radical* because it corrupts the ground of all maxims; it is, moreover, as a natural propensity, *inextirpable* by human powers, since extirpation could occur only through good maxims, and cannot take place when the ultimate subjective ground of all maxims is postulated as corrupt...[5]

4

In other words, radical evil is defined in such a way as to put in question our ability to save ourselves – an odd result for a thinker who makes human autonomy the heart of his philosophical vision. It is the logic produced by such a train of thought – set in motion by the aging Kant's utterly unfashionable lodging of the source of evil in the will, rather than in ignorance – that leads to his even more surprising language about divine aid, grace, and what he calls "supernatural cooperation" in his subsequent account of moral regeneration (p. 44; p. 40). Yet Kant does not cease to be Kantian, as exemplified by his own conclusion to the thought quoted above: "[Y]et at the same time it must be possible to *overcome* [radical evil], since it is found in man, a being whose actions are free" (p. 37; p. 32). Obviously, however, he saves his Kantian credentials only at the cost of appearing deeply ambivalent about the relationship between divine action and human autonomy, or between hope for salvation placed outside ourselves and hope placed in our own natural capacities. It is this ambivalence that finally makes Kant's vote in the referendum so problematic.

What follows is an attempt both to shed light on, and draw lessons from, Kant's views on radical evil and moral regeneration, with a particular emphasis on the delicate interplay between human freedom and transcendent action in the recovery from radical evil. Kant's position is a nest of tangles, but they are instructive tangles, especially for those concerned with reconciling traditional theological preoccupations with the characteristically modern demand for intellectual and moral autonomy. Kant's difficulties in successfully treating the topics at hand suggest ways in which the age is running ahead of itself while still bearing the weight of its Christian inheritance. As a result, no matter where Kant turns in his efforts to domesticate his own problem of radical evil, he meets with awkwardness. While a certain part of my aim in this study is simply to state his position as clearly as possible, my larger aim is to show that this awkwardness is not the result of philosophical shortsightedness or argumentative limitation, but of historical transition. Kant's problems are the problems of a thinker who is straddling worlds but who cannot possibly possess the historical perspective to assay the terrain causing his uncomfortable posture.

Moreover, despite the surprise expressed by Barth concerning the appearance of the doctrine of radical evil, there is an important sense in which it is no surprise at all, but rather the systematic working out of an issue already latent in the critical philosophy.[6] In the background here is the grounding perspective animating Kant's moral and religious philosophy, a powerful vision that is far more a matter of unspoken sensibility than of clear-cut conceptual commitment or explicit argumentation. We might say that, at its most general, comprehensive level, Kant's philosophical vision involves a kind of human–divine partnership in the creation of a moral universe; something such as this is, for Kant, the very point of reality. Moreover, the infinite approximation toward, if not the full realization of, this moral universe must be possible in fact as well as conceivable in principle, if certain "needs of reason" are not to be frustrated or revealed to be the product of mere subjective wish. For Kant, reason finally frames itself in the form of hope; reason's pervasive teleological tendencies are ultimately rendered in meaningful shapes, shapes that hint at why life is worth living. As a result, if serious questions can be raised concerning the actual possibility of the emergent moral universe embodied in reason's drive toward what Kant calls the highest good, then questions can be raised as well about the very process of rational thought that leads toward the postulates of practical reason themselves – freedom, immortality, and God. Doubt could only be thrown on one if it could also be thrown on the other.

But radical evil does in fact throw doubt on the approximation or actualization of the moral universe toward which Kant's philosophy moves – that is just the sort of thing evil does. Consequently, even though the doctrine of radical evil emerges within the critical philosophy due to implications arising out of Kant's own theory of freedom, it poses a genuine threat to his entire outlook: radical evil threatens to make the universe inexplicable and incomprehensible.[7] This is why Kant's efforts to respond to his own theory are so crucial, since a resolution of the problem is required if the rational hope that is at the center of his moral and religious philosophy is to be truly rational and if our sense of moral striving is not to turn out to be in vain. Because of Kant's deep-seated and unshakeable trust that the universe is not absurd – because, that is, of his conviction that our sense of moral obligation truly has purchase on reality, and does not just spin free – he is evidently satisfied that moral evil is overcome. But what is profoundly revealing is the fact that, in his explicit effort to spell out how this overcoming occurs, Kant seems to call into question the competence of human autonomy to deal with its self-made problem.

A cardinal indicator of this last point is the highly provocative vacillation that goes on as Kant attempts to sort out the exact relation between transcendent assistance and human autonomy in his depiction of the proper objects of human hope. It is almost as though he is intentionally previewing a century that will somehow manage to produce both a Kierkegaard and a Marx. Or, viewed retrospectively in terms of the received traditions with which he is working, it is as though Kant has not fully thrown off the thought forms of the Reformation even as he tries to do justice to the newly emergent claims of the Enlightenment, producing a mingling of idioms that is sometimes exasperating but always telling. When we discover, for example, that, at the key moment in his depiction of moral regeneration, Kant drops the vocabulary of his ethical rationalism and adopts the Johannine language of "rebirth" and "new creation" (p. 47; p. 43), we are at the heart of the lesson Kant is teaching us, however unwittingly. What is finally noteworthy is that not even Kant can smoothly and completely integrate the language of divine action and the language of human autonomy – the other worldly and this-worldly – a point helpfully compressed in Emil Fackenheim's remark that, for Kant, religion "culminates at the point at which the finite moral agent recognizes his radical inability to understand the relation between that which must be achieved by himself and that which can be expected only from God."[8] With the doctrine of radical evil and the related account of moral regeneration, we find Kant discovering the limits of his own Pelagianism. It may be that we also discover that he is at his most interesting when he is least Pelagian.[9]

The chapters that follow, then, constitute an attempt to chart a course through Kant's views concerning the nature and definition of moral evil, the relation of moral evil to human nature, the meaning of the expression "radical evil", and the process of moral regeneration. My ultimate aim is to highlight the vacillation in Kant's thinking that occurs as he attempts to work his way out of the doctrine of radical evil, with a view to understanding both the historical significance and theological implications of this vacillation. In a way, my account amounts to an explication of Kant's soteriology – a term not often associated with him – insofar as I am tracing his view of a condition from which he thinks we need to be saved, together with his account of how we are in fact potentially saved or delivered from the situation thus depicted. Kant's soteriology pivots on the terrible paradox that our fallenness is of our own doing – terrible, because within the Kantian framework this amounts to reason virtually turning against its own best interests, and freedom freely producing its own most severe debility. Kant concentrates the results of this paradox in a pair of claims: an evil that is "radical" involves the corruption of the means by which we might freely regenerate ourselves, meaning, as we have seen, that radical evil is "inextirpable by human powers" (p. 37; p. 32); but radical evil does not absolve us of our obligation to make ourselves good again, meaning, among other things, that even a fallen freedom is still freedom. Once fallen, we thus live under an impossible command that might be phrased this way: "Make yourself good again, even though the condition producing this imperative in the first place appears to make it impossible for you to do this." This vaguely tragic, Sisyphean dimension to Kant's total vision runs through the account of radical evil and moral regeneration, giving his mature anthropology a richness often missed in superficial portraits of Kant as the philosopher who says everything will be all right if we simply act "on principle."

The paradox compressed in Kant's impossible command is an instance of a series of telling wobbles that surface in Kant's account and that will help to organize my narrative. On the one hand, these wobbles simply denote a certain cumbersomeness, making even more problematic and difficult to follow a piece of writing that, though stylistically quite different from the three *Critiques*, possesses an organizational scheme that sometimes appears haphazard and makeshift. On the other hand, however, these wobbles convey what appears to be a deep ambivalence on Kant's part concerning the most important issues covered in his discussion:

1 Humankind has an "original predisposition to good" but a "natural propensity to evil." (pp. 26–32; pp. 21–27)
2 Radical evil is "innate" but "brought upon us" by our own freedom. (pp. 32, 38, 42; pp. 28, 33, 38)
3 We are morally obligated to deliver ourselves from radical evil, even though it is *"inextirpable* by human powers." (p. 37; p. 32)
4 We must "make ourselves" good again, but divine aid "may be necessary" to our actually becoming good. (p. 44; p. 40)

The progression of this wobbling from numbers one through four has the effect of recasting in fresh terms the instability already latent in Kant's treatment of the postulate of immortality in the *Critique of Practical Reason*, where his awkward ambivalence about this-worldly versus otherworldly dimensions of human hope finds initial expression. Moreover, all of the wobbling in the *Religion* has an idiomatic counterpart in Kant's oscillation between the language of his ethical rationalism and the language of the Bible. I am taking the view that this entire set of wobbles – including the idiomatic one – signals the tension between human autonomy and transcendent assistance with which Kant appears ultimately to be struggling and which signals the transitions through which the culture as a whole is moving. Viewing Kant's struggle is like watching a great thinker practicing to be Promethean, but he is doing so at a time when the shadows of the biblical heritage still fall heavily on the practice grounds. It is perfectly clear what Kant *wants* to do in the *Religion*, as in his moral and religious thought generally: he wants human autonomy to take over the role traditionally played by divine action in the creation of a good universe, with a corresponding displacement of the supernatural world by the noumenal realm where Kantian freedom enjoys its possibility. Kant's own desires in the matter are boldly signalled in the remarkably telling comment that "godliness is not a surrogate for virtue" (p. 185; p. 173). In principle, Kant wants human effort to inherit both the role and the prerogatives traditionally enjoyed by God, for he has a clear glimpse of the emerging insight, characteristic of a certain intellectual community in the modern West, that a full theory of autonomy is incompatible with any appeal to divine action. What is noteworthy is that not even Kant can quite pull off this transposition, and the reason he cannot do so is to be found in the cluster of difficulties produced by his own theory of radical evil. The theory of radical evil is finally symptomatic of the fact that Kant has not totally thrown off the habits of mind produced by Christian culture, yet these habits of mind are in many ways antithetical to his deepest philosophical instincts.

Kant thus ends up straddling two worlds.[10] One effect of this awkward posture is that, through the lens of radical evil, Kant perceives that a free will is not simply a problem for itself but is a virtual mystery to itself. However elaborate his explanatory apparatus may appear to be, Kant cannot fully understand his own position. *Religion within the Limits of Reason Alone* not only contains a revealing set of wobbles, it contains frequent use of the word "inscrutable" (*unerforschlich*) and an almost systematic employment of an argumentatively timely agnosticism. For Kant, the things we do *not* know are the big things, not the little ones: we neither know why we fall into radical evil nor exactly how it is that we get out again, given the unspecifiable mixture of human effort and divine cooperation needed for the salvation process. Any given individual – no matter how insightful or morally alert – does not even know for certain if he or she is good or evil, since Kant's account leaves profoundly opaque the deepest motivations not only of others, but of ourselves as well. Such a limitation on moral self-knowledge would seem to entail yet another infringement on Kant's own theory of freedom, since it suggests we can never be absolutely certain we are doing what we "ought" to do. As a result, the process of character-building begins to look like a game of Sartrean darts, with no sure thing either before or after the toss.

An ambivalent wobbling, a suggestive agnosticism, and hints of severe limitations on both self-knowledge and freedom thus provide the deep structure of Kant's account of radical evil and moral regeneration. Taken together, these themes imply that Kant's moral philosophy culminates in the suspicion that human reason is not master in its own house. In peculiar ways, Kant is both heir to the Reformation and precursor to Freud, as well as a proponent of Enlightenment. Stanley Cavell's insight, though intended for quite a different context, is nonetheless apt: "If Freud's unconscious is what is not available to knowledge (under, let us say, normal circumstances) then Kant's Reason projects a whole realm of the self or mind which is even more strongly unavailable to knowledge..."[11] Our common picture of Kant often keeps this side of his thinking from coming into full view, partly the result, no doubt (as Mary Midgley has shrewdly observed), of a tendency to "treat a few quotations from the rather dramatic opening sections of the *Groundwork* as his last words on both individuality and freedom."[12] Likewise, it is typically assumed that the fundamental tension in Kant's world view is between freedom and determinism (or necessity). In Ernest Gellner's memorable expression, Kant's philosophy is animated by two great fears: "The first fear is that the mechanical vision does *not* hold; the second fear is that it *does*."[13] With the emphasis here, studies of Kant's religious thought invariably concentrate on how he reconciles his moral theism with a scientific account of a physical universe that, taken by itself, would leave all human actions strictly predetermined and morality therefore impossible.

The lesson of this study, however, may be that a deeper and more troubling tension in Kant's world view is that between freedom and something more like original sin than Newtonian necessity. Freedom is more fundamentally in conflict with itself than it is threatened by a mechanistic universe. It is this tension, finally, that keeps Kant's vote in the referendum on otherworldliness from being clear cut. Whereas the first, more commonly addressed tension is what we might call a "conceptual" difficulty that is the natural spin-off of Kant's efforts to have both Newton and morality, the second tension is more existentially urgent and intrinsically tragic, for it is produced by freedom itself as a problem for itself. The first tension is something we *discover* as we try to make sense, simultaneously, of a physical universe and human action; but the second tension is something we *create* as, in a life filled with moral promise, we turn inexplicably against ourselves and subvert our original predisposition to good.

It is often said in connection with Kant's view of freedom that what makes us "human" for him is our ability to "oppose our ends to those imposed upon us by nature."[14] The chapters that follow constitute an attempt, not to repudiate, but to expand upon this common view. For the theory of radical evil suggests that what also makes us human is our ability to oppose not only the ends imposed upon us by nature, but also the ends that our own reason would freely give to itself.

I

Radical evil

1

Ivan and Kant

I wanted to discuss the suffering of humanity in general, but perhaps we'd better confine ourselves to the sufferings of children.

Ivan Karamazov

A thoughtful person is acquainted with a kind of distress which threatens his moral fibre, a kind of distress of which the thoughtless know nothing: discontent with Providence which governs the course of this world. This distress he is apt to feel when he considers the evils which oppress the human species so heavily and, apparently, so hopelessly.

Kant

Ivan's problem

In a famous passage in *The Brothers Karamazov*, Dostoyevsky has Ivan tell Alyosha about "a little girl of five who was hated by her father and mother, 'most worthy and respectable people, a good education and breeding.' " So they "subjected her to every possible torture," they "beat her, thrashed her, kicked her for no reason till her body was one bruise."

Then they went to greater refinements of cruelty – shut her up all night in the cold and frost in a privy, and... smeared her face and filled her mouth with excrement, and it was her mother, her mother did this. And that mother could sleep, hearing the poor child's groans![1]

On February 20, 1987, *The New York Times* ran an article with the headline, "Mother Accused of Rape Role."

A Bronx woman was arrested yesterday and charged with restraining her 6-year-old daughter while three men raped the girl on separate occasions and then gave the mother money or drugs, the police said... The sergeant said (the mother) was accused of "holding down her daughter's head while she was raped and sodomized."

"I don't believe," John le Carré's spy George Smiley once said, "that we

13

can ever entirely know what makes anyone do anything."[2] In no situation does this observation seem more fitting than in our experience of evil-doing, whether we confront it through the novelist's imagination or in our daily headlines. We may not be able succinctly and convincingly to define what we mean by evil, but we know it when we see it. What we typically do not know is what point or purpose moral evil could possibly play in some larger or overarching scheme of things, which is of course why the experience of evil is often connected with the loss of religious belief. It is this connection, after all, that Ivan wants to puzzle out in his anguished attempt to reconcile the notion of a loving, all-powerful God with a world filled with tortured children.

Imagine that you are creating a fabric of human destiny with the object of making men happy in the end, giving them peace and rest at last, but that it was essential and inevitable to torture to death only one tiny creature – that baby beating its breast with its fist, for instance – and to found that edifice on its unavenged tears, would you consent to be the architect on those conditions?[3]

And what if the "unavenged tears" were not merely those of a single baby, but of untold numbers of men, women, children, and animals populating a world very much like the one we in fact experience? What ultimate, providential end could such suffering serve? Just as Albert Camus would do in the following century, Ivan raises here the troubling possibility that any God that we *could* reconcile with our experience of evil in the world would not be worthy of devotion and worship but should instead invite rebellion. It is one thing to accept – Job-like – afflictions visited upon oneself while retaining faith in God, but quite another thing to rationalize someone else's pain, especially a child's. People far less reflective than Ivan or Camus have felt the pangs of religious skepticism due to this and similarly awful thought experiments.

In its starkest forms, moral evil is a kind of void in our experience, an absence of meaning that leaves us unable to configure our contact with the external world in narrative form. The revelation of the Nazi death camps at first produced numbness more than an articulate outrage, and a sustained Jewish response to the camps did not really take shape until well into the 1960s. Evidently, the experience of evil in such a degree points us not only in the direction of religious skepticism, but toward something utterly inexplicable in ourselves. It is not by accident that the word "monster" is often used following the capture of a true evil-doer, such as a former concentration camp guard. Our inability to explain, account for, or render in a meaningful narrative our experience of evil finally signals the inscrutability of human behavior itself and, especially, of our deepest motivations: moral evil rad-icalizes the difficulty already latent in the question, "Why does anybody do anything?"[4] This is perhaps why traditional efforts to explain the existence of evil in the world – such as the Genesis account of the fall – usually leave unexplored the question of the underlying motivation that produces evil. We give a name to the product of the illustrative narrative – "pride," "disobed-ience," "rebellion" – but not really an explanation. And, more recently, mod-ern social scientific attempts to "explain" what the theologians and myth-tellers can only hint at invariably end up sounding either utterly banal or grotesquely disproportionate to the lived experience of the victims of evil.

Almost a century before Ivan embarked on his tormented explorations of the human heart, Immanuel Kant remarked that "the deeps of the heart . . . are inscrutable" to us (p. 51; p. 46), and that a natural human tendency toward evil is both universal and utterly beyond all explanations. Kant can no more explain the behavior of the parents in Ivan's story than can Ivan himself. The surprise in this lies not only in the fact that a philosopher known for uncommon philosophical ambition should come up short in the exploration of such a fundamental matter, but also in the very fact that he takes moral evil with unflinching seriousness, refusing to explain it away as the product of a mere epistemological lapse. For in many ways, Kant and his Enlighten-ment peers are devoted to the notion that knowledge is not only power, but virtue as well, and that most of what we call evil in the world can be attributed to the drag effect of a received tradition of priestcraft and illegitimate royal authority. "Dare to know," Kant enjoins in his famous essay on Enlighten-ment. "Dare to use your own reason" and to come out from under your "self-incurred tutelage."[5] The obvious premise beneath this call to intellectual maturity is the claim that each one of us possesses sound reason and, conse-quently, full equality in the pursuit of the good life. In his own polite way, Kant is echoing Diderot's far less polite remark that he will not rest comfort-ably until the last king is hanged in the entrails of the last priest – until, that is, there are no more deceitful authority figures trying to tell him what to do. For both Kant and Diderot, true autonomy is humanity's authentic vocation and will emerge only as we recognize and confront traditional dogma – both religious and political – as instruments of oppression and social control.

The inner logic of this position normally includes the claim that what we call evil is the result of ignorance rather than the product of an intrinsically evil will. Plato rather than Augustine stands behind the Enlightenment call to intellectual maturity. Rousseau, in particular, will make the point explicit, as he compresses a lifetime of complaining into his complaint about what society does to a naturally good animal. And Rousseau will, of course, profoundly affect Kant. In particular, Rousseau will help Kant to get over his intellectual snobbery and to appreciate that a good heart – available to every-one – and not intellectual sophistication – available to only a privileged few – is the decisive insight into ourselves and our capacities as moral beings.[6] Rousseau helps Kant to recover in a fresh way the broadly democratic prin-ciple that was always at the heart of the pietism on which Kant had been raised.[7] Kant, after all, had ended in revulsion toward his official pietist training, due to what he took to be its encouragement of the hypocritical feigning of religious affects and enthusiasm. For by the time of his schooling at the Collegium Fridericianum in Königsberg, the school's originally pietest intention had degenerated into an emphasis on ostentatious techniques for undergoing and reporting the coveted experience of personal conversion, together with specific prescriptions for endless scrutiny of the heart.[8] Even the young Kant saw that the school's atmosphere encouraged a split between the sincerely felt ethical dimensions of religious piety and public conformity to the expected patterns of religious expression. Surely Kant's eventual emphasis, not only on the practical, non-dogmatic dimensions of religion, but on autonomy itself, must have deep psychological rooting in these early experiences of "interference from the spiritual discipline" and bondage to religious patterns grounded in external technique and aimed toward "ingrati-ation."[9] The point would still be on Kant's mind late in life, when, in his essay on theodicy based on the Book of Job, he says, "Job spoke as he thought, as he felt, and as every man in his position would feel."

His friends, however, spoke as if they were overheard by the Almighty whose behavior they were judging, and as if they cared more for winning his favours by passing the right judgement than for saying the truth. The dishonesty with which they affirmed things of which they should have confessed that they had no knowledge and with which they feigned convictions which in fact they did not have, contrasts with Job's free and sincere outspokenness, which is so removed from lying flattery that it almost borders on temerity.[10]

The principle of sincerity that Kant finds in Rousseau is thus decisive for the structure of his moral and religious viewpoint, for it is what helps him to work his way back to an appreciation of what is potentially common to us all, regardless of intellectual attainment. Kant "thinks he discerns in Rous-seau the will not to be peculiar and eccentric but to be altogether sincere."[11] So the surprise is that Kant can go so far with peers such as Diderot and Rousseau – for whom the "one great enemy" is the Christian doctrine of original sin[12] – and yet assume a position on moral evil that looks more Augustinian than Platonic. For Kant's position assumes this look quite unmistakably in his account of radical evil in *Religion within the Limits of Reason Alone*. Kant's friend Goethe would develop his own unflattering suspicions as to why Kant devised this doctrine, suspicions that he shared in a letter to Herder, saying that Kant "had criminally smeared his philosopher's cloak with the shameful stain of radical evil, after it had taken him a long human life to cleanse it from many a dirty prejudice, so that Christians too might yet be enticed to kiss its hem."[13]

As we shall see, it will not be necessary to agree with Goethe's disparaging view of Kant's motivations to agree that the parallel between radical evil and original sin is very real. In both cases, we are dealing with a debility that is brought upon us through our own act of will rather than through mere ignorance or lack of information. In neither case is moral evil a problem arising out of an insufficient data base, or even out of unfortunate environmental circumstances. Likewise, we are dealing in both cases with a debility that produces a fundamental alteration in our basic condition, rather than a merely momentary or episodic change in our outward behavior. The debility is deep and structural and not just signalled through an occasional lapse. Finally, in the case of both radical evil and original sin the debility in question is defined in such a way as to make it evidently impossible to save or renew ourselves through our own efforts. Precisely when we find ourselves facing the greatest obligation with which life confronts us, we discover we are crippled. Thus – and this is what must have irked Goethe – with this one doctrine, Kant puts both reason and freedom into question: reason, because of the seemingly irrational character of the act of will that throws us into radical evil; and freedom, because of the apparent impossibility that we can, through our own autonomous powers, save ourselves once we have fallen. Radical evil implies that reason is capable of turning against its own best interests, and that freedom has a limit point that may even return us to dependency on the priests. While Kant would of course shrink from this last potential implication of his own view, it gradually becomes clear why, for someone like Goethe, the theory of radical evil must represent backsliding of the worst sort, made all the more reprehensible by the enlightened credentials of its proponent.

Kant's metaphysical trust

Kant's theory of radical evil reflects his consideration of the issue over several decades and must be seen in the context of his total moral and religious outlook.[14] For his ultimate response to both Ivan and Goethe will be, roughly, that he does not take moral evil any less seriously than the former and is no less optimistic about humanity's progressive vocation than the latter. He takes moral evil with full seriousness, yet he does not end in despair; moral evil is a genuine threat to a coherent view of the universe, yet Kant's universe is finally coherent. In his universe, the "center *does* hold," but not because Kant falls into sentimentality. His ability to incorporate both radical evil and ultimate coherence in a single outlook reflects a deep metaphysical trust on his part, a trust that is perhaps the decisive dividing line between Kant and Ivan. Yet it remains true to say that radical evil is the most profound threat to Kant's total vision, which is no doubt the reason – as we shall see in more than one instance – that Kant is clearly breathing hard as he attempts to respond to his own problem. It will be useful, then, prior to my specific account of his theory of radical evil, to tease out certain features of Kant's background metaphysical trust that is both threatened by, and the counterbalance to, his willingness to take moral evil seriously.

Kant's moral and religious outlook did not emerge all at once and retain a single form throughout his maturity, and there remains some question as to whether his views were taking important new turns late in his life.[15] Yet there remains a unified vision to his total outlook which is what makes his view recognizably "Kantian," regardless of the disagreements commentators may justifiably have about the particular features of his view of God, or the exact relation between God and moral action, or the nature of the connection between human history and Kant's notion of the highest good. This unified vision can perhaps be expressed as the deep trust that reality as a whole is the scene of an ongoing, cooperative effort between humanity and God in the production of a moral universe. The vision is profoundly teleological and the goal is explicity moral. Regardless of whether this goal is conceived of as genuinely historical or as simply an ideal to be approximated but never truly reached, the ongoing movement toward this goal is assured in Kant's scheme by what he calls "needs of reason" that subtly transform certain logical features of his train of thought into a metaphysical content: the discovery of certain constraints on thought is simultaneously the discovery of certain features of reality that are both unknowable in any other way and legitimately postulated once we discover the constraints. This transformation from logic to metaphysics – from a *form of* thought to a *content for* thought – roughly describes Kant's postulation of freedom, immortality, and God in the *Critique of Practical Reason*, a process representing Kant's uncanny knack for producing generous metaphysical results from the most stringent epistemological starting point.[16] The limited yet sophisticated activity of "critique" thus yields a robust and basically optimistic vision of an emergent moral universe.[17]

The obvious point to be made, then, is that moral evil threatens the production of the moral universe toward which Kant thinks reason moves. The issue is deeply rooted in the structure of Kant's practical philosophy and in its tendency to move forward through the resolution of self-made antinomies. In this case, specifically, as one commentator has correctly pointed out, Kant's entire argument for the postulate of the immortality of the soul "arises out of a dialectical threat to the practical possibility of moral perfection in man" that comes to our attention through an antinomy of practical reason.[18] In effect, moral evil disputes the forms that Kant claims reason takes, and Kant cannot maintain his rationalist stance without taking some account of this threat. His eventual account of radical evil is thus not simply an effort on his part to grasp and articulate in systematic form the evil human tendencies that are a part of his experience of the world; it is an effort to confront a potentially devastating obstacle to the very theory of practical reason.

Another way of making this point in a manner that both illustrates Kant's tendency to move from logical form to metaphysical content and also underscores the dangers posed to his position by moral evil is to characterize his philosophy of religion as the sustained effort to think through the total product of moral action in a universe that "makes sense." The background aspect of "sense-making" here is both crucial and the thing most directly threatened by the reality of evil; we can perhaps think of it as Kant's streamlined way of carrying on the Leibnizian trust that we live in the best of all possible worlds. The decisive feature of Kant's metaphysical trust is his deep sense that, when moral striving is viewed as a totality (as he is attempting to do, for example, in the second *Critique*), we ultimately discover something like fairness and correct proportion as features of the universe. Something such as this is what Bernard Williams has in mind when he says that "Kantianism... offers... solace to a sense of the world's unfairness."[19] Precisely here is Kant's response to Ivan, for in a Kantian universe the spectre of tortured children cannot be the final image, nor is the Kantian God a perverse sadist. I can perhaps best clarify Kant's underlying trust that he lives in such a sense-making universe by isolating the crucial role played by this trust in his postulation of the existence of God.

Metaphysical trust and belief in God

It is well known that Kant does not hold up a claim about the existence of God as though such a claim could be a theoretical proposition, open to the give-and-take of debate such as we find in Hume's *Dialogues Concerning Natural Religion*. In moral and religious matters, Kant's strategy never relies on convincing us of certain truth claims that we could, in principle, either accept or reject. Instead, he typically attempts to draw out into the light of day certain convictions that he thinks no rational being would dispute, and he then goes on to fashion from these convictions a kind of "rational mosaic" designed to highlight both the indubitable content and the elegant "fit" or coherence of religious belief. Viewed in this light, Kant's philosophy of religion is like an extended footnote to his own claim that there exists a

practical knowledge which, while resting solely upon reason and requiring no historical doctrine, lies as close to every man, even the most simple, as though it were engraved upon his heart – a law, which we need but name to find ourselves at once in agreement with everyone else regarding its authority, and which carries with it in everyone's consciousness *unconditioned* binding force, to wit, the law of morality. (p. 181; p. 169)

We thus begin with the moral law and end with belief in God. The moral foundation here is clear and unmistakable, but the progression from the moral starting point to the postulation of God's existence does not proceed on purely moral terms. For a careful reading of the second *Critique* reveals that the obvious moral element in the postulation process is intimately connected with considerations that are not strictly moral in character, if we conceive of morality here on the narrow, deontological grounds of Kant's own moral theory. These considerations stem from the so-called "needs of reason" that shape the direction of Kant's thinking, needs that demand symmetry, correct proportion, and coherence.[20] The inner secret of Kant's philosophy of religion is the way it transforms these needs from being predicates of thinking alone to being predicates of reality as such: Kant moves from thought "making sense" to reality "making sense," all the while implicitly trading on the latter to give movement to the former. The postulation process culminating in the postulation of God's existence gains its life from just this movement. Clearly, such a process would be utterly illicit if the operative needs were purely subjective in nature, since we would then be generating metaphysical claims on the basis of mere inclination alone.[21] But Kant is convinced that the postulates arise "not for the sake of some arbitrary speculative design but only for the sake of a practically necessary end of the pure rational will, which does not here choose but rather obeys an inexorable command of reason."[22] The postulates become the appropriate content of a genuinely rational faith precisely because they are grounded "objectively in pure reason" and are "not based on inclination."[23] Belief in God is not simply subjectively satisfying, though it is that – it is objectively valid as well.

It is this confidence that, in his religious views, he is not simply trading off of a subjective wish that signals Kant's deep-seated metaphysical trust.

20

Kant is saying, in part, that truly rational thought is rational because it is constrained and shaped in ways that are independent of the thinker. There are several points in his philosophy of religion where this trust comes most prominently into play, but perhaps the most explicit point is his deployment of the notion of the *summum bonum*, or highest good, in his effort to postulate God's existence.

Kant conceives of the highest good as virtue and happiness existing in proper proportion.[24] Virtue in the Kantian sense means acting according to duty alone, rather than according to the whimsy of inclination; and happiness means the "state of a rational being in the world with whom in the totality of his existence everything goes according to his wish and will."[25] The difficulty is that the absolute virtue entailed by the concept of the highest good is a perfection "of which no rational being in the world of sense is at any time capable."[26] As a result, the realization of the highest good depends on the perfection of virtue which, in turn, relies on the "infinite progress" necessary to achieve what Kant calls "holiness."[27] Unless there exist the conditions conducive to this end, the reality of the highest good is threatened, which is to say that reason's "natural drive" toward totality is frustrated, a result that is for Kant rationally intolerable to the point of being virtually unthinkable. Therefore, if the highest good is to be realized, there must exist the conditions of the possibility of achieving perfect virtue, and the resulting medium for this infinite perfection could only be a non-sensuous, non-worldly mode of existence unrestricted by temporality. For Kant, then, "the highest good is practically possible only on the supposition of the immortality of the soul..."[28] In other words, the immortality of the soul "derives from the practically necessary condition of a duration adequate to the perfect fulfillment of the moral law."[29]

In this way, the postulate of immortality becomes the stepping stone for Kant's postulation of the existence of God. In effect, the duration provided by immortality suffices only to guarantee the condition for achieving complete virtue. But such a result satisfies merely one part of the highest good; there remains the proportioning of happiness to the virtue achieved. Any guarantee that happiness will truly arise in proportion to virtue must be based "on the supposition of the existence of a cause adequate to this effect."[30] A causality suited to this task will be characterized by the intelligence and will establishing initial relatedness to the task, together with the omnipotence and omniscience serving as the means of actually executing it. Such attributes leave us with what would, in Kant's historical setting, normally be meant by God.[31] Consequently, the requirements of the highest good allow us to

21

postulate, not only immortality, but a God who effects the proportioning of happiness to the virtue made possible by the postulate of immortality.

Now it is obvious why this should be called a "moral" argument, given the roles played by our initial apprehension of the moral law and by the governing concern for moral perfection. Yet other considerations not obviously moral in character also play a critical role in Kant's train of thought, and it is these considerations that betray the underlying metaphysical trust that is at once both severely threatened by the idea of moral evil and Kant's strongest weapon against the possibility that moral evil could somehow finally be victorious. Indeed, the entire argument for the existence of God can be taken as the complex unfolding of an implicit confidence in the rationality of the universe.

This view of the matter becomes clearer if we notice that Kant's argumentation is sustained both by the moral law's demand for virtue *and* by a certain rational demand for symmetry and proportion that, strictly speaking, has little or nothing to do with morality in the Kantian sense. Without this second feature, Kant's argument could not sustain the momentum necessary to yield the rational mosaic that is the final product of his practical philosophy. The point is that the overarching design of Kant's practical philosophy requires movement and dynamic progression for its final articulation and for what Kant takes to be its persuasiveness; such progression is precisely what we see in the development of three postulates, rather than just one. For all its importance in Kant's scheme, the moral law alone simply cannot account for all this movement: by itself, the moral law will at some point just "sit" there. The required dynamic element derives as well from the Kantian demand that the universe is ultimately a symmetrical and "fitting" place, a place where things (in the larger sense) finally "hang together." This is the whole point of the rational demand that virtue and happiness be properly proportioned. Kant's trust in the ultimate reasonableness of things becomes evident if we simply ask: "*Why* must virtue and happiness be proportioned?" Kant's answer to this question likewise entails the answers to the several troubling questions raised by Ivan, though – as we shall eventually see – Kant does not secure these answers by diluting the reality of moral evil.

My point for the moment is simply the suggestion that more is at work in Kant's moral argument for the existence of God than sustained reflection on the moral law. At work here is reflection on the moral law *in a universe that makes sense*, and this latent appeal to "sense-making" can be neither justified nor carried through on the narrow grounds provided by the moral law alone. Kant's moral argument reaches its climactic moment only through the dual appeal to the moral law *and* to something like symmetry or proportion.

22

This mixture of the moral and the non-moral is best appreciated by examining once again the key term in Kant's argument, his notion of the highest good. The idea of the highest good, Kant tells us, contains an ambiguity, since the concept of the "highest" can mean either the "supreme" (*supremum*) or the "perfect" (*consummatum*).[32] To be "supreme" means to be unconditioned, in the sense that there is no further term or condition to which the unconditioned is subordinate.[33] To be "perfect," on the other hand, means to be "that whole which is no part of a yet larger whole of the same kind."[34] It is crucial for Kant's purposes that this ambiguity in the idea of the highest be exploited, for otherwise he should be forced to conclude that virtue, the "supreme" good, constitutes by itself the highest good. Kant's earlier examination in the *Foundations of the Metaphysics of Morals* of the good will as the only thing we can call good without qualification[35] necessarily yields the conclusion that virtue alone is the supreme good, but this basic Kantian insight does "not imply that virtue is the entire and perfect good..."

For this, happiness is also required, and indeed not merely in the partial eye of a person who makes himself his end but even in the judgment of an impartial reason, which impartially regards persons in the world as ends-in-themselves.[36]

It is both important and extremely revealing to notice that the idea of happiness is only introduced because of what Kant takes to be the second sense of "highest," namely, the highest as the "perfect." Unlike virtue, happiness in itself is not intrinsically good; instead, happiness, in Kant's own words, "is required," by which he means required to "perfect" or "consummate" a rational ideal. Kant explicitly indicates the sense in which he intends the idea of the perfect by correlating it with the Latin term, *consummatum*, which derives from the verb (*consummare*) meaning to "sum up" or "complete." Consequently, the idea of happiness is incorporated into Kant's conception of the highest good, not in order to add moral weight to it, but to fill it out. The issue is not one of morality, but of proportionality.

Nothing in Kant's previous thinking had prepared us for the appearance of happiness in a positive or constructive light in his practical philosophy, and its appearance at this point is a matter of longstanding dispute and puzzlement. The questionable role played by happiness in Kant's conception of the highest good is only one of the reasons behind Allen Wood's accurate remark that nearly "all critics of Kant's moral arguments seem sooner or later to alight on the doctrine of the highest good as the weak point in Kant's defense of moral faith."[37] Obviously, Kant could not introduce the idea of happiness for its own sake, since this would immediately inject a note of heteronomy into his moral theory. That is, the quickest way to undermine

Kantian virtue would be for the moral agent to be motivated by the hope for happiness. Indeed, there is simply no *moral* reason for Kant to discuss happiness at all, except as a losing candidate for that which is good in itself, which is how the topic arises in the *Foundations*.[38] He introduces happiness now only because virtue alone cannot satisfy both senses of the concept of "highest": even absolute virtue, by itself, leaves us with a potentially imperfect ("disproportionate") universe. Kant's argument is capsulized in his claim that "to be in need of happiness and also worthy of it and yet not to partake of it could not be in accordance with the complete volition of an omnipotent rational being..."[39] Oddly, Kant seems here to be invoking the existence of God as a premise to help him reach happiness as a conclusion – which is seemingly to flip his argument in precisely the opposite direction from the one apparently intended. But even if we allow this reference to God "only for the sake of the argument,"[40] as Kant asks us to take it, his comment still leaves us without moral reasons for discussing happiness. For on the grounds of Kant's own moral theory, to be worthy of happiness (i.e., to be virtuous) and yet to be without it probably does not confront us with a genuinely moral issue. As always within the Kantian scheme, the consequences of actions are irrelevant to judgments concerning their morality, and this would presumably include the happiness or unhappiness of the moral agent. Whether or not something is a moral issue, by Kantian standards, turns on the quality of the will and the will's exercise of freedom in determining its own incentive. Whatever else its merits, Kant's easy (and unargued for) equation of "virtue" and "worthiness to be happy" is certainly not a *moral* equation by this Kantian standard. The spectre of an unhappy person of great virtue may be distressing and deeply poignant, but it hardly threatens the moral status of the person in question and offers us no direct information about the moral status of anyone else.[41] Morality is not threatened by such an unfortunate state of affairs; instead, the only thing threatened is "correct proportion." Without happiness in proportion to virtue, the universe will not suddenly be less *moral* – but it will be less *symmetrical*.

This view of the matter means that, if God's existence is postulated by Kant on the grounds that there must be a causality adequate to proportioning happiness to virtue, then God enters Kant's scheme by riding on the coattails of the principle of proportionality. Postulating God's existence hinges on the idea of happiness; yet happiness, we have just seen, satisfies a rational yet non-moral need. The believer does not assent to belief in God in order to be moral, but only in order to satisfy reason's demand for symmetry. On Kantian grounds, I cannot conceive of a universe in which, in the long run, the wicked will prosper and the virtuous or innocent – such as the little girl in Ivan's story – find only suffering and wretchedness. Strictly speaking, such a vision is not morally intolerable if, with Kant, we restrict considerations of morality to the mandates of the categorical imperative. Instead, such a vision simply does not "add up," it is "out of whack": it confronts us with an absurdity in the form of a grotesque disproportion. It is, after all, precisely the problem of disproportion with which Ivan is wrestling as he wonders aloud about creating a perfect world through the torturing of a single child.

As a good Kantian, then, I believe in God because I cannot conceive that the universe is absurd and asymmetrical. Just this Kantian trust fills the void produced by Ivan's despair. In Kant's own idiom, the possibility that virtue and happiness will *not* be correctly proportioned may be a sheer "logical" possibility, but it evidently never looms as a "real" possibility. This is presumably why Kant never addresses this potential outcome in his moral argument. The fact that Kant clearly feels no need to argue against the disastrous possibility that virtue and happiness will not be correctly proportioned – which is the flip side of his confident employment of the principle of proportionality in the course of his argumentation – simply shows how deeply ingrained his metaphysical trust is. Indeed, it is just this trust in the rationality of the universe that gives morality its point. In *this* universe, moral endeavor is ultimately meaningful and makes a positive difference. Belief in God and confidence in morality grow out of the same metaphysical soil.

Moral evil as metaphysical threat

Earlier in this chapter, I suggested that our experience of moral evil threatens our ability to make sense of the world. Into what sort of narrative does the torturing of little children fit? If we could conceive of such a narrative, would a sensitive person be able to *live* by it? Should not the capacity of a narrative to incorporate Ivan Karamazov's little girl as part of an intelligible plot lead responsible people to repudiate the narrative as morally reprehensible and unacceptable? What if our experience of evil and innocent suffering is so profound as to negate, in advance, the countervailing weight that a benevolent deity might provide?

Such questions – which are of course variations on the several questions associated with the traditional problem of theodicy in the West – help to clarify the issues that evidently separate Ivan and Kant. Kant can tell himself a rational story that both presupposes and confirms a reasonable universe in which things work out, while Ivan can only sharpen his own anguished question and torment his brother with demented yet morally powerful hypotheses. Whereas Kant resolves the problem of moral evil by assuming at the outset that the universe is somehow fair and symmetrical and then working back from there, Ivan *confronts* the problem of moral evil by eliminating any such assumption at the outset and then trying to work his way forward. We might simply say that Ivan takes moral evil seriously, while Kant does not, diluting it in some way that represents that tendency of the Enlightenment to underestimate or diminish the truly demonic. We could say that Ivan has someone very much like Kant in mind when he protests, "I don't want harmony... too high a price has been placed on harmony."[42] Perhaps Kant is simply begging the question being raised by Ivan.

Yet whatever the difference may be between Ivan and Kant regarding a larger metaphysical confidence, it does not seem adequate simply to say that Kant takes moral evil less seriously than Ivan. His imagination is no doubt less vivid, but it is not by accident, as we shall see, that his view culminates in a theory of *radical* evil. Kant's position is interesting in large part because he manages to retain his rational narrative while simultaneously depicting evil as profoundly real, lodged mysteriously in the free will and capable of breaking out at any time in ways that defy all explanations. Moral evil is the riderless horse in Kant's total vision; it cannot be domesticated, yet its wildness does not destroy the vision. These same points all hold for his account of moral regeneration as well. Kant's metaphysical trust may be deep, but it possesses utterly no predictive value.

Indeed, in terms of the history of Kant's philosophical development, the theory of radical evil signals his departure from an earlier, largely Leibnizian optimism, where moral evil becomes rationalized as instrumental towards the production of a greater good.[43] His position during this earlier period was not entirely consistent, for at precisely the same time that Kant would espouse an instrumentalist view in one writing,[44] he would remark elsewhere that "evil is not a means to goodness" but "arises as a by-product" of our struggle between reason and instinct.[45] Still, we can trace a fundamentally Leibnizian position from Kant's pre-critical *Considerations on Optimism* of 1759 (four years after the Lisbon earthquake) up through some of his writings on the philosophy of history in the mid-1780s. Although it is true that his Leibnizian confidence appears to weaken – or at least to change tone – over the course of this period,[46] it remains fair to say that throughout this period Kant typically finds a positive construction to place on evil: evil ultimately plays a role in the production of good.

For example, what Kant calls the "unsocial sociability of men" in his "Idea for a Universal History from a Cosmopolitan Point of View" (1784) takes root in the same appeal to our selfish natures as his later account of radical evil will. Our common tendency to subordinate moral duty to selfish desires produces "antagonism in society" and the cynical expectation that others are similarly self-interested.[47] But instead of elaborating a negative set of conclusions from this pessimistic starting point (as he will in the *Religion*), Kant goes on to argue that it is precisely our selfish natures that compel us, over time, to organize civic arrangements in increasingly rational ways. Political improvement occurs through the pressure of our having to come to practical terms with our naturally selfish and competitive original circumstance: we move from "barbarism to culture" and "thereby change a society of men driven together by their natural feelings into a moral whole."

Without those in themselves unamiable characteristics of unsociability from whence opposition springs – characteristics each man must find in his own selfish pretensions – all talents would remain hidden, unborn in an Arcadian shepherd's life, with all its concord, contentment, mutual affection... Thanks be to Nature, then, for the incompatibility, for heartless competitive vanity, for the insatiable desire to possess and to rule! Without them, all the excellent natural capacities of humanity would forever sleep, undeveloped.[48]

Kant is playing Hobbes, but Hobbes with progressive, teleological tendencies. Were it not for our selfishness, civil society would not progress.[49]

With the doctrine of radical evil in the *Religion*, the mood really is different. Here, as one commentator has fairly said, "we find ourselves in a different intellectual universe: we hear... of forces of evil which are to be defeated rather than utilized."[50] Or as we might say in the present context: here we find Kant's metaphysical trust put to its most severe test. Consequently, the metaphysical trust separating Kant and Ivan may well produce a rational narrative, but – oddly – it is not really a teleological one. Instead, it is a narrative much more like the Protestant Christian depiction of fall, justification, and reconciliation, minus the intellectual saving grace of a full-fledged doctrine of providence. Kant edges closer to Ivan precisely by breaking his earlier link between moral evil and a rationalizing teleology: the account of evil cannot be absorbed by a larger vision of purposefulness, but can only be counterbalanced by a theory of moral regeneration that is itself just as inscrutable in its workings as the original fall it is meant to offset. Kant's metaphysical trust never really translates into an "explanation" that would answer Ivan's questions. This result goes hand in hand with Kant's increasing tendency late in life to take seriously some of the more sinister implications of his own theory of freedom. The strains of agnosticism and episodes of philosophical flat-footedness that we continually confront in the *Religion* are ample evidence of this telling break from the Leibnizian way of dealing with moral evil. Kant's theory of freedom lets loose human possibilities that will not submit to conceptual control.

What Kant's view does do, however, is produce the series of wobbles I alluded to in my Introduction to this study, culminating in his oscillation between appeals to human autonomy and to divine action in his account of the salvation process. In some sense, Kant's effort to take moral evil seriously results in at least the appearance of a limitation placed on human autonomy, insofar as autonomy seems incapable of saving itself. The issue is a complex one, because this limitation arising in connection with moral regeneration goes together with a limitless and truly unfathomable freedom at the point that Kant depicts the fall into radical evil: perversely, freedom seems to have more leeway in the direction of the fall than in the direction of moral recovery. Kant is thus pressing in both directions at once, indicating in the account of evil that freedom eludes conceptual domestication, while hinting, in the account of moral regeneration, that freedom reaches a limit when it attempts to correct its own fallenness.

Moreover, we shall finally see that the difficulties associated with the wobbling in Kant's overall account are vastly compounded by the fact that his strategy for recovering from radical evil delivers his entire philosophy of religion into a subterranean yet vicious circularity. The circularity arises out of that feature of his argumentation that most explicitly distinguishes Kant from Ivan, namely, Kant's appeal to symmetry and correct proportion. For, as I have just tried to show, his appeal to symmetry is what ultimately licenses the postulation of the existence of God – the good Kantian finally gets to God because of the confidence that we live in a universe that makes sense. Reason will not be frustrated in its efforts to think out all the necessary entailments of the highest good. God turns out to be one of those.

But, as we shall see in part II of this study, in his account of moral regeneration Kant will appeal to God and divine action in order to assure that there *is* symmetry in the universe. Kant clearly appreciates that to end with radical evil would be to end in despair, futility, and a deep sense of contradiction, for if radical evil were to be the last word, then rational beings would be saddled with a sense of obligation to overcome evil but with no rational hope that such a moral triumph could actually occur. By Kant's own account, this would be the situation in which we would find ourselves if we were entirely dependent upon our autonomy, given the crippling produced by his definition of radical evil. However, Kant's whole point is that it *is* rational to hope for recovery: moral conversion *can* occur, even the most wicked among us may be regenerated. It is not futile to hope that we can act on our sense of moral obligation, which means in turn that the symmetry of the universe is assured. The oddity is that this assurance is provided by appeal to God, in the form of God's inscrutable cooperation and assistance in the regeneration process. Our own sense of moral failure and weakness is offset by the hope of a divine supplement to our imperfect efforts – this, roughly, is the heart of Kant's theory of moral regeneration.

The circularity here is palpable: whereas the postulation of God's existence in the second *Critique* relies on appeal to a symmetrical universe, the guarantee of that same symmetrical universe in the face of radical evil relies, in the *Religion*, on appeal to God. A latter-day Ivan may begin to suspect that Kant wants to have it both ways.

With these complicated matters as both background and preview, then, it is time to look more closely at Kant's actual definition of moral evil.

2

Kant's definition of moral evil

> When the will abandons the higher, and turns to what is lower, it becomes evil – not because that is evil to which it turns, but because the turning is perverse.
>
> St. Augustine

> No one can say with certainty why this man becomes good, that man evil.
>
> Kant

Overview

Kant claims that moral evil is the subordination, within a maxim, of the incentive of moral duty to the incentive of sensuous inclination or "self-love" (p. 36; p. 31). He further claims that *radical* evil is the freely-willed choice of an evil "ground" of maxim-making that results in the subordination of the moral incentive to the sensuous as a regular, ongoing policy in one's successive acts of maxim-making (p. 37; p. 32). He develops these claims in the context of a sort of contest within human nature between what he calls an "original predisposition to good" and a "natural propensity to evil," a set of terms that embodies the insight that, for Kant, the "human will is the locus of countervailing incentives, the ordering of which constitutes the moral 'self'."[1] Indeed, *Religion within the Limits of Reason Alone* is structured in large part in a manner designed to play out what Kant calls the "conflict of the good with the evil principle for sovereignty over man," leading eventually to the "victory of the good over the evil principle" – with these two expressions serving, in fact, as the titles of Books Two and Three of the *Religion* (pp. 57, 93; pp. 50, 85).

Kant's way of depicting this contest yields the important and rather surprising claim that radical evil is "innate" in human nature, for the propensity to evil is, he tells us, "entwined with and, as it were, rooted in humanity itself" (p. 32; p. 28). The claim that radical evil is innate takes Kant onto strange ground and – appropriately enough – surrounds him with odd bed-fellows. "A member of the British Parliament once exclaimed," Kant suddenly tells us, that " 'Every man has his price, for which he sells himself.' "

If this is true . . . if there is no virtue for which some temptation cannot be found capable of overthrowing it, and if whether the good or evil spirit wins us over to his party depends merely on which bids the most and pays us most promptly, then certainly it holds true of men universally, as the apostle said: "They are all under sin – there is none righteous (in the spirit of the law), no, not one." (pp. 38–9; p. 34)

Here Kant is not invoking the familiar idiom of Leibniz and Wolff, or the customary problematics of Hume and Rousseau. He has instead stepped into another world and is signalling his shift by quoting from the unlikeliest of conversation partners: Robert Walpole and St. Paul.

As we shall see on more than one occasion, Kant's claim concerning the innateness of radical evil is deeply problematic, and it is finally not clear how he can justify it or how he can possibly make sense of the idea of an "innate" exercise of freedom. It is one thing to speak of moral evil as the potential product of an act of maxim-making. Indeed, one could even say that Kant is simply deducing moral evil transcendentally, since his theory of freedom clearly serves as the necessary condition of its possibility: a theory of moral evil depicts one of the ways in which freedom can relate to the moral law, namely, in a way that subordinates the moral law to the incentive of self-love.[2]

But it is quite another thing to claim that this immoral exercise of freedom points to something innate. A transcendental argument concerning the possibility of moral evil could well be a natural elaboration of Kant's theory of freedom.[3] By contrast, the suggestion of the innateness of an underlying radical evil appears to shift us away from inquiry into freedom's possibilities to the idea of a limitation on freedom. But of course Kant does not stop with the potential limitation, as though he has cast us into an Augustinian pit from which there is no possible escape short of outside help. Since the propensity to evil neither eliminates the obligation to make ourselves good, nor fully destroys our ability to do so, Kant's position culminates in a comment that, through its very equivocalness, conveys the complexity of his viewpoint:

This evil is *radical*, because it corrupts the ground of all maxims; it is, moreover, as a natural propensity, *inextirpable* by human powers, since extirpation could occur only through good maxims, and cannot take place when the ultimate subjective ground of all maxims is postulated as corrupt; yet at the same time it must be possible to *overcome* it, since it is found in man, a being whose actions are free. (p. 37; p. 33)

To a great extent, Kant's theory of radical evil and the related account of moral regeneration constitute an extended commentary on this quotation. As he surveys these matters, Kant both draws on his earlier writings and develops fresh insights into the relationship between human nature and moral agency, erecting an extremely complicated terminological scaffolding in the process. The complexity of the material requires a piecemeal approach to Kant's language, and a good place to start is his notion of maxim-making and its relation to his definition of moral evil.

Maxim-making

Early in the *Religion*, Kant claims that

the source of evil cannot lie in an object *determining* the will through inclination, nor yet in a natural impulse; it can lie only in a rule made by the will for the use of its freedom, that is, in a maxim. (p. 21; p. 17)

A maxim is for Kant a special kind of principle, one that guides or informs action; in effect, a maxim is a "practical principle." Acting according to a maxim is equivalent to willing the action "as an instance of a concept."[4] The centrality of the maxim to Kant's delineation of the formal structure of the moral life is evident in the role it plays in Kant's categorical imperative: "Act as though the maxim of your action were by your will to become a universal law of nature."[5] The very idea of a maxim is fundamental to Kant's efforts to determine how reason can be practical, as well as to his attempt to delineate a theory of moral evil. The theory of the maxim is Kant's specific device for showing how the will can be independent of natural determination.

Moreover, discourse about maxims is Kant's way of accounting for those practical principles by which one actually does act, as opposed to those principles by which one ought ideally to act. This is presumably why Kant calls a maxim "the subjective principle of volition."[6] In effect, a maxim is the guiding principle that I could state to myself were I to reflect upon the overall policy determining a given act – e.g., "I should enrich myself by whatever means possible," "I should at all times tell the truth," "I should always put the interests of my family before the interests of strangers." This distinction between guiding principles by which I actually act and those by which I ought ideally to act arises, because Kant understands a person's maxim necessarily to be subjectively valid (it really *is* my practical principle) even though it may or may not be objectively valid (embodying the universaliz-ability requirement of the categorical imperative). A maxim is thus a subjective determining ground of the will, and its relation to the objective demands of the moral law determines the maxim's morality.

Despite Kant's familiar insistence that the morality of an act should not be judged by its end product or results, there is an important sense in which the language of ends remains pertinent to his conception of a maxim. At one point in *The Metaphysics of Morals*, Kant flatly states that "every maxim contains an end."[7] The relevant sense of "end" here is of course not the material result of a given act; rather, it is the goal or "good" that is being served or honored by the maxim in question – be it personal enrichment, respect for the truth, concern for one's relatives, or something else. The maxim *embodies* this end, and the capacity to fashion maxims – be they moral or immoral – is what keeps us from being creatures of sheer whim or perpetual childlike spontaneity. By embodying ends, maxims make manifest general life policies that give a distinctive cast to a moral agent in its successive acts, while simultaneously signaling the agent's ability even to have such policies.

Obviously, the notion of a maxim is a major component in Kant's general account of the will. This is because the will, for him, is the faculty that acts according to a conception of law in its efforts to bring about certain ends[8] and – as we have just seen – every maxim contains an end. In effect, maxims articulate the ends determining the will in its successive acts. The "will can be appraised as good or evil only by means of its maxims," Kant tells us (p. 29; p. 24). A morally good will is reflected through maxims that contain the moral law as their end. In such cases, that which is already objectively valid (the moral law) is made subjectively valid through the production of a maxim: I make the moral law my personal practical principle, thereby effectively "incarnating" the moral law through my will. The condition of the possibility of the production of a moral maxim is thus the agent's capacity for respect for the moral law. This capacity reveals the important insight that the moral law can in fact serve as an incentive in the agent's free production of maxims.

Alternatively, a genuinely free agent may choose to produce maxims containing some end other than the moral law. When this happens, the maxims do not cease to be subjectively valid (they still really are the agent's practical principles), but they do cease to be objectively valid (which is to say, they are immoral maxims). In such cases, the agent has succumbed to sensuous inclination, or the law of self-love, as his or her primary incentive. This is the point of Kant's remark that moral evil resides in a maxim.

Maxim-making and moral evil

We can begin to see that moral evil will have its most specific locus in the link between freedom and maxim-making. Part of the importance of the *Religion* resides precisely in the fact that, in this book, Kant works out this linkage and its implications in a more sustained way than anywhere else, thereby filling out features of his moral philosophy that had previously been sketchy or ambiguous. In one very specific respect, the *Religion* deepens Kant's account of moral evil and maxim-making by denying that some maxims simply have a morally good content while others have a content that is evil. The moral character of a maxim, Kant tells us, is not a matter of content at all, but of form. His point is not really a change or alteration of his basic critical teaching so much as it is a deepening of a central insight running through the *Foundations of the Metaphysics of Morals* and the *Critique of Practical Reason* – namely, the insight that the morality of an act is determined by the form of our willing, and not by the maxim's material content or by the material result of our willing. It is this insight, after all, that accounts for the purely formal character of Kant's categorical imperative. His position finds succinct expression in the *Critique of Practical Reason*:

If a rational being can think of its maxims as practical universal laws, he can do so only by considering them as principles which contain the determining grounds of the will because of this form and not because of their matter.[9]

The account in the *Religion* examines the formal structure of volition with a particular concern for the incentives informing a given maxim. The reason we cannot simply sort maxims into two camps – those with a moral incentive and those with an incentive that is sensuous – is that for Kant *every* maxim contains both moral and and sensuous incentives (p. 36; p. 31). This standpoint is in keeping with Kant's general view of human nature as simultaneously rational and finite, but he had never before made the point so clearly and explicitly in connection with the issue of maxim-making. Since a rational yet finite being is always affected by both moral and sensuous incentives – by the moral law and the law of self-love – any given maxim must necessarily be a mix of the two types of incentives. We do not suspend, bracket, or somehow ignore one incentive in the course of fashioning maxims; to conceive of the maxim-maker as driven solely by one sort of incentive or the other would be to falsify our real situation. Consequently, the question of the moral worth of a given maxim cannot simply be the question of whether the moral law, or a sensuous impulse, furnishes the incentive. For to pose the issue this way – in light of the presence always of *both* types of incentives

– would be to fall into the contradiction that the same person "would be at once good and evil" (p. 36; p. 31).

Moral evil, then, must reside not in the content of a given maxim, but in the form. Kant describes the issue in terms of the process of "subordination" (*Unterordnung*) – that is, in terms of the question concerning which of the two types of incentives the moral agent "makes the condition of the other" (p. 36; p. 31). The metaphor of subordination is telling for the way it connotes the suppression of the one sort of incentive by the other, but without involving the complete destruction or elimination of the defeated incentive. We can perhaps further refine Kant's point here and say that, whereas the distilled product of moral evil resides in the form of a maxim, *moral evil itself is a property of the act of will that freely subordinates one incentive to another, the moral to the sensuous.* That is, moral evil finally resides not so much in the form of the maxim as in the free act that creates or makes real that form. This way of putting the matter is in keeping with Kant's concern to show that, in the moral realm, freedom becomes manifest through the form of our willing and not through an empirical content. Moreover, at the time of the *Religion*, moral evil is for Kant definitely not a "lack" or a privation, but a positive reality: it *becomes* a reality, moving from not being to being real, in the course of maxim-making.[10] This fundamental point, which runs through the first two books of the *Religion*, marks a significant departure from the view that Kant espoused a decade earlier in his university lectures on philosophical theology, where he suggested that evil can be viewed as the "incompleteness in the development of the seed toward good." Evil itself "has no special seed," Kant said in that earlier context, for "it is only a negation, and consists only in a limitation of what is good."[11]

By the time of the *Religion*, Kant's views have evidently changed. Indeed, we can perhaps approach the very idea of "radical evil" as Kant's effort to locate and describe the evil "seed" he had earlier rejected. Far from being a mere limitation or negation, moral evil is a specific variety of free "doing" that gets crystallized in a maxim. Since the catalyst is an act of the will, evil is not a static mode of "being"; and since this will is, for Kant, truly autonomous, evil is not to be thought of as a fixed "essence" simply given with human nature. The structure of moral agency that frames Kant's effort to depict moral evil is given added complexity by the distinction he invokes, when speaking of the will, between *Willkür* and *Wille*. The free production of an evil maxim is an act of *Willkür*, by which Kant means the faculty of choice that is subject to both rational and sensuous incentives.[12] Kant means to denote by that aspect of the will he calls *Willkür* our actual capacity for agency, in contrast to the wholly rational *Wille*, which is the source of our respect for the moral law and very close to what must be rationality itself for Kant. That is, if *Wille* could act, it could only act out of respect for the moral law. But it cannot act; it can only provide an imperative of duty to *Willkür* which, in turn, can elect to subordinate this rational incentive to the sensuous. "The Will [*Wille*] itself has no determining ground; but insofar as it can determine will [*Willkür*], it is practical reason itself."[13]

Kant's distinction between *Wille* and *Willkür* no doubt conveys a note of arbitrariness, and the question of the exact relationship between these two aspects of a supposedly unified will is never satisfactorily addressed by Kant.[14] Bernard Carnois has noted that the problem of the coexistence in one being of "a law-giving will side by side with free choice appears so difficult to articulate and resolve within the framework of his philosophy that Kant himself never seems to have addressed it."[15] Part of the difficulty, as Carnois has shown in his effort to adduce a coherent theory of freedom in Kant's philosophy, is that Kant's use of the terminology of *Wille* and *Willkür* not only evolved over time but was not always employed consistently:

In the *Grundlegung*, *Wille* designates both autonomous will and free choice. Starting with the second *Critique*, however, the will endowed with free choice is more and more frequently called *Willkür*, the term Kant will employ almost constantly in the *Religion*. But it sometimes happens that we find *Willkür* where we would expect to see *Wille*, and vice versa.[16]

However, it is often the case with Kant's writing that a strained or awkward claim is best decoded, not with a view to resolving its tensions, but with a view to the argumentative dividends that it pays. In the case of the distinction between *Wille* and *Willkür*, the dividends are readily evident, especially if we view the distinction in the context of the problem of moral evil. For by discriminating in this way between aspects of an ultimately single and unified will, Kant is more able to explain how it is that we remain rational (and thus free, responsible, and accountable) even when we act immorally. The distinction between *Wille* and *Willkür* thus enables him, among other things, to insist that we never become wholly "devilish," actively repudiating the moral law and living beyond its reach (p. 35; p. 30). Immoral acts should not be viewed as the forfeiture of our freedom, a circumstance that would make it potentially (and ironically) impossible to attribute immorality to us. Moreover, we cannot conceive of an autonomous will that could will to give up its autonomy without falling into stark contradiction. In other words, Kant's depiction of the two aspects of the will helps him to avoid the trap of only being able to impute virtue or a brutish, amoral heteronomy to the moral agent. Even when it is subordinating the moral law to sensuous inclination,

Willkür remains subject to the incentive provided by *Wille*. Moral evil is not equivalent to the destruction of the rational capacity.[17]

Consequently, Kant tells us, even "the most wicked" person "does not, under any maxim whatsoever, repudiate the moral law in the manner of a rebel" (p. 36; p. 31). Kant effectively means here that such a person *cannot* repudiate the moral law, because of the presence of *Wille*. The fact that a wicked person can fail to give priority to the moral mandate arising out of *Wille* is an act of *Willkür*, but this does not amount to the destruction of a latent moral potentiality. As we shall see in connection with Kant's account of moral regeneration, this point takes on considerable importance as Kant tries to explain how it is that we retain the capacity to overcome an evil that is radical.

The "predisposition to good" and the "propensity to evil"

A distinctive feature of *Religion within the Limits of Reason Alone* is the way Kant interweaves closely-defined details of his moral philosophy – such as his account of maxim-making – with sweeping generalizations about human nature. The first two of the four Books of the *Religion*, in particular, amount to a Kantian treatise on human nature. The account of radical evil arises out of a more general Kantian concern for how we freely mobilize and order our natural stock of human potentialities. Kant's description and assessment of these potentialities both dictates much of the total action of the book and draws his rationalist ethical idiom into surprisingly close contact with the idiom of Christian orthodoxy. Because of what he says about human nature, for example, the *Religion* as a whole can just as easily be read as a Kantian soteriology – surprisingly orthodox in many of its features – as it can be read as a reduction of religious belief to moral action, which is the reading the book mainly invites.[18]

It is in connection with the theme of human potentialities and basic human nature that Kant introduces his troublesome terms "predisposition" (*Anlage*) and "propensity" (*Hang*). We have an "original predisposition to good," Kant tells us, together with a "natural propensity to evil." The burden of the first two Books of the *Religion* is to examine these fundamental features of human nature and their relationship to one another. One might further say that the burden of Kant's entire moral–religious philosophy is to chart the careers of these two features of human nature in a universe that is presumed to be rational.

Broadly construed, the point of Kant's language about the original predisposition to good and the natural propensity to evil is to enable him to argue that evil arises from what we freely do with what we are naturally given, rather than from what we are naturally given taken by itself. Obviously, Kant cannot make any natural human characteristic the root cause of evil, for evil could then be said to be necessitated by something given in human nature, severing the connection between moral evil and freedom of the will. He in fact criticizes the Stoics (whom Kant otherwise clearly admires) for locating the source of evil "in the merely undisciplined natural inclinations" (p. 57; p. 50). The source of evil must be something for which a rational agent can be held accountable (p. 35; p. 30). Put differently: moral evil is not contained analytically in the sheer concept of "rational being" or "human nature." At the same time, the source of moral evil must have an intrinsic connection with what is unique to rational beings, if Kant is not to see his account of moral evil dissolve into a mere aspect of a general theory of natural evil. For Kant, perhaps more than for any other modern thinker, there has to be a constitutive difference between the reprehensible acts we confront in Ivan's examples and the tragedies associated with natural disasters such as earthquakes, diseases, and floods. Furthermore, any convincing account of moral evil must keep in view our finite, sensuous nature, taking care not to ascribe to us the sort of "holy will" that would be immune to natural human drives and incentives, thereby robbing virtue of its merit by making it automatic.

As a result, Kant must walk a fine line between attributing moral evil to something naturally given in human nature and attributing it to some force or capacity utterly irrelevant to basic human nature. The purpose of the vocabulary of predisposition and propensity is to enable him to walk this fine line.

The term "predisposition" is Kant's way of talking about basic human nature as it is prior to any actual exercise of freedom. We are not "really" what we essentially are until we exercise our freedom; the idea that we "make ourselves" is close to being the animating center of Kant's entire philosophical anthropology. But we are surely *something* prior to that point, and the notion of an original predisposition enables Kant to map out what that is. Kant's aim, in effect, is to take a kind of anthropological inventory, and in so doing he specifies three original predispositions: the predispositions to animality, humanity, and personality (pp. 26–8; pp. 21–3). The three correspond, roughly, to: physical "self-love" (providing for our preservation as a species); a self-love that is both physical and rational (producing the inclination "to acquire worth in the opinion of others"); and "the capacity for respect for the moral law" as a sufficient incentive for the will (pp. 26–7; pp. 22–3). [19]

The key here is the predisposition to personality. Personality is virtually synonymous with what Kant – both in the *Religion* and elsewhere – calls "moral feeling" (p. 27; p. 23).[20] Moral feeling is evidently the product of *Wille* and represents a peculiar crossbreeding of the rational and affective in Kant's ethical theory. It is an interesting instance of Kant's drawing together a theory of the logical structure of moral volition and the moral psychology of the agent. We may perhaps think of moral feeling as the form taken by the moral law when the moral law presents itself as an incentive for the agent's *Willkür*: the moral law gains purchase on a rational yet finite being in the form of moral feeling.[21] Lewis White Beck has made the interesting point that, strictly speaking, the moral law taken by itself is never our incentive, for a "law is just not the sort of thing that can be an incentive."[22] Instead, it is the *consciousness* of the moral law that is our incentive, and this consciousness is mediated to us in the form of moral feeling.

Moral feeling is thus synonymous with respect for the moral law, (pp. 27–8; p. 23)[23] and "personality," as we have just seen, is the capacity for respect for the moral law as a sufficient incentive for determining the will. Kant normally calls feelings "pathological," even when the feeling in question is one that would seem to be intrinsically good or desirable, such as the feeling of love.[24] His concern in so doing is the protection of the purity of the incentives of practical reason: even seemingly positive feelings are, in effect, polluted by their empirical, as opposed to rational, origin.[25] Olivier Reboul has suggested that "respect" is for Kant the only "practical" – as opposed to pathological – feeling, due to the fact that it is absolutely disinterested. The absence of disinterestedness is for Kant the polluting factor in acts of maxim-making, which is what lies behind Reboul's dictum that "heteronomy is the triumph of impurity over disinterestedness."[26] This disinterestedness elevates, as it were, the feeling of respect to the point where, in this one case, a certain feeling plays a constructive, if not decisive, role in Kant's depiction of the incentives of practical reason.

The predisposition to personality thus gives us the potential to be truly rational beings in our moral conduct, while the two other predispositions are Kant's ways of giving full credit to our finite, fallible side, understood both in strictly sensuous and in social terms. All three predispositions – and not merely the predisposition to personality – are good in themselves (p. 28; p. 23). Kant goes further even than this and states that natural "inclinations, *considered in themselves, are good*" (p. 58; p. 51). Although it remains true to say that Kant's moral philosophy continues the Platonic–Augustinian denigration of the bodily and sensual – a codifying of the moral good in terms calling for the subordination of, if not the total suppression of, what is physical and instinctual – he never flatly states that the body is bad.[27] Moral evil is never understood by Kant as sheer sensuality running amok by its own steam. Instead, moral evil must always involve the free act that subordinates the moral law to sensuous inclinations. "Evil could have sprung only from the morally-evil (not from mere limitations in our nature)..." (p. 43; p. 38). Kant's account of the predispositions thus exemplifies his view of our potentialities as rational yet finite creatures. These potentialities have very clear limits on both ends of the spectrum, for Kant specifies that we cannot become purely animal-like (operating solely by sensuous inclination) or truly devilish (actively repudiating the moral law so that it could no longer be an incentive) (p. 35; p. 30), any more than we could reasonably expect ever to have a genuinely "holy" will (*Wille* without *Willkür*).[28] All three predispositions remain in place, effectively channeling our potentialities in ways that are roughly fixed.

Goodness or evil are thus the result of what we do with these potentialities. Though the potentialities are fixed – in the sense that we cannot be held accountable for them – what we do with them is not fixed. The original predispositions effectively constitute the hand we are initially dealt, while what we make of this hand, or how we play it, depends upon the way we ourselves introduce the wild card of freedom. The concept of the predispositions enables Kant to exploit the difference between saying we are "created *for good*" (which he endorses) and saying we are "already actually good" prior to any act of freedom (which he denies) (p. 44; p. 40).

It is just here that Kant's notion of a "propensity" comes into play. There is considerable confusion over just what he could possibly mean by this term, produced in large part by his tortured basic definition of a propensity as "the subjective ground of the possibility of an inclination" (p. 28; p. 23).[29] The force of the term "subjective" here is to connote the element of free choice (*Willkür*) attending the idea of a propensity, an element of choice clearly lacking in the case of the predispositions. That is, whereas we have no choice in the matter of what our original predispositions will be, there will be choice (and thus potential culpability) in the matter of at least some of our propensities. At the same time, however, there is evidently both a limit in the range of our potential propensities and a link between our given sensuous nature and those propensities Kant labels "physical" propensities (p. 31; p. 26). Both of these features of Kant's theory – especially the second – create severe gray areas in the matter of the connection between freedom and the propensities. Similarly, if the only kind of "inclination" we can conceive of is the kind arising out of our sensuous nature, it is not clear how Kant can intelligibly connect that term with the element of freedom attending the idea of a "subjective ground" as it appears in his basic definition of a propensity. Freely electing certain inclinations, and not others, in *this* sense would be roughly equivalent to freely deciding what aspects of the "predisposition to animality" we wanted to feel affected by.

Clearly, Kant cannot simply mean physical, sensuous inclinations in his initial definition of propensity. The term "inclination" here has to connote something broader – involving the general idea of an "incentive" – for Kant's subsequent account of the propensity to evil to make sense.[30] That is, what we are perhaps seeing here is Kant's attempt to show how we *can* be held accountable for an incentive structure that has at least part of its basis in something for which we *cannot* be held accountable, namely, our sensuousness. Moreover, Kant seems on the whole to be less interested in elaborating a general theory of propensities (along the lines of his general theory of predispositions) than in utilizing the concept of a propensity in order to zero in on one particular "subjective ground of the possibility of an inclination." The particular subjective ground in question is the one lying behind our general tendency to deviate from the moral law – this general tendency, rather than episodic or occasional and disconnected lapses, is what interests Kant. The entire account of radical evil toward which Kant is moving is in fact based on the insight that there is an inevitable pattern connected with our willing of evil maxims, and the notion of the propensity is Kant's way of transcendentally delineating this pattern without allowing its inevitability to turn into outright necessity.

Consequently, now we find Kant saying that the "propensity to evil must consist in the subjective ground of the possibility of the deviation of the maxims from the moral law" (p. 29; p. 24). If we are not simply to ignore his initial definition of a propensity as the subjective ground of the possibility of an *inclination*, we have to consider the relation between "inclination," in that context, and "deviation of the maxims from the moral law" in this second formulation. Again, what I think we are seeing – although admittedly not very clearly – is Kant trying to theorize a bridge between our sensuous nature and moral culpability, a bridge that leaves sensuousness blameless, when taken by itself, while still managing to refer to it in the account of moral evil. This approach on Kant's part makes a kind of sense, since, as we have already seen, evil consists of the subordination, within a maxim, of the incentive of the moral law to that of sensuous inclination. We now learn that the idea of a propensity suggests the way in which sensuous inclinations get the upper hand, so to speak, in the formation of maxims. To be sure, the propensity to evil does not explain how or why the subordination of the moral to the sensuous occurs; indeed, one of the chief aims of this entire study is to underscore the complete mystery associated with the exercise of an evil will in Kant's account. Yet the propensity to evil does explain the sheer potentiality that is required for there ever to be moral evil in the world. This is significant, since Kant's theorizing about our original predispositions leaves a gap in respect of just this potentiality, in light of his insistence that all of our predispositions are good in themselves. That is to say: Kant's theory of the predispositions accounts for all of our potential in life, *except* for our potential to become morally evil.

In the light of the obvious importance of the notion of a propensity for Kant's total account of radical evil, it is unfortunate in the extreme that he does not spell out more explicitly the meaning of the term. He does give an example of what he means, but the example – besides having a repugnant content – appears to transfer us out of the moral realm and into the physical or natural realm in a way that diminishes the example's explanatory power. A propensity, Kant tells us, is a tendency "to crave a delight which, when once experienced, arouses in the subject an *inclination* to it."

Thus all savage people have a propensity for intoxicants; for though many of them are wholly ignorant of intoxication and in consequence have absolutely no craving for an intoxicant, let them but once sample it and there is aroused in them an almost inextinguishable craving for it. (p. 28n.; p. 24n.)

Kant goes on to remark that between "inclination, which presupposes acquaintance with the object of desire," and the term propensity, there is the term "*instinct*, which is a felt want to do or to enjoy something of which one has as yet no conception (such as... the sexual impulse)." And "beyond" inclination there is "a further stage in the faculty of desire, *passion* (not *emotion*, for this has to do with the feeling of pleasure and pain), which is an inclination that excludes the mastery over oneself" (pp. 28–9n.; p. 24n.).

Kant is evidently trying to devise a kind of calculus of sensuousness here. An interesting feature of this set of comments is the fact that the terms "inclination" and "propensity" mean – in this context, at least – virtually the same thing, the difference between them being that, in the case of an inclination, one has actual "acquaintance with the object of desire." A propensity evidently *becomes* an inclination when one "meets" whatever is craved. In one way, this distinction helps to clarify the point of Kant's original definition of a propensity as "the subjective ground of the *possibility* of an inclination." Viewed another way, however, Kant's position here does not seem to keep adequately sorted out the physical aspects of the idea of a propensity from the moral aspects, a confusion that is compounded by the example of a propensity for intoxicants. For as we have seen, if the only sense of "inclination" packed into his definition of a propensity is a purely physical, sensuous inclination, it is a feature of human nature that would have related analytically to the predisposition to animality. In such a case, there could be no legitimate task of a *subjective* ground of the possibility of an inclination, if the force of the term "subjective" here is to connote our free act. The predisposition to animality, after all, is simply a sophisticated device for packaging all our natural sensuous impulses under a single rubric. It would make no sense to speak of a subjective ground of the possibility of something naturally given.

Kant seems to need more argumentative maneuvering room than his initial definition of a propensity has afforded him. His problem emerges out of his effort somehow to couple the insight that a propensity relates to the possibility of an inclination with the insight that a propensity is something that can be regarded as having been "acquired," "brought upon" ourselves, (p. 29; p. 24) and for which we are "accountable" (p. 35; p. 30). Despite the fact that he has embraced the idea that a propensity relates to the possibility of an inclination, he needs to keep adequate space between these terms if he is to make a case for a propensity toward moral evil. For by his own terms, an "inclination" toward evil would mean, in effect, that we had already "met" evil prior to any free act.

Kant helps his case when he admits that a "physical propensity" can involve no moral culpability, claiming that the notion of a "physical propensity" directed "towards any use of freedom whatsoever – whether for good or bad – is a contradiction" (p. 31; p. 26). This admission seems to wreak havoc with his original connection between a propensity and the possibility of an inclination. The contrast case to a "physical propensity" is what Kant calls "a subjective determining ground of the will which *precedes all acts*" (p. 31; p. 26). Kant will explicitly call the propensity to evil a propensity in this sense, even paraphrasing it at that point as *peccatum originarium* (p. 31; p. 26). The term propensity in this fresh sense seems to be a way of talking about our incentives, or incentive structure. Obviously, at least some of the conceptual difficulties are dissolved away once Kant drops the reference to inclinations in his account of the idea of a propensity. But it is not clear that we are any closer to grasping why Kant should be proposing that there is something natural and inevitable about the propensity to evil.

Nonetheless, it is possible to grasp and chart out some of Kant's more general aims regarding the idea of the propensity to evil. For in light of the Kantian premise that our sensuous, embodied existence by itself carries no moral blame, his notion of a propensity can perhaps be viewed as a conceptual probe into the moral dimensions that eventually do arise out of our sensuous condition. The terms "inclination," "instinct," "passion," and

"emotion" finally do have moral relevance and suggest a kind of scale, meas-
uring the relationship between sensuousness and freedom. One cannot
freely elect to eliminate the sexual instinct, any more than one can decide to
keep the pupil of the eye from reacting involuntarily to the light. But one can
evidently exercise considerable freedom in channeling or deploying sexual
drives, just as one can get in out of the sun. Through moral discipline, one
gains a measure of control over the inclinations arising naturally out of
instincts, and the careful cultivation of one's propensities is the chief agent
in this disciplining process. The term "propensity" suggests the premise of
a certain control over one's inclinations, just as – by Kant's definition – the
term "passion" is an inclination out of control, "an inclination that excludes
the mastery over oneself."

The concept of a propensity, then, is part of a complex network of discrimi-
nations evidently intended to help Kant to plot out the several ways in which
our finite, sensuous side abuts on the moral life. His position is a kind of
polite preview of the Freudian project, in the sense that – upon inspection –
a presumably rational being turns out to be subject to a vast and powerful
array of dynamic, hidden, and natural forces, forces that can blind even the
most intelligent and insightful person to his or her true motivations in public
life. The key difference between Kant and Freud is of course Kant's commitment to a full-blooded theory of autonomy. In light of Kant's mapping out
of the ways our sensuousness bears on the moral life, then, we might propose
that the term propensity is (unlike, say, the terms "instinct" or "passion") a
Kantian device for depicting the way in which we can exercise some responsibility over, and thereby be held accountable for, our sensuous inclinations.
We cannot *help* having inclinations, and thus moral evil cannot simply be
attributed to the bald fact that we have them; but the moral life ultimately
consists of a contest within the will between the rational and the sensuous
in a process of subordination, as the will freely creates its own incentive
structure. The notion of a propensity is Kant's way of fashioning a corridor
between sensuousness and the moral life in a way that preserves both
freedom and our real condition as beings possessing the predisposition to
animality, for which we cannot be held accountable. In other words, the term
propensity is Kant's way of guaranteeing that his analysis of human nature
preserves some sort of accountability with respect to the sensuous life, which
is otherwise a life that is simply "given" by nature.

It remains true, however, that Kant's specific example of what he calls
"savages" and the propensity for intoxicants no doubt begs the question at
stake by remaining confined to a purely physical propensity. Aside from this
example, Kant only speaks of the propensity to evil. It may be that he in fact

44

means to draw an analogy between a craving for more intoxicants and a craving for more evil, once it has been tasted.[31] But the analogy would then be an extremely selective one, since it is not offset by another analogy depicting a propensity for good. There is thus some confusion – or what one commentator has aptly called a "lack of symmetry"[32] – in Kant's account of moral motivation as it crystallizes in his theory of the propensities. There is no intrinsic reason why the notion of a propensity should have only a negative or evil connotation. Yet Kant does not correct this asymmetry by suggesting what a positive or morally beneficial propensity might be. One might respond by suggesting that our capacity for being moral has already been provided for in what Kant has said about the predispositions. But this response would then only raise the question of why what Kant is attempting to chart out in the account of propensities was not initially integrated into his theory of the predispositions.

There is, moreover, a further difficulty injected by Kant's discrimination among "three distinct degrees" of the "capacity for evil" (p. 29; p. 24). Kant designates these as: "frailty," or weakness of will; "impurity," or the tendency to keep the moral incentive from being self-sufficient by diluting it with other incentives; and "wickedness," which is the explicit reversal of the proper ethical order of the incentives determining the will (pp. 29–30; pp. 24–5). Kant elaborates on these three degrees only in the barest way. His account leaves unclear whether he is saying that the propensity to evil itself comes in these degrees, or if only "wickedness" is an expression of this propensity. Furthermore, given Kant's insistence that both the moral and the sensuous incentives are present in *all* acts of maxim-making, the point of his idea of "impurity" – the "propensity for mixing unmoral with moral motivating causes" (p. 29; p. 24) – is not at all clear. If he means the tendency to subordinate the moral to the sensuous, then the idea of the impurity of the will simply collapses into what Kant calls wickedness. But if he means the competing presence of both kinds of incentives, then Kant seems to be casting in a pejorative light what he elsewhere proposes as the normal and natural situation in which all rational beings who are also sensuous beings find themselves (p. 36; p. 31). We might say that, insofar as Kant's account of radical evil appears only to involve what he is here calling "wickedness" (*Bösartigkeit*), it is not at all clear what the point of the other two degrees of evil is, or whether they are in fact examples of "moral" evil.[33]

One thing that is clear is Kant's insistence that the sheer propensity to evil is not evil itself any more than a given predisposition or inclination is evil in and of itself. Such a result would be too much like associating moral evil with a natural property. Instead, this propensity is the sheer tendency to

45

subordinate the moral law to sensuous inclination in the fashioning of our maxims: by itself, it always remains in *potential*. Whether or not we actually *do* deviate from the moral law in this way is not predetermined but depends in each instance upon a discrete act of freedom. As Kant explains, by the notion of a propensity "we understand a subjective determining ground of the will which *precedes all acts* and which, therefore, is itself not an act" (p. 31; p. 26).[34] Kant clearly believes that all rational beings do in fact succumb to the propensity to evil, but the absence of genuine argumentation for this crucial point is one of the most outstanding features of the entire *Religion*. At the crucial moment in his account, Kant offers a purely empirical argument for the claim that we are "evil by nature."

He is evil *by nature*, means but this, that evil can be predicated of man as a species; not that such a quality can be inferred from the concept of his species (that is, of man in general) – for then it would be necessary; but rather that from what we know of man through experience we cannot judge otherwise of him, or, that we may presuppose evil to be subjectively necessary to every man, even to the best. (p. 32; p. 27)

We shall have occasion to look more closely at Kant's claim regarding the universality of moral evil in chapters 3 and 4 in connection with the more direct account of radical evil. For now, it is simply worth noting the peculiarity of this appeal to experience, one which cannot possibly support the argumentative weight Kant seems to be placing on it. Invariably – but not necessarily – a capacity for evil in principle becomes the production of evil in fact. But Kant can hardly appeal *to* a matter of fact to make this case.

Somewhat clearer is the reasoning behind Kant's linkage between the propensity to evil (whether or not it is universal) and individual accountability. Since moral evil must ultimately arise out of freedom (instead of from a fixed human nature), Kant observes that propensities – unlike predispositions – can be brought upon ourselves, which, as we have seen, can only mean that we have some control over our inclinations (p. 29; p. 24). Moreover, because Kant thinks that the propensity to evil is universal ("this propensity can be considered as belonging universally to mankind..." [p. 29; p. 24]), he is finally led to the seemingly paradoxical judgment that evil is both freely elected and "innate" (pp. 21, 32, 42; pp. 17, 28, 38), a view that would appear to rob either "freedom" or "innateness" of its point.[35] In any case, it is because of this claim concerning "a *radical* innate *evil* in human nature" (p. 32; p. 28) that Kant flatly states that "man is evil by nature" (p. 32; p. 27), thereby giving peers such as Goethe good reason for worry. Yet Kant himself is evidently satisfied that he has avoided making the phrase, "evil by nature," synonymous with the phrase, "evil by necessity," since he has reached his conclusion through an account of human potentialities – all of which require specific acts of freedom to pass from potentiality to actuality. "We are accountable," Kant tells us, "for the propensity to evil..." (p. 35; p. 30).

Summary

The account of human nature informing Kant's view of moral evil thus consists of a series of delicate balancing acts. His method in the execution of these balancing acts might fruitfully have been more nuanced, for it is sometimes unclear where balancing shades off into self-contradiction. Kant's main problem is that his basic definition of moral evil turns on the threefold idea that: sensuous incentives gain the upper hand in the formation of maxims; sensuousness is naturally given, and we are therefore not to be blamed for feeling the effects of our sensuousness; we can exercise freedom over the ways in which sensuous incentives affect us, and perhaps even over what sensuous inclinations we actually have. Kant tells us at one point that "inclinations merely make difficult the *execution* of the good maxim which opposes them" (p. 58n.; p. 51n.). One implication of this comment is that inclinations never make the execution of the good maxim "impossible." Another implication Kant draws out himself: "genuine evil consists in this, that a man does not *will* to withstand those inclinations when they tempt him to transgress" (p. 58n.; p. 51n.). The self-legislating capacity that is at the center of Kant's positive conception of freedom is, in large part, the capacity to suppress, control, and re-order what is naturally given to us as sensuous beings. The latent pathos running through this depiction of our earthly circumstance concerns not only the inevitable struggle the moral life thus becomes for each one of us, but the fact that Kant is on his way to arguing that it is a struggle that we will all inevitably lose.

In tracing out this position, Kant is not only on the way to a distinctive theory of radical evil, but he is distinguishing his position on moral evil from the other available options in late eighteenth century European culture.[36] As long as Kant emphasized a basically Leibnizian instrumentalist view of evil, he was not offering an original and independent standpoint so much as he was serving as a prestigious representative of one of the positions already current by the time he reached intellectual maturity. His account in *Religion within the Limits of Reason Alone* will set him apart and – most telling of all – please no one. For some interpreters,[37] Kant's position in the *Religion* does not signal a fundamental change in point of view so much as it represents a long-needed systematic working out of certain implications of his theory of the will. While such an interpretation helpfully locates an undeniable continuity between the views in the *Religion* and certain features of Kant's earlier position, it seems to undervalue the very real change in sensibility introduced by the first two books of the *Religion*. These are not writings that fit comfortably within the Enlightenment, nor are they the predictable follow-up effort to smooth out rough features of the *Foundations of the Metaphysics of Morals* and the *Critique of Practical Reason*. Both the basic position and, especially, the tone of the *Religion* are sufficiently different as to make it extremely problematic to place too much emphasis on continuity. But it must be said that it is just as difficult to pinpoint the reasons for a change in Kant's point of view on the matter of moral evil, a change that one would suspect might be forced by life experience, but regarding which Kant is characteristically reticent.[38]

The odd ground Kant is carving out for himself is amply attested to by the fact that he eventually finds himself offending both Goethe *and* the Prussian censor – a feat probably achieved by no other thinker of the day. The offense to Goethe, as we have seen, is produced by the similarities between Kant's view and the traditional doctrine of original sin. Here, Kant sets himself apart from a host of Enlightenment peers by lodging moral evil in the will, rather than finding its source in ignorance or societal pressures. This has the effect of producing a divide between Kant and the more characteristic Enlightenment thinker who would view humanity's "natural benevolence" (to use Voltaire's expression) as the true basis of religion – a position, as Norman Hampson once characterized it, that had "come a long way from original sin."[39] For all the influence on Kant of Rousseau, there is a very clear parting of the ways between the two thinkers on the question of evil. Kant flatly rejects Rousseau's notion that an originally good human nature is corrupted by society, as though culpability resides in something that overrides individual accountability.[40] Kant's approach has the effect of turning our attention to a failure in one's own individual will. By contrast, in playing out the broadly Platonic tradition that associates evil with ignorance – thus making evil always corrigible in principle – Rousseau would turn our attention to our surroundings. Alter our educational and civic arrangements – design them against the background assumption of an inherently good and innocent creature that wants only to flourish in creativity and community – and people really will become "better." It has been said of Rousseau that an "essentially pagan affirmation of the natural goodness of man" is a "central doctrine and premise" of his thought, and that he "emphatically and repeatedly rejected" the orthodox Christian notion "that man is originally evil but that his natural state of innocence was destroyed by original sin."[41] In terms of this comparison, it is noteworthy that Kant is closer to the Christian view than to Rousseau's. By rejecting Rousseau's lodging of moral culpability in one's social surroundings rather than in one's own will, and by arguing that both virtue and evil are independent of environmental circumstance, Kant marks out a major cultural divide that continues to influence life in the modern West and which is near the surface of countless debates over public policy. Though it has been said, with respect to his appearance and reality distinction, that Kant was a kind of closet Platonist all his life,[42] he is clearly no Platonist on the question of evil. Moral evil for him is the unaccountable and free process by which one sort of incentive overwhelms another in the process of moral agency. No mere epistemological flaw, evil is a deep predicate of the free will and, for just this reason, is utterly mysterious.

From Goethe's standpoint, Kant's position is almost criminally regressive. From another standpoint, however, we can appreciate that Kant's evolution away from Leibnizian instrumentalism is of a piece with his general philosophical repudiation of the stagnant forms in which Leibnizianism had come to expression in Kant's day in the philosophy of Wolff.[43] In the years following the great Lisbon earthquake of 1755, there would be much discussion of the general problem of evil, but not really much fresh reflection on the more specific question of moral evil. A work such as Voltaire's *Candide* might appear to be an exception, though in comparison with Kant's *Religion* it appears less like an examination of moral evil than an account of ignorance coupled with a debunking of false optimism. In addition to Kant's own earlier rationalist–Leibnizian instrumentalist view, the available options on the specific question of moral evil (as opposed to physical or natural evil) mainly consisted of the two extremes of the orthodox Christian conception of original sin and variations on the environmental account represented by Rousseau.[44] From the standpoint of the former view, we inherit the sin of Adam and thus come into the world already needing grace. Alternatively, from the standpoint of the latter view, we enter the world in innocence or with a natural benevolence and commit evil only to the extent that we are corrupted by an environment too influenced by the ideology and social machinery produced by the first standpoint. This second view would be a natural expression of most forms of deism, which tended to find their inspiration in Locke's *tabula rasa* – applied, in this case, to human nature itself. Consequently, in the view of the vast majority of Kant's natural conversation partners, both clarity about human nature and prospects for cultural progress rely heavily on expunging the destructive effects of the first, largely Christian view, for "submission to organized religion is a betrayal of man's true estate."[45]

In the case of the question of moral evil, then – as in the case of his transcendental revolution in philosophical method generally – Kant is both filling a vacuum and fashioning a hybrid position.[46] Moral evil is the positive result of something we do, and not merely the absence of good or the unfortunate effect of the accidents of environment. We are not the passive or ignorant recipients of events beyond our control in the production of moral evil, but the active producers.

At the same time, however, we retain both the power and the obligation to overcome moral evil: we should not passively await the effects of grace. We have, after all, an "original predisposition to good" and do not "inherit" the sin of Adam or anyone else. "In the search for the rational origin of evil actions, every such action must be regarded as though the individual had fallen into it directly from a state of innocence" (p. 41; p. 36).[47] Both Christianity *and* Enlightenment optimism have rightful claims in the formulation of the problem of evil. Just as evil is not merely the regrettable product of ignorance and circumstance, it is not the premise for a full-blown theory of divine grace either. It is not really an eclecticism coming to expression here in Kant's position so much as it is the inevitable result of his lifelong immersion in both pietism and Wolffian rationalism, producing within a single viewpoint the competing demands for what is personal and highly individualistic on the one hand, and for what is abstract and rather coldly universal on the other.[48] The potentially paradoxical – and certainly unstable – character of his view is aptly captured in the notion that moral evil for Kant is the product of a *rational act*. Such a formula really is the net effect of Kant's account of free agency and maxim-making, the fall-out of his effort to connect freedom to the process by which the moral incentive is subordinated to the sensuous in the formation of an evil maxim.

Consequently, Kant's position not only distinguishes his from the alternative views of the day, but it assures that the problem of moral regeneration for the individual can never be offset or superseded by any general account of social or historical progress. This is to say that the strong role played in his theory of moral evil by personal, individual accountability and responsibility can never be absorbed into a wider narrative concerning moral progress viewed at the corporate level. Such a wider narrative may hint at the ways in which history may move in a progressive direction, but it cannot account for how an individual moral agent may convert from evil to virtue. This is a crucial point, because it so happens that much of the second half of the *Religion* is devoted to precisely such a theory of moral progress, conceived in terms of what Kant calls the "ethical commonwealth" and the gradual approximation of the "kingdom of God on earth."[49] Commentators have pointed out for a long time that the *Religion* appears stratified along two tracks, the one concerning the individual, personal moral and religious life, the other concerning our moral and religious lives as lived out at the social, corporate level.[50] As we shall see in the course of tracing out the specific problem of radical evil and its consequences, there can be no easy appeal to the corporate level as a solution to the *individual's* task of moral regeneration. Such is the bitter consequence of Kant's highly individualistic account of the freedom of the will and accountability in moral matters. One implication of this result is that Kant's own effort to view history teleologically and propose a general theory of cultural progress is made vastly more difficult – if not undermined altogether – by what he has to say about radical evil.

3

"This evil is radical..."

What comes out of the mouth proceeds from the heart, and this defiles a man.

Matthew 15:18

Radical evil and the disposition

The cumbersome terminological scaffolding that stands in the background of Kant's view of radical evil can be misleading. It can create the impression that the theory of radical evil is a somewhat isolated and highly technical component within Kant's total ethical theory, a component that Kant momentarily sets off for special attention to fill out a picture potentially left incomplete by the *Foundations of the Metaphysics of Morals* and the *Critique of Practical Reason.*[1] But the theory of radical evil is not a corrective to the earlier ethical writings, but a crucial part of Kant's larger vision of the creation of a moral universe. As I have been suggesting, Kant envisions reality as a meaningful arena of human–divine cooperation in the creation of a morally good universe. Insofar as moral evil is a threat to the realization of this universe, it is a threat to the very meaning of life; even more, then, will an evil that is *radical* exist as a threat. Consequently, however cumbersome his account of this issue may be, the account is absolutely central to Kant's effort to define and justify his most comprehensive vision of the destiny of rational beings.

We have seen that Kant means by moral evil the subordination, within a maxim, of the incentive of moral duty to the incentive of sensuous inclination, or self-love. This subordination occurs through the free exercise of the will. To express the matter rather crudely, one could further say that *radical* evil means *always* subordinating the moral to the sensuous in our acts of maxim-making. Yet Kant's real point in connection with the adjective "radical" is finally not so much a quantitative as a qualitative one. Kant's deeper point is conveyed by his comment that, because of radical evil, the "cast of mind" is "corrupted at its root" (p. 30; p. 25), producing a "foul taint in our race" (p. 38; p. 34). He works his position out with the help of his notion of the "disposition" (*Gesinnung*), as well as through further elaboration of the term "propensity": his account of the disposition enables him to explain how one's entire cast of mind comes to moral ruin, guaranteeing evil maxims without eliminating the role played by freedom in the act of maxim-making; and his delineation of a propensity to evil ultimately licenses Kant's seemingly self-contradictory claim that we are evil "by nature" (p. 32; p. 27). Taken together, the roles played by the disposition and the propensity to evil produce the very real similarity between Kant's theory of radical evil and the Christian doctrine of original sin.[2]

Kant's notion of the disposition not only lies behind the adjective, "radical," but it begins to answer some of the questions produced by his view of the relation between moral evil and maxim-making. A moment's reflection suggests that to appreciate that it is the form and not the content of a maxim that determines its moral character is not yet to apprehend how and why we become morally evil. Consequently, one emerging question concerns the connection between freedom and the form of a given maxim. By turning our attention away from the content of a given maxim to its form, Kant is directing our attention to the autonomous act by which the moral agent subordinates one sort of incentive to another. Evil, like virtue, somehow arises out of this process of subordination and becomes real or actual insofar as it becomes a property of this process of free election. It is precisely because Kant draws this connection between moral evil and a specific, free, and active process of subordination that he departs from the tradition, popular among other Enlightenment figures, that construes evil in terms of either ignorance or the mere absence of good.

But what can be said about this process of subordination? How is the form of a given maxim determined? What can be said about the connection between freedom and the form of a given maxim? What accounts for moral evil?

Kant will of course never answer the last of these questions, since an answer would involve "explaining" an exercise of freedom. But he sheds considerable light on aspects of the other questions through his account of the disposition, giving point to the expression, "radical evil," in the process. Moreover, his account of the connection between the disposition and radical evil is precisely what creates the difficulties associated with the process of moral regeneration. The "fall" of the disposition turns out to constitute both an evil that is radical *and* a moral problem from which we appear to be unable to save ourselves through our own freedom. This is because a moral regeneration occurring through our own powers could only find its resource in a good disposition; but such a resource is of course unavailable because it is precisely the existence of an *evil* disposition that produces the need for moral regeneration in the first place. In effect, a "fallen freedom" has created the awful paradox that it is morally obligated to save itself but cannot: a fallen freedom faces a seemingly impossible command. The disposition thus becomes the crucial term in Kant's account of fall and salvation and thereby merits special scrutiny.

Together with his claim that moral evil resides in the form, and not the content, of a given maxim, Kant offers the related claim that the form of the maxim is freely determined by "an underlying common ground, itself a maxim" (p. 20; p. 16). The underlying common ground of *all* of our maxims is what Kant calls the subjective disposition: the disposition, Kant tells us, is "the ultimate subjective ground of the adoption of maxims" (p. 25; p. 20). If a given disposition in fact belongs to a rational being, it must further be understood as unified (not fragmented or chaotic) and as applying to the individual's total exercise of freedom (p. 25; p. 20). Yet as itself a kind of maxim, the disposition is not produced by or grounded in anything other than freedom, since for Kant the whole point of a maxim is that it is a practical principle made by a free will. The force of the term "subjective" in Kant's definition of the disposition as the "ultimate subjective ground of the adoption of maxims" is to underscore the required element of freedom.

The disposition is thus a kind of "mega-maxim" – or, as Kant himself sometimes terms it, the "supreme maxim" (*die oberste Maxime*) (p. 31; p. 26) – that arises out of a free act and gives characteristic tendencies or patterns to our various acts of maxim-making.[3]

The supposed *unity* of the disposition, together with the fact that it serves as the ground of the production of maxims, is what lies behind the expression, "radical evil." If individual maxims are the formal locus of moral evil, and if all maxims find their source in a unified ground that has become wicked, then moral evil pervades the entire being of the moral agent in a "radical" way: "This evil is *radical* because it corrupts the ground of all maxims... [T]he cast of mind is thereby corrupted at its root (so far as the moral disposition is concerned)" (pp. 37, 30; pp. 32, 25). Moreover, the unity of the disposition is what allows us (in principle, if not in fact) to characterize the moral agent by a single, unambiguous moral valuation, despite the potential diversity of the agent's phenomenal acts. That is, as the "supreme maxim" (p. 31; p. 26) the disposition accounts for any distinctive tendencies characteristic of a given moral agent's lower-order acts of maxim-making, including the tendency to fashion immoral maxims. We infer something about a person's disposition from the types of acts we associate with that person over time. When, in ordinary discourse, we refer to someone as having a good or a bad "character," we are – from the Kantian standpoint – addressing the question of that person's disposition. A morally sound disposition (that is, a person of "good character") regularly produces actions based upon maxims in which the incentive of sensuous inclination has been subordinated to that of the moral law. Kant himself seems to join in this common human tendency to evaluate the moral character of the people one meets in everyday life, but he reminds us that, again from his standpoint, such evaluations (even of oneself) are the product of inferences and not of theoretical knowledge.

[F]or outer experience does not disclose the inner nature of the disposition but merely allows of an inference about it though not one of strict certainty. (For the matter of that, not even does a man's inner experience with regard to himself enable him so to fathom the depths of his own heart as to obtain, through self-observation, quite certain knowledge of the basis of the maxims which he professes, of their purity and stability.) (p. 63; pp. 56–7)

Or, as Kant had earlier phrased it in the *Critique of Pure Reason*, the "real morality of actions, their merit or guilt, even that of our own conduct, remains entirely hidden from us."[4]

Analyzing the disposition

Obviously, it could be fairly claimed that Kant's concept of the disposition raises as many questions as it settles. Here – as virtually everywhere in efforts to explicate Kant's views on moral and religious matters – the challenge is to connect up an arid and technical terminology with recognizable features of our own moral experience. We can perhaps provisionally think of the disposition as the knot in the thread that is unraveling in Kant's hands as he attempts to specify the locus of moral evil: it is his way of halting the regress we embark on when we press the question of what "causes" evil in a situation defined by the Kantian linkage among moral evil, maxim-making, and freedom.

The crucial feature of the disposition that potentially helps it to be this knot is its unity. Whereas there can be no accounting for the fact that a given disposition is either virtuous or wicked, we can, thinks Kant, account for the fact that the disposition is a unity. Here, he draws off of the metaphysical implications of his phenomena–noumena dichotomy. Since the disposition is the seat of our moral character, it cannot be rendered or thematized in public, phenomenal terms, for there can be no mixing or integrating of the moral and the phenomenal in a way that would allow freedom to "appear." This means in turn that the agent's disposition, due to its noumenal and thus profoundly private quality, eludes all descriptions involving temporal order or transformation through time. In short, the disposition deflects in principle all attempts at periodization; consequently, it can only be described as a "unity." In Kant's words, the "subjective moral principle of the *disposition*... is not susceptible to division into periods of time, but can only be thought of as an absolute unity" (p. 70n.; p. 64n.).

We therefore have, on the one hand, a single, timeless disposition that constitutes the definitive feature of one's moral condition and, on the other hand, the worldly manifestation of the disposition in countless acts of maxim-making. One thing that obviously needs to be accounted for here in any assessment of the problem of moral evil is the exact relationship between the free act by which the moral agent chooses his or her disposition, and the free acts arising out of the disposition in individual acts of maxim-making – the relationship, that is, between the choice of the supreme maxim and the choice of any particular maxim in an everyday moment of moral decision-making. If this distinction cannot be sustained, it is not clear how Kant can deduce the very notion of the disposition as something distinct from lower-order maxims. Kant comes closest to addressing this distinction by demarcating two different senses of the word "act" in relation to moral choice:

The term "act" can apply in general to that exercise of freedom whereby the supreme maxim (in harmony with the law or contrary to it) is adopted by the will, but also to the exercise of freedom whereby the actions themselves (considered materially, i.e., with reference to the objects of volition) are performed in accordance with that maxim. (p. 31; p. 26)

We can take this "act"–"act" distinction to mean that the term "act" (*Tat*) can apply to the exercise of freedom in the adoption of the disposition and that it can apply as well to the exercise of freedom by which particular maxims are chosen in accordance with the general policy established by the underlying disposition. Notice that this distinction at least hints at the possibility that the intelligible, moral self is dual – or even multiple – with the self potentially lodged both in the act by which I adopt my disposition, and in the act (or acts) by which I choose to follow out the moral structure of the disposition. Such a possibility is of course ironic, in light of the fact that Kant has introduced the distinction as part of a strategy to defend the idea of the unity of the moral agent. Kant is on extremely slippery terrain here, for he wants simultaneously to defend three claims in the course of working out the distinction between "act" and "act": the claim that the moral agent is characterized by a freely chosen ground that "unifies" the agent's moral structure in terms of a specifiable principle; the claim that the moral worth of discrete acts of willing is pre-established by this background structure; and the claim that discrete acts of willing are free acts of *Willkür*. Obviously, if Kant presses the second claim too hard, the third is jeopardized. Alternatively, if he underplays the second and emphasizes the third, then the point of the distinction between "act" and "act" gradually becomes vague, or its introduction begins to seem arbitrary, as though the distinction is offered only for the sake of being able to say that the moral agent is ultimately unified and not fragmentary or chaotic.

However, the distinction does help to underscore the fact that moral self-hood in the deepest, Kantian sense consists of something more like "agency" than like a static "essence." That is, the "act"–"act" distinction discloses that, for Kant, the definitive feature of the moral self is *already* a kind of willing, and not an essence that is logically prior to an original act of willing. The problem is how to discuss this primordial agency in a way that protects it *as* agency (instead of transforming it into a fixed essence), while simultaneously avoiding having this agency dissolve into formless chaos, unrelated to any structure that could underwrite moral valuation. Kant is, as it were, attempting here to get "behind" the self so as to gain a foothold in the structure of the will that will enable him to impute evil or virtue to the moral agent, but the foothold itself cannot be "fixed." In the process, the very idea of moral selfhood is rendered in terms of the sheer capacity for agency.[5]

Although this way of viewing the matter may get us closer to isolating what it means for a moral agent to "choose" a "character," it hardly settles the question of the relation between the disposition and individual acts of maxim-making. For Kant's distinction between two sorts of "acts" does not so much account for this relationship as it re-emphasizes the problem, since Kant offers no principle of integration of the two senses of "act." This result is problematic, for at stake here is just the issue Kant wants to put to rest with his employment of the notion of the disposition: namely, the issue of the unity of the moral agent.

This theme of unity is of considerable importance to any coherent account of "fall" and regeneration, so problems Kant has at this point will haunt his entire scheme. Especially in light of Kant's enormous emphasis on personal autonomy and accountability in moral matters, it is crucial for him to be able to attribute an enduring, single personal identity to someone who falls into radical evil and becomes morally regenerated.[6] It must be assumed that part of his point in having the disposition ground all discrete acts of maxim-making is to avoid the sheer indeterminacy that would obtain if individual acts of maxim-making were construed as simply spontaneous, disconnected, and utterly unrelated to any common ground.[7] Indeed, there is the strong possibility that the concept of the disposition – which has been called "the most important single contribution of the *Religion* to Kant's ethical theory"[8] – was introduced in this late work for the express purpose of enabling Kant to show more convincingly how we can impute moral blame to a single rational being over time. If the moral life were a series of spontaneous acts, not connected by any overarching moral policy (as provided for by the Kantian disposition), all efforts to describe in enduring terms someone's moral worth would be crippled. Likewise, the impossibility of attributing moral guilt, over time, to the *same* moral agent would potentially make the idea of moral regeneration incoherent.

The role played by the disposition in helping Kant to avoid the dangers of indeterminacy in moral matters thus suggests the intimate and significant connection between the doctrine of the disposition and the Kantian doctrine of autonomy. Autonomy is sometimes characterized as freedom in the "positive" sense – involving the ability to prescribe laws to oneself – in contrast to freedom in the "negative" sense – involving only the absence of empirical determination and restraint.[9] Individual acts of maxim-making are not scattered disjointedly, their range limited only by the degree of external constraint imposed on the moral actor, as they might be, for example, in a Humean account of moral agency. Instead, individual acts of maxim-making enjoy intelligible internal relations to one another by virtue of the unifying function of the freely adopted disposition. Just as autonomy (in contrast to mere freedom from empirical determination) is the capacity to prescribe laws to oneself, the underlying moral disposition involves our latent tendency to adopt characteristic and enduring courses of action that could be formulated in a general principle. We might go so far as to say that the point at which the theory of autonomy and the theory of the disposition cross is very close to what might constitute a Kantian theory of personal identity.[10] A more negative implication emerges, however, if we remind ourselves that Kant never really integrates the two senses of "act" in his account of the relationship between the choice of a disposition and the subsequent choices of lower-order maxims. For this failure ironically suggests that, precisely in his effort to account for the unity of moral agency, Kant inadvertently introduces a fresh division, a result that evinces the general tendency of the critical philosophy to multiply Kantian "selves" – the "empirical" self, the "noumenal" self, the "transcendental ego" – without ever systematically showing how they all finally relate to one another.[11] If we keep in mind that Kant must ultimately show that, in the course of moral regeneration, the "self" that is saved or regenerated is the same "self" that had fallen – for otherwise there would be no moral symmetry to the salvation process – then the importance of a Kantian theory of personal identity becomes readily apparent.

The connection that Kant draws between the disposition and the continuity and regularity of our moral endeavors makes it tempting simply to conceive of the disposition as the static "basis" of maxim-making. Kant's tendency to invoke the metaphor of a "ground" when referring to the disposition increases this temptation. Yet we have already seen that, upon inspection, this "ground" turns out to be a form of agency, requiring its own motivational source, rather than a fixed essence. Moreover, it is important to recall that Kant calls the disposition *itself* a maxim (pp. 20–1; pp. 16–17). This is because Kant wants to avoid at all costs a theory of the production of maxims that ultimately locates the source of our maxim-making in a "natural impulse" (p. 21; p. 17) or in any other given attribute of human nature for which the moral agent could not finally be held accountable. The "ultimate ground of the adoption of our maxims... must itself lie in free choice" (*Willkür*), Kant insists (pp. 21–2; p. 17), and the term "maxim" is, for all practical purposes, a philosophical device for protecting the requisite element of freedom. Thus, the disposition is both the ground of our maxim-making *and* itself a maxim, yet one that cannot be further analyzed or accounted for. A free act – the making of a maxim – rests on another free act – the making of the supreme maxim. Kant really never gets any further than this in his search for the foothold determining moral selfhood.

Consequently, whereas the notion of the disposition as an underlying "ground" initially gives the source of moral evil the appearance of something static, we see on closer inspection that the real problem facing Kant at this point is the threat of infinite regress. For if Kant is going to tell us that freely produced maxims have a certain underlying ground which is also freely produced, we will inevitably ask what the "ground of the ground" is (and so on). Otherwise, it is not clear why Kant cannot simply suspend his analysis at the point where the determination of the form of any particular maxim is described. In what turns out to be something close to a guiding motif in the *Religion*, Kant deals with the possibility of a regress by invoking a systematic agnosticism in his effort to account for the ultimate ground of maxim-making and the source of evil. The "ultimate ground" determining our moral status is, Kant tells us, "inscrutable to us" (p. 21; p. 17). The moral disposition constituting this ground is unified and freely chosen, for otherwise we would be forced to say that the ground underlying the production of maxims is "caused," robbing morality of its point (p. 25; pp. 20–21). But no more can be said regarding this underlying ground: "we are unable to derive this disposition, or rather its ultimate ground, from any original act of the will in time" (p. 25; p. 21). The disposition is the product of a noumenal free act, outside of time, regarding which nothing of a theoretical or cognitive nature can be said.

We are very close at this point to the heart of the sheer mystery connected with anyone's becoming virtuous or evil. Kant will take us no further back than the foundational "act" by which I choose my supreme maxim and freely establish the incentive structure influencing all my subsequent acts of maxim-making. One thing here that is noteworthy is the very fine line between a true locus of moral agency and complete, chaotic indeterminacy: if we concentrate our attention on the role that the primary act plays relative to the derivative acts, we have a sense of a theory of the unity of agency; if, on the other hand, we concentrate on the question of how or why that primary act is itself freely undertaken, we are left with a dizzying sense of contingency. Kant is here talking about the free will giving itself its incentive. By virtue of the incentive it gives itself, the will's general policy regarding maxim-making will be established and the moral agent's characteristic stance toward a world of other moral agents will be determined.

But Kant has left no bootstraps – either to describe or to pull on – in the accounting of this basic moral act. It is almost as though he needs a further "self" behind the self that undertakes this primary dispositional act to account for the motivation of this act.[12] Likewise (as we shall see in part II of this study), a similar motivational source of the primary act is needed to account for the act producing moral regeneration. For a fallen disposition – a supreme maxim devoted to the primacy of the sensuous, selfish incentive – appears utterly incapable of initiating the regenerating act.

Kant is of course blocked in here: if he provides something like a self behind the self to account for the primary act, the problem of infinite regress once again looms; and if he says too much about the motivation behind the primary act, he runs the risk of "explaining" it in terms of its "causes."[13] But, at a minimum, what might have been helpful would have been a further accounting of the relationship between *Willkür* and the primary dispositional act. Kant has compressed together – quite literally, in one extremely important and compacted paragraph in the *Religion* (pp. 31–2; pp. 26–7) – his distinction between two senses of "act," his link between the primary sense of "act" and the choice of the disposition, his definition of the disposition as a "supreme maxim," and his association of the primary "act" with the propensity to evil. Just here, more than at any other single point, Kant is analyzing the free choice to become radically evil. It would seem to be a natural moment for him to clarify, to the extent that his own ground rules might permit, the role played by *Willkür* in the primary dispositional act and to say whatever he can about the incentive structure informing *that* act. Unfortunately, what we get instead is an exemplification of Kant's frequent tendency throughout his philosophy to exhibit the way his technical terms relate to one another, rather than to show what their joint deployment could actually mean.

The conundrum we are left with, then, is this: the primary dispositional act determines the basic motivation of *Willkür* and sets the moral tone of the secondary acts of maxim-making characterizing a given agent's exercise of *Willkür*;[14] but it is *Willkür* itself that is responsible for this primary act. This is the net effect of Kant's unwillingness to lodge the source of our moral nature in anything given rather than chosen. It is perhaps inevitable, then, that his moral philosophy ends in mystery. Yet it would appear that Kant is obligated to tell us more, since this entire account of the will giving itself an incentive structure is occasioned by Kant's claim that we invariably give ourselves a structure that is evil. His ability to make such a claim seems incompatible with his self-professed *inability* to tell us anything more about the primary dispositional act. That is, his ignorance or agnosticism on the second point would appear to make it impossible for him to make the first one.

Ultimately, the net effect of the things Kant does not explain to us is to put in question the explanatory power of his concept of the disposition. Kant's use of the metaphor of "ground" in his depiction of the subjective disposition turns out to be especially unhelpful and misleading, since it simply begs the question of the "ground" of the "ground." I suggested at the beginning of this section that we might provisionally think of the disposition as the knot in the thread running through Kant's hands as he attempts to specify the locus of moral evil in the account of moral agency. But upon inspection, it turns out that there is no knot, only slack, in the form of a fathomless freedom. Consequently, the term "disposition" in Kant's moral philosophy does not really characterize a fixed point within human nature that is disclosed in the course of moral valuation. Instead, the term simply plays the role of a useful fiction designed to protect two of Kant's most important insights: the ultimate unity of moral agency and the indecipherable character of freedom. Insofar as Kant is marshalling these ideas in order to argue that evil is both radical and universal, his position finally yields the insight that moral evil is utterly unaccountable. It is hard to avoid the conclusion that the complex conceptual and terminological gridwork attending his account of radical evil is somehow incommensurate with such an unhelpful result.

Radical evil and the "nature of man"

We have seen so far that the expression "radical evil" depends upon Kant's notion of the disposition. We have further seen that, in trying to relate moral evil to maxim-making, the disposition, and freedom, Kant has effectively made the following claims:

1   Moral evil arises in acts of maxim-making.
2   Maxims have their common ground in the disposition, or supreme maxim.
3   The choice of the disposition is, like the choice of any maxim, free.
4   Because the choice of the disposition is free, we cannot finally inquire into or explain it definitively.

This set of claims is fairly obscure to begin with. The really troubling issue, however, is the emerging possibility that Kant is running together the question of whether we could ever *know* the ultimate determining ground of the will with the quite different question of what the ultimate determining ground of the will *is*. By systematically claiming we can never know what the ground is (it remains "inscrutable" to us), Kant assumes the correctness of the view that the ultimate ground of the will is freedom. But of course it is precisely because of the prior assumption that the moral agent is free that Kant claims that we cannot finally "know" the determining ground of the will.

Clarifying Kant's problems in argumentation at this point is not merely a stale philosophical exercise but bears immediately on his important and provocative claim that radical evil is "innate." The connecting link between Kant's account of the disposition and his claim that we are innately evil – or, as he puts it, evil "by nature" (p. 32; p. 27) – is his account of the expression, "nature of man." Kant takes pains to explain the notion of "nature of man" in a manner that removes any hint of determinism from the term "nature," which of course is just the opposite tactic from the one we normally associate with his use of the term. In this context, in which he is trying to account for the "indwelling of the evil principle with the good, or... the radical evil in human nature" (p. 19; p. 15), Kant defines "nature of man" as "the subjective ground of the exercise (under objective moral laws) of man's freedom in general" (p. 21; p. 16). In other words, "nature" in this narrower, anthropological sense must be compatible with freedom. What we are thus getting here is what Bernard Carnois has described as "an astonishing reversal of Kant's terminology" where the term "nature" receives a meaning "altogether different from that which ordinarily is attached to it and comes to designate freedom" rather than determinism.[15]

By "nature of man," then, Kant means the ground of the exercise of our freedom, a definition which of course puts this expression in close contact with his concept of the disposition. In parallel with his claim that the disposition should itself be understood as a kind of maxim (and thus understood as arising out of freedom rather than out of a fixed or given attribute), Kant says that this "subjective ground of the exercise of our freedom" must itself be "an expression of freedom" (p. 21; pp. 16–17), for otherwise we fall into the trap of finding a "cause" for freedom. His aim throughout these early passages in the *Religion* is to hold together the claim that moral evil is intertwined, root-like, with our very nature with the claim that we are responsible, through a free act, for moral evil. He wants to be able to say that we are evil by nature without simultaneously adopting the claim that evil is a "given." Being evil by nature is a "nature" we freely elect.

However, if we fit together these remarks about the nature of man with Kant's account of the disposition – as Kant himself seems to be inviting us to do – we discover something very close to an equivocation that puts into question Kant's entire effort to say what he evidently wants to say. Again, the problem is the way he trades on an epistemological point – the "unknowability" of freedom – in order to make what amounts to the key metaphysical point – the notion that we are evil by nature due to a natural propensity to adopt an evil disposition. The flaw comes more clearly into view if we look once again at the way Kant spells out the implications of the connection between freedom and moral evil, a link he absolutely has to forge if the evil he is discussing is rightfully to be called "moral" evil.

We have seen that Kant has said that the ultimate ground determining our moral status is "inscrutable" to us. His point is that, since the source of either evil or virtue is freedom, any attempt ultimately to explain or account for a given moral character is automatically futile, since freedom never admits of a theoretical explanation. To "explain" a free act would be to specify its antecedent conditions; such an explanation would gain its explanatory power only at the cost of eliminating freedom. Thus, says Kant, "it must not be considered permissible to inquire into the subjective ground in man of the adoption of this maxim rather than of its opposite."

If this ground itself were not ultimately a maxim, but a mere natural impulse, it would be possible to trace the use of our freedom wholly to determination by natural causes; this, however, is contradictory to the very notion of freedom. (p. 21; p. 17)

Because the source of moral evil is the free act by which the moral agent fashions maxims, we can never specify the ultimate ground of evil. Embarking on the search for this ground, "we are referred back endlessly in the series of subjective determining grounds, without ever being able to reach the ultimate ground" (p. 21; p. 18). When Kant says that the ultimate ground of moral evil is "inscrutable to us," he means it is unknowable in principle precisely because the ground of evil is not something naturally caused or sensuously conditioned.

What becomes evident here is the possibility that Kant is using the claim that the source of moral evil is freedom as a premise in generating the further claim that the source of moral evil is unknowable. The peculiarity of this line of argumentation gradually becomes clear: the peculiarity is that the conclusion of Kant's train of thought appears to deny his ability to know his own major premise. If the overriding epistemological issue here concerns a demand for agnosticism regarding the ultimate source or ground of evil, then Kant can hardly argue this case on the basis of a claim about what the source of evil is. If the conclusion flatly states the unknowability of P, then P forfeits any chance for candidacy as a premise in the argument designed to reach that conclusion.

The deeper problem here, as I indicated earlier, is that Kant refers to the *source* of evil and to our potential *knowledge* of the source of evil in a thoroughly equivocal manner. For the most part he is simply assuming that freedom is the ground of evil and then offering his related comments regarding our inability to know or discover that ground. At the same time, however, the entire account of radical evil occurs in the context of Kant's concern to avoid attributing moral evil to sheer natural impulse or sensuous inclination, a view that would absolve us of responsibility for the evil thus portrayed. That is, throughout the first two Books of the *Religion*, Kant is not simply *assuming* that freedom is the ground of evil, he is *arguing* the case as well, in light of his full recognition that a natural, sensuous ground of evil would be disastrous for his position. His effort, for example, to distinguish the predisposition to good from the propensity to evil is partly an effort to avoid associating moral evil with the sheer fact that we are sensuous beings, but to associate it instead with a free response to our sensuousness. Viewed in this light, Kant's appeal to the "inscrutability" of the ground or source of moral evil subtly takes on the status of a major reason why this ground must indeed be freedom. Nothing in our "knowable," phenomenal experience of sensuous inclinations and sheer bodiliness finally accounts for moral evil. Consequently, the unknowability of the source of evil buttresses the attribution of evil to freedom; the intertwining of the two issues indicates that they are intended to be mutually reinforcing:

That the ultimate subjective ground of the adoption of moral maxims is inscrutable is indeed already evident from this, that *since this adoption is free*, its ground (why, for example, I have already chosen an evil and not a good maxim) must not be sought in any natural impulse, but always again in a maxim. (p. 21n.; pp. 17–18n., emphasis added)

The disposition, i.e., the ultimate subjective ground of the adoption of maxims... itself must have been adopted by free choice, for otherwise it could not be imputed. But the subjective ground or cause of this adoption cannot further be known. (p. 25; p. 20)

What is noteworthy here is the way the agnostic note struck by Kant is discreetly enlisted to help him make the connection between evil and freedom. He is virtually compelled to argue in this way, for it is simply not clear that he has any reason for claiming that freedom is the ground of moral evil other than his own systematic need to salvage individual accountability and culpability in moral matters. Kant can no more explain the "fall" than could Augustine, his long-windedness in the matter notwithstanding.

But if the unknowability of the ground of evil is helping Kant to argue that the ground of evil is freedom, then the argumentative flaw here becomes altogether clear. For it is only because of the prior assumption that freedom is the ground of evil that Kant is able to argue the unknowability of this ground. Any appeal to the unknowability or inscrutability of the source of evil in the attempt to strengthen the link between evil and freedom must fail, since the appeal depends for its persuasiveness upon the prior assumption of what is supposedly open to question. Freedom itself is what *produces* the inscrutability.

My own view is that Kant's argumentative trouble stems mainly from his wanting to say that radical evil is both freely elected and "innate." In effect, the awkwardness of his philosophical posture is mirrored in this hybrid claim. The key to the sense of an "innateness" that preserves freedom is Kant's notion of propensity which, as we saw in the previous chapter, serves as a kind of terminological corridor between our sensuousness (which is simply given, or innate) and the moral life (which is freely fashioned). That is, the term "propensity" is at least in part a device for showing that, though we bear no responsibility (and thus no culpability) for the fact that we happen to have natural inclinations, we do bear responsibility for the way we relate the incentives arising out of the inclinations to the rational incentive. Kant's survey of the complex interrelationship between what is given and what is free thereby makes equivalent the following three claims: we have a "natural propensity" to radical evil; we are evil "by nature"; and radical evil is "innate."

The way in which Kant draws his most specific connection between the propensity to evil and the idea of innateness both confirms that he is saying radical evil is innate and also lifts into view his apparent working criteria for the very idea of innateness. The propensity to evil, he tells us, is

entitled a simple propensity and innate, because it cannot be eradicated (since for such eradication the highest maxim would have to be that of the good – whereas in this propensity it already has been postulated as evil), but chiefly because we can no more assign a further cause for a corruption in us by evil of just this highest maxim, although this is our own action, than we can assign a cause for any fundamental attribute belonging to our nature. (pp. 31–2; p. 27)

There seem to be two criteria for innateness embedded in this comment, both of which appear to be peculiar: innateness entails something that "cannot be eradicated," and innateness involves something for which we cannot "assign a further cause." The second of these does not seem to be a genuine criterion so much as it appears to be an admission that we no longer know what we are talking about. To say that something is innate because we cannot trace back its causality any further has the look of that same equivocation between an anthropological claim and an epistemological limitation that we just surveyed. At a minimum, it is not clear how Kant can legitimately make a claim about something as crucial as innateness on the basis of an appeal to agnosticism. But as we have seen – and as we shall have occasion to see again – the argumentative structure of the *Religion* is heavily dependent on precisely this timely use of the argument from ignorance.

Alternatively, the idea that one criterion of innateness is the impossibility of eradication initially appears quite plausible. We would have no trouble saying that other features of our lives – such as the need for food – were innate in this sense. However, the question here does not concern whether this is a helpful criterion of innateness, but whether it is a criterion that fairly applies to the propensity to evil. And here Kant seems to be on slippery ground, as signalled by his parenthetical expression linking the impossibility of eradication with the notion that the propensity has "already been postulated as evil." What is troubling here is the fact that *Kant* has "already" postulated the propensity as evil in the course of his argument. Apart from his having done so, there would appear to be good grounds for supposing that we were not compelled to give in to the propensity to evil, for if we were, how could we be morally culpable? Kant himself re-opens just this line of thought when he maintains we cannot be held responsible for our natural inclinations, yet we "are accountable... for the propensity to evil" (p. 35; p. 30). That is, when he wants to underscore our accountability for the propensity to evil, he seems to be distinguishing the propensity from what is innate, rather than identifying one with the other.

Moreover, there seems to be an asymmetry with respect to the exercise of freedom in Kant's suggestion that the propensity cannot be eradicated once it is postulated as having become evil. For it is only by virtue of its having been a propensity freely chosen that moral culpability attends the choice; but the "eradication criterion" evidently entails the idea that this free act cannot be freely undone or reversed. The result of the act leaves us with something innate, in the sense of "impossible to eradicate." We have willed our way into bondage. This view may in fact be precisely what Kant is arguing for, but it obviously means that the difficulties associated with the whole question of moral regeneration – severe enough as it is – are vastly compounded by Kant's way of making the point that the propensity to evil is innate. Just as problematic is the heavily compromised position in which Kant's own doctrine of autonomy finds itself, if he is here setting limits to what freedom can accomplish.

There is consequently a frustrating conceptual logjam at the point where Kant wants to link innateness and the propensity to evil. Quite simply, it is never clear why Kant thinks radical evil is universal, or the propensity to evil innate. At the point in the *Religion* where Kant makes these claims most explicit, he turns to empirical examples, as though offering a familiar "long melancholy litany of indictments against humanity" will simply make manifest what we somehow intuitively know about the race (p. 33; p. 28). But of course there is utterly no way that Kant, above all, could legitimately generate a claim about an intrinsic feature of human nature from even the lengthiest list of empirical examples. The elaborate explanatory apparatus of the first two Books of the *Religion* thus turns out to be considerably misleading. We seem to be getting a detailed account of both the source and the nature of moral evil, designed to lead to the eventual conclusion that radical evil, arising out of the disposition, is innate in human nature. As it turns out, however, most of Kant's key concepts – such as "disposition" – have virtually no explanatory power when it comes to accounting for radical evil and its source. Instead, the key concepts can best be thought of as mere placeholders on the road to the Kantian insight that "there is then for us no conceivable ground from which the moral evil in us could originally have come" (p. 43; p. 38). The free act of *Willkür* out of which radical evil arises can never be trapped conceptually.

The implications of Kant's account for the moral agent are really quite startling. This is because the entire thrust of Kant's approach would seem to put in question the agent's capacity to have moral self-knowledge that is adequate to the Kantian demand that we make ourselves virtuous.[16] The unfathomability of freedom connects – virtually analytically – with the unknowability of one's subjective disposition. Such a result totally jeopardizes the moral agent's ability to exercise a truly informed capacity, which raises serious questions about culpability as well as about agency itself. The inability truly to know my own disposition (because it is noumenal) would seem to saddle me with a moral obligation which I am only partially equipped to meet. The Kantian insight that I "ground" my own act of giving myself a dispositional ground begins to look like the frightening possibility that the choice of a disposition is a hit-or-miss matter of sheer chance or blind luck.

This is the starkest form of indeterminacy threatening Kant's account of moral agency. What is ironic is the fact that it is just this problem – the threat of the potentially fragmented, unrelated, and purely contingent nature of the acts of freedom constituting the agent's moral make-up – that the theory of the disposition was itself meant to avoid. Instead, that theory exemplifies the problem: intended to save moral agency from sheer indeterminacy, the disposition cannot save itself. Meant to ground individual acts of maxim-making, the disposition cannot do the same chore for itself but renews the threat of indeterminacy with fresh strength.

Coming to expression through this maze of difficulties is the radical nature, not only of evil, but of Kant's theory of freedom and the exercise of *Willkür* that is the expression of that freedom. The Kant of the textbooks often seems to provide us with a mathematically precise universe, dependable transcendental footholds, a theory of moral obligation firmly grounded in the moral law, and an ambitious authorship designed to explain how all these fit together. Yet, as the account of radical evil suggests, the free will that is at the heart of Kant's theory of human nature has the look of something raw and arbitrary – the look, that is, of something surprisingly close to the world that Ivan describes. What separates the two is not the issue of belief in God, for that is subordinate in Kant's case to the compelling force of the moral law just as it is subordinate in Ivan's case to the experience of evil and suffering in the world. What separates them is Kant's clear-cut normative sense regarding how we "ought" to exercise our freedom, together with some background metaphysical commitments assuring him that truly moral action relates intelligibly to the wider moral–religious universe and makes a genuine difference in the promotion of the highest good. What finally separates Kant and Ivan is the former's confidence that the human experience of "ought" has purchase on reality. The universe is neither blind nor indifferent to our discrete acts of freedom.

It remains to be seen how Kant tackles the very severe difficulties that emerge once this freedom is exercised in a way that produces a radically evil disposition. What we have not really settled, however, is the puzzling question of why Kant should end up claiming that freedom will be *universally* exercised in this way. The question of why Kant claims that radical evil is universal must finally have at least part of its answer in Kant's deep suspicion of our bodies. For although he is careful not to blame moral evil on the sheer fact of our bodiliness, it is still the case that moral evil arises out of the competition for control of character between sensuous and rational incentives: rationality would have no competition if it were not embodied. The universality of radical evil is thus connected with the givenness of our bodily, sensuous condition. Consequently, even though Kant does not want to lodge specific responsibility for radical evil in the fact of our bodiliness, it seems true to say that his claim of the *universality* of radical evil is underwritten by this fact. We might say that the body provides freedom with its opportunity to go wrong. To be sure, the free will and not the body is the wrongdoer. But what is at stake here is not the sheer definition of moral evil, but the grounds for Kant's claim that the fall is universal, if not exactly "original" or primordial. Taken by themselves, discrete acts of human freedom undertaken by countless multitudes of moral agents provide no connecting thread that would account for this universality. Considered purely in terms of countless discrete acts of freedom, Kant's moral universe is a scene of innumerable idiosyncracies. The connecting thread is provided by the body – every moral agent has one. What is more, the definitive feature of a moral agent is the struggle to subordinate the incentives that emerge *because* we are embodied to the incentive arising out of reason.[17]

Radical evil can thus be viewed as the final result of Kant's latent resentment against the body, his philosophical chagrin that pure reason must cohabit with sensuousness. There is, after all, a profound connection between transcendental method and the "disembodied" standpoint – as though we "get it right," philosophically, only to the extent that we bracket (if not escape altogether) the conditions of our embodiment, as well as the effects of history. Kant cannot preserve a sense of our worth and dignity as moral beings while simultaneously taking what Nietzsche called a "skin-covered" view of the world: to preserve human dignity, he has to separate out the two viewpoints.[18] This is perhaps the chief lesson to be learned from the famous conclusion to the *Critique of Practical Reason*, where Kant contrasts consciousness of self as a physical being with consciousness of self in relation to the moral law. "The former view . . . annihilates, as it were, my importance as an animal creature," whereas the latter view "infinitely raises my worth as that of an intelligence by my personality" – that is to say, by my capacity to respect the moral law, which is a capacity that lifts me out of bodily determination. The "moral law reveals a life independent of all animality and even of the whole world of sense," Kant concludes with evident pride.[19] The remarkable thing is that Kant should think the linkage between human dignity and disembodied existence to be such a good thing. In so doing, he amply confirms and helpfully illustrates Sabina Lovibond's suggestion that the "demand for a standpoint *outside history* from which to deliver judgements of value is linked with the demand for a standpoint *outside the body* from which to survey reality: for an embodied creature necessarily exists in time."[20] It comes as no surprise, then, that conceiving of the moral life in terms of time is the one thing, above all, that Kant cannot seem to do.

II

Moral regeneration

4

A "change of heart"

> How indeed can we expect something perfectly straight to be framed out
> of such crooked wood?
>
> Kant

Are we devils?

The complexity of Kant's theory of radical evil guarantees that the question
of moral regeneration will confront us with a maze of difficulties. The fundamental problem is clear: if radical evil is a corruption of the underlying disposition, and if the disposition is itself the source of moral regeneration, then
the obligation to undertake moral regeneration appears to rest on an impossibility. On the other hand, if we simply admit our moral incapacity and put
our trust in divine grace, then any resulting regeneration would not be a
genuinely *moral* regeneration by Kant's standards, for the crucial element
of autonomy would be missing. We thus seem stuck between debility and
demand – between a corruption brought upon us by ourselves, and an obligation nonetheless to heal ourselves through a free but unspecifiable act.

Because of the way Kant has set the context for his account of moral regeneration, it is important to sort out the question of the sheer possibility of moral
regeneration from the question of its actual process. The sheer possibility of
moral regeneration is implicit in Kant's interesting comment that, though
our fall into evil is radical, it does not mean that we have become "devils."
Devilishness would mean the intentional, outright rejection of the moral law
for its own sake; it would mean the rejection of the moral law precisely
because it *is* the moral law. As such, devilishness would mark the limit point
beyond which no moral regeneration would be possible. Thus, Kant's claim
that we are *not* devils is simultaneously his claim that a moral capacity continues to reside in us, notwithstanding the fall into radical evil. Kant appeals
more than once to the idea of a "seed of goodness" remaining in even the
most wicked person, a seed that cannot be entirely "corrupted."[1] As long as

this is the case – as long, that is, as the will retains even the slightest sensitivity to the moral law as an incentive – we remain under the obligation to make ourselves good again.

However evil a man has been up to the very moment of an impending free act... it was not only his duty to have been better [in the past], it is *now* still his duty to better himself. To do so must be within his power. (p. 41; p. 36)

The capacity to experience moral obligation is at the same time the awareness that we are free to act as obligated, an insight that remains continuous with one of the deepest features of Kant's entire moral philosophy. Duty, Kant reminds us, "demands nothing of us which we cannot do" (p. 47; p. 43).

Kant's rejection of devilishness is thus the condition of the possibility of moral regeneration. However slim this possibility may be in a given case, and however murky the actual process, the capacity to experience moral obligation guarantees the possibility itself. Several things are at work in Kant's train of thought here, and the manner in which they work together is what keeps the theory of radical evil from being the depiction of a totally lost and desperate condition from which there is no escape. Kant is depending in part on a distinction that he invokes at one point between "wickedness" of the heart and the "perversity" of the heart (p. 37; p. 32). He warns against calling the depravity of human nature produced by radical evil "wickedness," if by that we mean a disposition "to adopt evil *as evil* into our maxim" as the controlling incentive (p. 37; p. 32). Here, the term "wickedness" is synonymous with the term "devilishness," which is confirmed by his calling the adoption of evil *as* evil into one's maxim "diabolical" (p. 37; p. 32). The point is potentially confusing, however, since he has earlier posited wickedness – along with "frailty" and "impurity" – as one of the "three distinct degrees" of moral evil, all of which can be predicated of rational beings (pp. 29–30; pp. 24–5). Wickedness of the sort that is not pure devilishness Kant calls *"perversity [Verkehrtheit]* of the human heart, for it reverses the ethical order [or priority] among the incentives of a *free* will" (p. 30; p. 25). Likewise, when he takes wickedness in the same sense as devilishness, Kant distinguishes both terms from what he again refers to as "perversity" of the heart (p. 37; p. 32). Wickedness as the diabolical is too much; wickedness as perversity, however, conveys just that "turning around" or reordering of incentives in a "perverse" order, the subordinating of the moral to the sensuous, that constitutes evil itself. At the same time, a heart that is perverse (rather than diabolical) "may coexist with a will which in general is good" (p. 37; p. 32), meaning that even a radical perversity of the human heart does

74

not eliminate the possibility of salvation. The problem is the perversion of a good will, rather than its destruction and subsequent absence.

A further ingredient in Kant's train of thought emerges as an implication of his view of the diabolical. By denying that we can reject the moral law for its own sake, Kant is evidently setting a limitation to freedom. He appears to be generating this important anthropological claim out of a fundamentally logical insight: freely willing to reject the moral law would be equivalent to exercising reason for the sake of being irrational. Consequently, we might characterize the rejection of devilishness as the result of Kant's structuring of certain limitations into human volition without thereby predetermining it in its successive acts,[2] a distinction that is obviously crucial for his theory of freedom. To say – as in the case of Kant's rejection of devilishness – what the will cannot do is not the same as to predict what it will in fact do. Freedom is preserved even as it is limited.

Another way of making this point is to say that, although the will can become evil, it cannot forfeit its rational character. Kant is indicating we become evil through an act of *Willkür*, but *Willkür* neither destroys *Wille* as the fully rational aspect of the will, nor does it ever totally lose the capacity to be affected by the rational incentive produced by *Wille*.[3] The inability to repudiate the moral law for its own sake implies the continuing, if perhaps weakened, presence of *Wille* as an incentive for the will as it fashions its principles. It thus seems accurate to say that the indestructability of *Wille* provides the metaphysical possibility of moral regeneration. This is no doubt the point of Kant's insistence that the moral renewal of the underlying disposition is not the restoration of something that has been *lost*, but the purifying of something that has been *corrupted* (p. 46; p. 42).

Placed in historical perspective, then, we might say that Kant's position is similar to that of Erasmus in his celebrated debate with Luther over the freedom of the will. The "freedom" at stake in that earlier debate is the freedom to take some sort of initiative or constructive step in the salvation process, an issue fundamental to the crisis over grace and works that occurs in the early sixteenth century and that finds a partially secularized variant in Kant's own account of moral recovery. The question up for debate concerns just how much has been destroyed by original sin. For Luther, sin destroys even our free will; subsequent to the fall and apart from grace, the will is best characterized as being in complete "bondage."[4] By contrast, Erasmus – without ever arguing that we fully earn salvation or actually merit grace – maintains that sin does not totally eliminate our capacity to turn toward God and open ourselves, in however limited a fashion, to the effects of grace. In a comment that foreshadows the position toward which Kant is moving, Erasmus maintains that

God credits us precisely with this, that we do not turn our hearts away from his grace, and that we concentrate our natural abilities on simple obedience. This proves at least that man can accomplish something, but that nevertheless he ascribes the sum total of all his doings to God, who is the author whence originates man's ability to unite his striving to God's grace.[5]

Cross-threading their idiom with Kant's, we could say that Luther is claiming that our fall includes the destruction of *Wille*, while Erasmus believes *Wille* remains intact. To take the latter view is not necessarily to claim that we achieve our salvation on our own, but only that we have the capacity to take a constructive step toward salvation. The historical continuity between Erasmus and Kant marks the continuity between Renaissance humanism and Enlightenment optimism regarding human effort and the accompanying suspicion of passively awaiting the effects of a freely bestowed grace.

Kant thus orchestrates his rejection of devilishness together with fresh variations on his familiar insistence that an obligation to act in a certain way entails the ability to do so. In a key comment that simultaneously conveys the apparent hopelessness of our condition and yet the promise of moral recovery, Kant says the following:

This evil is *radical*, because it corrupts the ground of all maxims; it is, moreover, as a natural propensity, *inextirpable* by human powers, since extirpation could occur only through good maxims, and cannot take place when the ultimate subjective ground of all maxims is postulated as corrupt; yet at the same time it must be possible to *overcome* it, since it is found in man, a being whose actions are free. (p. 37; p. 32)

We have already had occasion to note this important comment in connection with Kant's ultimate lodging of radical evil in the disposition as the "ultimate subjective ground of all maxims." What is of particular interest now is the very last part of this comment. Given the fall into radical evil, extirpation (or regeneration) cannot occur. Yet "at the same time it must be possible to *overcome*" radical evil, "since it is found in man, a being whose actions are free."

Upon first reading, this comment simply seems to be self-contradictory: Kant is evidently claiming both P and not P. We could continue to level the charge of self-contradiction even while appreciating that Kant's theory of autonomy obligates him to attach the second, rationalist claim to the first, quasi-Reformation claim. But the comment as a whole is not quite as self-contradictory as it at first appears. Kant is not, after all, saying that it is both

76

impossible and possible to extirpate radical evil through human powers. Rather, he is saying that it is impossible to extirpate it yet possible to "overcome" it, which connotes a final delivery from radical evil while remaining vague about just how the delivery is to be accomplished. The word that Greene and Hudson have translated here as "overcome" is *überwiegen*, which literally means "to outweigh." The possibility of having some circumstance or set of actions "outweigh" radical evil maintains the promise of moral regeneration while conveying something quite different from the term "extirpate." To succeed by "outweighing" the opponent is potentially to succeed by getting the help of another body, but in a manner that still utilizes the bulk and energies of one's own body. Whatever Kant's actual intentions may be, his language regarding the sheer possibility of moral regeneration implicitly sets the stage for his theory of divine cooperation, but without thereby jeopardizing the element of human autonomy that keeps his position Kantian.

The element of autonomy is assured by Kant's concluding reference to "a being whose actions are free." By adding this phrase, Kant both implicates the moral agent in the "outweighing" and offers a further gloss on the rejection of devilishness. Once again, Kant can always postulate freedom whenever the moral law retains any effectiveness as an incentive. His statement of the possibility of moral regeneration is not really self-contradictory so much as it implicitly allows for the exercise of freedom without eliminating the potential additional "weight" that divine aid might provide in the regeneration process. As Kant puts it at one point, moral regeneration

must be within our power, even though what *we* are able to do is in itself inadequate and though we thereby only render ourselves susceptible of higher, and for us inscrutable, assistance. (p. 45; pp. 40–1)

Despite a corrupt disposition's inability simply to renew itself through its own resources, then, the lingering "seed of goodness" assures the sheer logical possibility of moral renewal, while some as yet unspecified act or set of acts will transform this logical possibility into a real possibility. Kant's rejection of devilishness guarantees the former, while his actual theory of moral regeneration will chart out the transition from the former to the latter.

The nature of moral regeneration

Generally speaking, moral regeneration or conversion for Kant means the transformation of the underlying disposition – or supreme maxim – from evil to good. More strictly speaking, this means a reversal of the incentive structure of the disposition and, thus, an alteration in the will itself, brought about *by* the will. As we have just seen, Kant's rejection of devilishness arises out of the insight that radical evil is not the total loss of the capacity to be influenced by the moral incentive, but rather the corruption or perversion of the moral disposition. Accordingly, when Kant addresses the issue of moral conversion, he speaks in terms of the "restoration to its power of the original predisposition to good" (p. 44; p. 40), a restoration that involves establishing the "purity" of the moral law as "the supreme ground of all our maxims" (p. 46; p. 42). The metaphors of "power" and "purity" here refer to the relation of the moral incentive to the sensuous: moral conversion "un-perverts," as it were, the relation between these incentives as they compete for the position of superiority in the process of maxim-making; the moral incentive regains "power" over the sensuous, thereby manifesting the "purity" characteristic of an incentive that is *"adequate* in itself for the determination of the will"* (p. 46; p. 42).

Whereas Kant's most direct language regarding moral conversion emphasizes the role played by the two sorts of incentives as they compete for control of the disposition, it seems quite accurate to suggest that the entire theory of moral conversion turns on Kant's notion of the predisposition to personality. Along with the predispositions to animality and humanity, the predisposition to personality constitutes, as we have already seen, the cluster of potentialities lying behind our original predisposition to good. With specific respect to our moral timbre, the predisposition to personality is decisive, as it constitutes "the capacity for respect for the moral law as *in itself a sufficient incentive of the will"* (p. 27; pp. 22–3). Kant states that the good will is that which incorporates into its maxim the "moral feeling" arising out of the predisposition to personality (p. 27; p. 23). Radical evil thus implies a weakening of this feeling, while moral regeneration constitutes its return to full strength and impact.[6]

Unfortunately, though perhaps not surprisingly, Kant's actual account of moral regeneration itself is more noteworthy for what it leaves unsaid and unexplained than for what it clarifies. His discussion of the matter is both shaped and constrained by three systematic features of his overall philosophical position: his ethical rigorism, which requires that any given moral agent be either virtuous or evil rather than some sort of mixture of the two (a position further reenforced by his theory of a single, unified disposition) (p. 22; p. 18); his phenomena–noumena dichotomy which not only enforces a rigid dualism between virtue's public "empirical character" and virtue's hidden "intelligible character" (p. 47; pp. 42–3), but which makes it impossible to show how we can speak of the moral disposition in the temporal terms seemingly entailed by the very idea of a conversion; and his theory of freedom, which prohibits in principle the "explanation" of any act of freedom, such as would be involved in a moral conversion.

These severe constraints must be borne in mind when we reach the pivotal moment in Kant's narrative and encounter his extraordinary appeal to biblical language. Just prior to this moment Kant has reminded us of the difference between a "gradual reformation" in our observable, public conduct and a singular, noumenal or intelligible change in the hidden "ground of all maxims" that must be posited if both his ethical rigorism and his phenomena–noumena dichotomy are to be preserved (p. 47; p. 42). In addition, he invokes his familiar distinction between becoming *legally* good and becoming *morally* good (p. 47; p. 42).

Against the background of these contrasts, Kant then describes the process of moral regeneration. The change or alteration

cannot be brought about through gradual *reformation* so long as the basis of the maxims remains impure, but must be effected through a *revolution* in the man's disposition (a going over to the maxim of holiness of the disposition). He can become a new man only by a kind of rebirth, as it were a new creation (John III, 5; compare also Genesis I, 2), and a change of heart. (p. 47; p. 43)[7]

Later in the *Religion*, Kant will supplement this Johannine way of expressing the matter with the Pauline metaphor of "laying off of the old man and putting on of the new" (p. 74; p. 68).[8] In thus appealing to biblical language in these ways, Kant is effectively admitting that, at the point of moral regeneration, his own concepts fail him. They are bound to, for the reasons I have noted. The either/or character of his ethical rigorism drives him toward the metaphor of a "revolution," while the absence of any principle of integration between the noumenal–moral and the phenomenal–temporal commends the appropriation of the Johannine language of "rebirth" and "new creation." It seems not merely incidental that the idea of an instantaneous rebirth comes directly from the Königsberg catechism on which Kant was raised.[9] Evidently, his catechism – rather than sophisticated conceptual technique – helps him to depict the moment when radical evil is overcome.[10]

Kant had similarly invoked biblical narrative in his discussion, earlier in the *Religion*, of the fall into radical evil, where the Genesis account served some of his needs even as he distanced himself from other implications of its use.[11] In neither case – whether it be the transition from an originally good disposition to a freely chosen evil one, or the recovery from evil to virtue – can the relevant shift or alteration be rendered conceptually (let alone explained), since a purely contingent act of freedom is present in both instances. Indeed, the fact that these transformations are finally beyond all explanation actually yields Kant a cleverly employed argumentative dividend. Just at the point where Kant himself questions the very possibility of moral regeneration – by asking, "how can a bad tree bring forth good fruit?" (p. 45; p. 40) – he reminds the reader that the fall into evil is similarly inexplicable. This reminder effectively serves as an appeal to the inscrutability of the one (the original fall) as grounds for the sheer possibility of the other (the restoration of virtue). Since the former is inscrutable yet, in Kant's view, an undeniable fact of our moral experience, the inscrutability of the latter does not rule out its possibility. Since the "lapse from good into evil (when we remember that this originates in freedom) is no more comprehensible than the re-ascent from evil to good, the possibility of this last cannot be impugned" (p. 45; p. 40). Such an insight coheres with Kant's general tendency in the depiction of moral conversion to put what we cannot claim to know to positive use. The account gains an odd sort of argumentative strength from Kant's agnosticism.

Kant's appropriation of biblical language may make sense because of the inherent strictures produced by his own systematic position, but it is note-worthy in a deeper sense as well. The Kant who invokes the Johannine notion of "rebirth" or "new creation" is also the Kant who, elsewhere in the *Religion*, raises "the question as to whether morality should be expounded according to the Bible or whether the Bible should not rather be expounded according to morality" (p. 110n.; p. 101n.). Insofar as Kant's answer to his own question is unmistakably clear, producing the subordination of scripture to morality, the remark nicely serves as a symbol of the modern turn in biblical hermeneutics: instead of the text being authoritative over human consciousness, human consciousness (represented in this case by Kantian morality) controls the text, dictating what it can or should mean. As a rule, Kant's view of the Bible – as his view of historical religions in general – rests on the principle that a genuinely *religious* interest in text or tradition must be mediated through the moral consciousness. He does not rule out other kinds of interest, such as a strictly historical interest, but merely argues the futility of seeking a truly religious dividend through any but a moral reading of the text. "We must not quarrel unnecessarily over a question or over its historical aspect, when, however it is understood, it in no way helps us to be better men" (p. 43n.; p. 39n.).

In other words, Kant's most fundamental and characteristic position regarding biblical materials is highly reductionistic. The text is there to serve morality, not the other way around. Consequently, human subjectivity as the locus of moral awareness in the world takes command over the text. The implicit assumption here is that biblical materials are under a kind of conceptual control, with Kant's own conceptual apparatus always in position to explain or account for any given use or reading of the Bible, or to adjudicate between competing readings.[12] The point of Kant's reductionism is that any potential moral lesson or insight that we might derive from the Bible could, in principle, be stated quite adequately apart from any appeal to scripture: the conceptual apparatus yielding the moral meaning is both logically independent of, and superior to, the text. Scripture makes manifest a moral consciousness that derives its validity from the universal structure of reason, and not from what scripture itself offers us. Not only priority, but autonomy is transposed from scripture to the moral self.[13]

The extraordinary thing is that this entire hermeneutical principle undergoes a dramatic reversal in the account of moral regeneration, the only case of its kind in Kant's entire moral and religious philosophy. Instead of the philosophical conceptuality standing poised and ready to explain or translate more adequately a given scriptural account, the scriptural account is called upon because the conceptuality has exhausted itself. Kant cannot say directly what moral regeneration is, yet he has to posit its possibility if his moral universe is to remain intact. The stakes are very high at this moment, Kant's maneuvering room very limited – and it is the Bible that helps him out. From within his straitened position, Kant reaches out to biblical language to announce what his concepts necessitate but cannot describe. He is not really signalling a change in his moral view of religion or some sort of return to an orthodox conception of salvation so much as he is confronting a fresh sense in which radical evil may produce a limitation on reason. At the very least, it is more than a little noteworthy that Kant is driven to this non-reductionistic and – whatever his actual intentions in the matter – virtually confessional appeal to scripture by the problem of moral evil in human life. The moral failing disclosed by radical evil is mirrored in a severe intellectual limitation. In the specific instance of the discussion of moral regeneration, Kant's response to this limitation is to quote from the Bible.[14]

Despite Kant's conceptual failure, it remains possible to characterize moral regeneration in at least one way that remains within his purely conceptual terms. This is the characterization that is entailed by Kant's rejection of devilishness. As we have seen, the rejection of devilishness is the rejection of the idea that radical evil is the complete destruction of the rational capacity and of the attendant ability to be influenced by the moral incentive. A true devil would be beyond the reach of all moral feeling; a wicked rational being, however, "even the most wicked," does not "repudiate the moral law in the manner of a rebel" (p. 36; p. 31) but retains the capacity to be influenced by the moral incentive and, presumably, to experience remorse. To say these things is simply to say that *Wille* remains intact. Consequently, we might further say not only that *Wille* provides for the sheer metaphysical possibility of moral regeneration, but also that moral regeneration itself is a spontaneous act of *Willkür* that responds to the moral incentive continuously present in *Wille*. How and why this should occur is as puzzling as the question of why we fall into radical evil in the first place. After all, the whole point of an evil that is "radical" is that *Willkür* is motivated only to subordinate the moral incentive to the sensuous, not elevate it.

The peculiar thing is that the ever-present possibility of moral regeneration entailed by Kant's rejection of devilishness does not have a counterpart in the case of the moral agent who has in fact undergone regeneration. Although it is always possible, in principle, for a fallen agent to be renewed, it is evidently not possible for a renewed agent to "fall back again," for Kant speaks of the renewed disposition as arising out of "a single *unchangeable* decision" (pp. 47–8; p. 43, emphasis added). It is not clear how to take this claim, nor is it easy to argue against it. For, as Jean-Louis Bruch has pointed out, if, following conversion, there is in fact a second fall, Kant can simply claim that the conversion was not authentic, something which Kant was predisposed to claim in any case, based on his lifelong experience with Königsberg pietists.[15] Presumably, Kant's point is that the moral act implicit in the process of moral regeneration is so prodigious, and the resulting alteration in the disposition so strong, that he does not need to entertain the possibility of a relapse. Obviously, however, this position seems at odds with the pessimism regarding our propensity to evil that had informed Kant's depiction of an evil that is "radical." More importantly, the impossibility of a relapse appears to compromise his theory of freedom, by implying a way in which freedom cannot be exercised.

"Before and after": moral conversion and personal identity

We are not yet to the thorny problem of just how moral regeneration occurs, the issue that most explicitly brings into view Kant's problematic references to divine grace and "supernatural cooperation." But it should be obvious that the sheer definition of moral regeneration, taken by itself, opens up extremely difficult metaphysical questions, together with an assortment of complex considerations related to moral psychology and personal identity. Assuming the ever-present possibility of moral regeneration, how could it ever occur to a moral agent who has become radically evil to attempt to return to virtue? Does not the very definition of radical evil guarantee that any incentive to embark upon a moral recovery – produced, say, by passing feelings of remorse – will be vitiated by a supreme maxim devoted to the general policy of self-love? Does the moral agent suddenly appreciate that its own interest is somehow promoted by a moral conversion, so that the wicked person is subtly lured out of selfishness by an initially selfish motivation? If radical evil is a corrupting underlying act that transmits corruption through each derivative act, what can break into this chain and reverse the situation? And if moral regeneration is a true "rebirth," in what sense is the regenerated agent the "same" person as the evil one?

Numerous conceptual issues embedded in Kant's position are behind these questions. But perhaps the chief culprit producing this conceptual turbulence is what we might call the "before and after" feature of the transition from radical evil to a renewed disposition. Such a feature is of course mandatory if Kant is to speak convincingly of a true "conversion," allowing him to discriminate between the agent as fallen and as regenerated; yet that same feature is virtually unintelligible from the standpoint of the very philosophy that demands it. Kant himself captures the latter point rather bluntly in the *Critique of Pure Reason*:

In respect of the intelligible character, of which the empirical character is the sensible schema, there can be no *before* and *after*. . . . Reason . . . acts freely; it is not dynamically determined in the chain of natural causes through either outer or inner grounds antecedent in time.[16]

Like any other moral act, the dispositional act is not to be understood in terms of causal determinants, which is to say that the pure intuition of time can play no role in our conception of such an act. In other words: the dispositional act producing moral renewal stands in no possible relation to time.

This severing of the connection between time and the moral life is the price Kant must pay in order to protect his theory of freedom. In the background here, of course, is Kant's response to Hume's view of causality, conveyed most directly in Kant's Second Analogy of Experience in the first *Critique*.[17] In the Second Analogy, Kant is concerned to demonstrate the a priori status of our knowledge of causality, thus saving Newtonian regularity from the embarrassing implications of Hume's empiricism. A crucial feature of his position is the claim that all events that we experience in terms of a temporal sequence are also subject to the strict law of causality that Kant is seeking to vindicate: temporality (or the idea of temporal sequence) and causality are folded together as Kant offers his most formal reply to Hume.[18] In thus promoting this agenda, Kant makes it impossible, in his terms, to predicate freedom of any series of events we experience temporally; their being experienced temporally necessarily implicates those events in the causal nexus.

This is quite a satisfactory result for Kant, since, in the context of the *Critique of Pure Reason*, his chief concern is the defense of causality, not of freedom.

However, the Second Analogy leaves it abundantly clear that Kant will be able to salvage a theory of freedom only by sealing it off from temporality. And, indeed, his refusal to reintroduce any sort of splice between freedom and time, or between morality and our experience of ourselves and the world in temporal terms – a refusal fateful for German philosophy in the next century – is subsequently ratified by his formal depiction of his phenomena--noumena dichotomy[19] and by his account of what he rather confusingly calls "causality through freedom."[20] Kant explains that causality through freedom possesses a strictly "intelligible" character, which is Kantian code for "outside of time." The causality of freedom finds its source in pure reason which, "as a purely intelligible faculty, is not subject to the form of time, nor consequently to the conditions of succession in time."[21] If the causality of freedom assumed temporal form, it "would itself be subject to the natural law of appearances, in accordance with which causal series are determined in time; and its causality would then be nature, not freedom."[22] In other words, when experience is thematized temporally, "there is no freedom."[23] Instead, there is the positivist's fondest dream, for if

we could exhaustively investigate all the appearances of men's wills, there would not be found a single human action which we could not predict with certainty, and recognise as proceeding necessarily from its antecedent conditions.[24]

It is probably correct to say that Kant does not have a primary concern to promote as a foundational claim the non-temporal character of freedom and, therefore, of morality. Instead, as is often the case with his transcendental mode of argumentation, Kant finds himself adopting a position on a certain issue (freedom) because of what is necessarily entailed by his exploration into the conditions of the possibility of some other issue (causality). If causality is to be saved, then freedom cannot connect with time. But a commitment to causality does not dispute the sheer *logical* possibility of freedom, for "causality through freedom is at least *not incompatible with* nature."[25] Kant's theory of practical reason will give him sufficient excuse to cash in on this bare logical possibility of freedom, while his phenomena–noumena dichotomy will provide the metaphysical compartments necessary for depicting the peaceful coexistence of a free will and Newtonian determinism.

However understandable this orchestrating of large themes may be as we grasp Kant's post-Humean intentions, his position is fateful for some of the most central issues arising out of his moral and religious thought. For with this position, Kant has utterly crippled his ability to make clear sense of any instance of moral and religious "change," of any alteration in one's moral conditon or religious state that occurs in sequential terms. The effects of his account of the Second Analogy seep down into the smallest conceptual passages relevant to the individual's experience of duty and of episodes of moral decision-making, and they flood into the larger channels formed by Kant's progressive view of history and by the impact of teleological pressures on his efforts to grasp the career of freedom in the most comprehensive terms, as reason demands. When Kant utters his famous words, "If now one asks, What period in the entire known history of the church up to now is the best? I have no scruple in answering, *the present*," he has at his disposal no concepts for making sense of the idea of religious progress implicit in his own comment (p. 131; p. 122).[26]

Nor does he have an obvious way of making sense of the "before and after" of the process of moral conversion. Kant's theory of moral conversion or regeneration culminates in the paradox that an act having no relation to time produces a moral agent who is materially different "after" the act from "before." A related paradox resides in the ethically peculiar implication that the dispositional act producing moral regeneration stands in no relation to any previous act by the moral agent.[27] In other words, the absence of any mediating principle that would integrate the moral and the temporal leaves Kant unable to give sense to any notion of continuity, over time, in the life of the moral agent. Kant can string no metaphysical "thread" through the successive moments of the agent's life, considered morally; he cannot show how a "previous" act or moral condition would be relevant to a "present" act. Thus, there is a certain sense – not at all trivial – in which *every* free act is for Kant a "conversion." This odd possibility is the net effect of freedom's aloofness from all empirical determinants, which, by definition, fall into a causal pattern. Kant comes close to making this very point himself when, in the *Metaphysics of Morals*, he says that virtue "is always in progress and yet always beginning from the beginning."[28]

Moreover, the same principle that establishes the ever-present possibility of moral regeneration – the principle that even the most wicked person is not a devil, but is free to change morally at *any* time – makes it impossible to explain how the "same" moral agent can be guilty (or virtuous) over time. It is simply not clear how to attribute a persisting identity to the agent, considered as a free being. For the very thing that makes the agent's freedom what it is is the absence of the connectedness characteristic of empirical conditions – the absence, that is, of the skein of empirical determinants that, in principle, Newton could chart out for us with complete certainty. But Kant offers no alternative principle of connectedness pertaining to the intelligible world where the moral life has its day, no moral analogue for the kind of connectedness we attribute to events in the natural world. We can never be truly articulate about how the moral agent's moral condition at one moment relates to the agent's condition at another moment.

The implications of this cluster of difficulties for Kant's efforts to depict moral regeneration are ominous indeed. Obviously, if the regenerating dispositional act effectively stands in no relation to any previous act, then the problems associated with our natural question concerning why an evil agent would bother to attempt moral regeneration are considerably deepened. Kant cannot show how anything occurring in the agent's life subsequent to the original fall into radical evil is relevant to any potential "future" moral choice, including the choice to adopt a good disposition. In other words, Kant can shed no light whatsoever on the issue of *motivation* in relation to moral conversion. For the very concept of motivation is virtually analytic with the idea that past experiences, acts, and attitudes bear on a present moment of decision-making in connected and explicable ways. Kant, however, has no means of making the connection. Kant's dilemma is made especially clear if we imagine the situation he lands in if we were simply to posit the needed connection as a kind of thought experiment, enabling ourselves to speak, say, of a moral agent who cultivated the "habit" of performing his or her moral duty over time, including the duty to achieve moral regeneration. For "a *habitual* disposition to perform one's duty would not be a moral one" on Kantian grounds, even if such a disposition consistently results in actions that are in accordance with moral principles. "For the efficacy of such a disposition rests upon its connection with a certain class of actions in the past, and Kant has no conceptual means for conceiving of this relation other than the 'natural' causal principle of necessary succession according to a rule."[29] The lesson is clear: the same principle that allows us to attribute a continuing identity over time to the moral agent makes it impossible for us to characterize the agent's acts as moral. Coming to expression in this dilemma is the fundamental tension – if not sheer incompatibility – between Kant's career-long effort to forge a satisfactory theory of personal identity and his effort, only late in his career, to devise a solution to the problem of moral regeneration posed by his theory of radical evil.

This ruinous result for any effort to explain why an evil agent would attempt to become good again is further reinforced by a striking logical implication of Kant's position. For, as one commentator has put it, in light of the irrelevance of time to freedom and morality, "the person at the point of making the second choice [i.e., to become good again] is numerically indistinguishable from the same person at the point of making the first choice [i.e., to adopt an evil disposition]."

There is no reason whatsoever for the person to make a different choice on the second occasion than on the first occasion. It is as if one person at one occasion made two choices of incompatible supreme maxims... Only if we allow past experience to have an influence on the present decision can this be avoided.[30]

Radical evil and moral regeneration are linked in ways that find no parallel linkage in the moral agent viewed over time. The whole problem of moral renewal or conversion gradually concentrates itself in the question of how we are to understand the difference between the moral agent in his or her first, wrong choice and the agent at the point of the second, virtuous choice.[31]

This way of formulating the problem reveals that Kant's position on moral regeneration masks a build-up of enormous competing pressures concerning the problem of personal identity: on the one hand, the very idea of regeneration or conversion – reinforced by Kant's ethical rigorism and by his appeal to the biblical motifs of "rebirth" and "new creation" – suggests two distinct moral agents, a fallen and a redeemed one; while on the other hand, morality's noumenal insulation from the effects of time suggests just one moral agent, due to Kant's inability to discriminate between "before and after" when he considers the agent as an intelligible, rather than empirical, being. In the first instance, the resulting conceptual problem concerns the integration of the two different selves under a theory of personal identity that allows us to say that the regenerated agent really is the "same" person – in some sense – as the guilty one. For if we cannot do this – if, that is, we end up with two metaphysically distinct agents – it ultimately becomes unclear how we are intelligibly to relate the issues of fall and regeneration. One term needs the other, a need that is met by its being the same person who undergoes both. And in the second instance, the problem concerns showing that the agent was sufficiently different at one point (in time?) than at another for the very idea of conversion to have meaningful application. In addition, demonstrating this difference would be necessary if Kant is not to end up with the self-contradictory thesis that the same person "simultaneously" adopts both an evil and a good disposition.

What is gradually coming into view here is the assortment of conceptual costs Kant must bear as he solves the problems posed by radical evil. As we shall see in the next two chapters, these costs skyrocket as Kant goes beyond simply characterizing moral regeneration to explaining how it actually occurs. For it is in depicting how moral regeneration occurs that Kant needs to offset a fallen freedom with appeals to grace, atonement, and supernatural cooperation. However guarded these appeals may be, the mere fact that Kant turns in such a direction leaves his theory of freedom in a potentially compromised position and severely qualifies any characterization we may wish to give to the connection between purely human efforts and moral regeneration. In Kant's handling of the problem of moral regeneration, we have the confluence of a characteristically modern concern for the autonomy of the moral subject and the biblical tradition's preoccupation with divine action exercised for the sake of the salvation of a fallen humanity. Kant clearly wants to jettison the latter, but his own theory of radical evil makes this impossible. The question then becomes how he accounts for moral regeneration without compounding the problems for human freedom that even his qualified references to God produce.

5

Moral regeneration, human autonomy, and divine aid

And now there opens up before him the abyss of a mystery regarding what God may do . . . , whether indeed *anything* in general, and if so, *what* in particular should be ascribed to God.

Kant

Suppose we were ignorant of what God does and suppose we were convinced only of this: that, because of the holiness of His law and the insuperable evil of our hearts, God must have hidden some supplement to our deficiencies somewhere in the depth of His decrees, something we could humbly rely on, if only we should do what is in our power, so as not to be unworthy of His law. If that were so, we should have all the guidance we need, whatever the manner of communication between the divine goodness and ourselves might be.

Kant

Overview of the problems

However difficult it may be to explain what moral regeneration is, the difficulties are enormously compounded when we attempt to account for how it occurs. For just here Kant is delicately walking a fine line between autonomy and grace, free will and providence, appealing to the human dimension so as to have the result be a truly *moral* regeneration, while referring in vague but substantive ways to divine action so as to underwrite the possibility of what radical evil seems to make impossible. As I have been indicating all along, this is where Kant's position will wobble most severely, signalling his awkward posture between a modern commitment to autonomy and a received tradition framed in terms of biblical imagery. He is struggling to free himself of the latter in order to do justice to the former, but is prevented from doing so because of his own theory of radical evil. The resulting interpretive problems that emerge at this point are quite considerable.

For example, it is not entirely clear how to understand the epistemological status of Kant's comments about grace and divine aid. This is because much of what he has to say about such topics is packed into the "General Observations" appended to each of the four books of the *Religion*, which are intended to afford Kant the opportunity to discuss matters that "do not belong within" a religion of pure reason "but border upon it" – what he calls, *"parerga"* (p. 52; p. 47). He includes among such topics "works of grace," "miracles," "mysteries," and "means of grace." Whatever Kant's excuses, it is frankly odd to find him discussing such topics – an oddity that is hardly mitigated by the fact that none of the four topics "exhibits a close connection to the topic of the book to which it is appended."[1]

Reason, conscious of her inability to satisfy her moral need, extends herself to high-flown ideas capable of supplying this lack, without, however, appropriating these ideas as an extension of her domain. Reason does not dispute the possibility or the reality of the objects of these ideas; she simply cannot adopt them into her maxims of thought and action. (p. 52; pp. 47–8)

With specific respect to the idea of grace, this position yields the result that "we can admit a work of grace as something incomprehensible, but we cannot adopt it into our maxims either for theoretical or for practical use" (p. 53; p. 49).

The tone of such comments is apparently modest, but their actual effect is to give Kant considerable maneuvering room. As we shall see in this and the following chapter, it is quite difficult to gain clear focus on the fine line that Kant means to draw here. But his approach in this instance, is, I think, a good example of an extremely important general tendency in the *Religion*. For implicit in Kant's strategy concerning the *parerga* is a motif that, despite its latency, is one of the most powerful driving forces in the entire book – namely, his exploitation of what he originally announces as a limitation of reason and cognition for positive, constructive purposes. Kant more or less "backs into" discussions of seemingly forbidden or philosophically irrelevant topics, and then, once there, he devises solutions to difficulties produced on the purely philosophical level. The key move, obviously, is the move that gets him on the initially forbidden ground.

The suspicion thus arises that his appeals to such notions as grace are more heuristic than theologically robust, more strategic than substantive. In this particular case, my own suspicion is that Kant knows he needs the added room provided by appeals to grace in order to handle the problems posed by radical evil. To what extent this possibility might actually shape *Religion within the Limits of Reason Alone* is impossible to say. All we can say is that Kant's cautionary, limiting language does not offset the fact that he is, after all, providing himself with an excuse to talk about grace and supernatural action – a result that by itself would be alarming to a certain sort of deist.[2]

Moreover, it is not at all clear that Kant abides by his own strictures as he goes on to make use of the notion of divine aid in his account of moral conversion. As we shall see, when it suits him, Kant clearly appears to be employing "for practical use" the possibility of divine assistance, something he had denied he would be doing (p. 53; p. 49). For example, he will characteristically warn against the "persuasion that we can distinguish the effects of grace from those of nature (virtue) or can actually produce the former within ourselves," labeling such a view "fanaticism" (p. 174; p. 162). Yet he will immediately add the comment that to

believe that there may be works of grace and that perhaps these may even be necessary to supplement the incompleteness of our struggle toward virtue – that is all we can say on this subject. (p. 174; p. 162)

This heavily qualified comment bears an ironic resemblance to the final judgment of Hume's Philo, following his lengthy debate with Cleanthes about the possibility of moving from experience of order in the world to belief in God, in the *Dialogues Concerning Natural Religion*: "[T]he whole of natural theology... resolves itself into one simple, though somewhat ambiguous, at least undefined proposition, *that the cause or causes of order in the universe probably bear some remote analogy to human intelligence.*"[3] But of course whereas Philo means to water down – to the point of negating – the claims of natural theology, Kant takes up his own seemingly watered down version of the appeal to divine action and exploits it in order to help solve the problem of moral regeneration. Kant openly admits that his qualified summary is "all we can say" – but it turns out that "all we can say" is actually quite a lot. Kant's attempt to surround his comment with modesty does not offset the fact that the view thus expressed produces generous results for a thinker presumably wed to a purely moral theory of religion.

Kant's most important safeguard against both overemphasizing the role played by divine aid and making theoretical claims impossible to support by critical principles is his tendency to address the possibility of divine aid as an object of rational hope. This feature of his account of moral regeneration not only reflects Kant's explicit and longstanding interest in the question, "What may I hope?" – evidently taken as *the* religious question[4] – but suggests the way his reasoning in resolving the problem of radical evil repeats much of the reasoning previously present in the postulation process in the second *Critique*. Although the goal now is to exhibit both the logical and the real possibility of moral regeneration (rather than of immortality and God), Kant's thinking in both cases is moved along by certain needs or demands of reason that signal the controlling role played in his vision by something like correct proportion or symmetry. Once again, Ivan Karamazov would no doubt want to ask if this way of solving the problem of moral evil is in fact to beg the very question at stake by demonstrating the triumph over evil simply by assuming at the outset that the universe is fair and proportionate. The point at which the dividing line between Kant and Ivan is due to an argumentative difference, or due instead to pre-argumentative differences in something like "animal faith," is difficult to specify exactly. What seems clear is that the difference between them is highlighted most explicitly, not by Kant's theory of radical evil, but by his account of moral regeneration, which theoretically vindicates both God and human autonomy without, presumably, making evil itself any less real.

As we shall see in the course of this chapter and the next, a further difficulty in the interpretation of Kant's view of moral regeneration arises out of the fact that his account folds together several issues that ought ideally to be kept separate. The effect is to leave his reader either confused or actually misled regarding just what it is that produces – or is capable of producing – moral regeneration. A good example of this is Section One of Book Two, in which Kant offers what amounts to his christology, couched in terms of what he calls the "personified idea of the good principle" (pp. 60ff.; pp. 54ff.). Throughout this section, Kant equivocates between simply discussing the "objective reality of this idea" and actually employing this idea for the purpose of explaining how moral conversion occurs. One might put the point more positively by saying that, in this section of the *Religion*, Kant is implicitly acknowledging that one cannot discuss radical evil ("original sin") without also discussing christology, and that one cannot discuss the latter without discussing the doctrine of justification. This is a perfectly natural theological principle; the problem is that it is not clear from the discussion how it can be a *Kantian* principle. This section, perhaps more than any other single place in Kant's entire philosophy of religion, hints at the possibility that Kant's commitment to radical evil forces his position back to some sort of reliance on a specific historical occurrence – in the form of Christ's breaking the "power" of the evil principle to hold us against our will (pp. 82–3; p. 77) – in the resolution of his own problem. The doctrine of radical evil potentially suggests that the full articulation of Kant's philosophy of religion ironically and covertly hinges on an appeal to an historical moment, while every other feature of his position tends to subordinate history to the imperializing tendencies of a universalizing rationality. Of course, Kant does not finally capitulate to this pressure that his own doctrine has produced, since the resulting compromise for reason would be too extreme. Instead, he works laboriously to integrate a theory of atonement with his coveted principle of autonomy, with the help of a rather convoluted theory of punishment for past sins. But the instability in his position is very real and serves as a telling preview of subsequent christological debates over whether Jesus simply makes manifest certain truths that are logically separable from his person, or whether instead his actual appearance as an historical event is decisive for salvation. The surprise, perhaps, is that Kant should even be implicated in such a set of questions at all. He would not have to be, were it not for his own theory of radical evil.

Hoping for help

Kant opens the "General Observation" appended to Book One of the *Religion* with the following comment:

Man *himself* must make or have made himself into whatever, in a moral sense, whether good or evil, he is or is to become... Granted that some supernatural cooperation may be necessary to his becoming good, or to his becoming better, yet, whether this cooperation consists merely in the abatement of hindrances or indeed ,in positive assistance, man must first make himself worthy to receive it. (p. 44; p. 40)

This comment sets the stage for Kant's account of what is evidently a human–divine partnership in the process of moral regeneration. Kant then progresses past his own stage settings and further defines the issue posed above by moving the key question to center stage: "But if a man is corrupt in the very ground of his maxims, how can he possibly bring about this revolution by his own powers and of himself become a good man?" (p. 47; p. 43).

It is in his answer to this question that Kant comes closest actually to characterizing moral regeneration, while also making explicit the role of God in the regeneration process. As Kant works out his answer, he weaves together several topics in a complicated pattern: an emphasis on "hope"; a delicate moral psychology, designed to provide a fully rational assurance that divine aid is forthcoming while guarding against allowing this assurance to engender passivity or moral laxity; and considerable reliance on his dualistic tendencies, especially the dichotomies between the phenomenal and noumenal and between a sensible and an intellectual intuition. Kant manipulates these several threads with a view to showing how radical evil is overcome.

Theologically considered, the result is a conflation of the doctrines of justification and sanctification, the mingling of the latter with the former made inevitable by the demands posed by Kant's views on freedom and moral accountability. Somewhat ironically – in light of the connections often drawn between Kant and Luther – this theological result represents, if anything, a return to a pre-Reformation view of justification, with its characteristic emphasis on both the capacity and the willingness (however slight) of the believer to respond to the divine initiative.[5] In Kant's terms, *Wille* always remains intact: it is our indestructible resource for moral acting, however sinful our condition may become.

In two separate but similar sections of the *Religion*, Kant puts these themes to use (pp. 47ff., 67ff.; pp. 43ff., 60ff.). The accounts are not only difficult, but confusing as well. This is because in the first instance, as we saw in the previous chapter, Kant has framed the issue in terms of the question, "how can [a corrupt agent] possibly bring about this revolution by his own powers," yet he simply skips over the answer to this specific question and describes what the change is like, not how it occurs. The resulting equivocation reveals that Kant is actually explaining nothing. And the second instance is the point in the text where Kant runs together the question of how moral regeneration is possible with his christological question of whether the "personified idea of the good principle" is possible. The net effect of these sudden plot alterations is to make it extremely difficult to isolate Kant's actual comments on moral regeneration and divine aid.

Insofar as we can isolate the first step in this position, however, it seems to occur in the following comment:

> [I]f a man reverses, by a single unchangeable decision, that highest ground of his maxims whereby he was an evil man (and thus puts on a new man), he is, so far as his principle and cast of mind are concerned, a subject susceptible of goodness, but only in continuous labor and growth is he a good man. That is, he can hope in the light of that purity of the principle which he has adopted as the supreme maxim of his will, and of its stability, to find himself upon the good (though strait) path of continual *progress* from bad to better. (pp. 47–8; p. 43)

Notice to begin with how Kant begs his own question (concerning how someone with a corrupt disposition can become good again) by simply assuming at the outset of his answer that this transformation has already occurred. Just *how* someone "reverses, by a single unchangeable decision, that highest ground" of one's maxims (i.e., the disposition), is exactly what we want to understand, rather than what we can assume as a premise for discussing something else. Presumably, Kant cannot really answer this question without setting a free act of *Willkür* into an explanatory framework – but he is the one who has fashioned the question as though he is going to tell us.

What he does tell us, though, goes to the heart of the problem concerning divine aid or grace. The important point seems to be this: Kant is clearly less interested in the metaphysical question of whether or not God is actually "acting" on my behalf than in the psychological question of the potential effect the *possibility* of such aid might have on my motivation. For I begin with a twofold problem that could destroy at the outset any motivation to overcome radical evil. First, since I begin in evil, I begin with a disposition that will systematically rebuff all attempts at moral regeneration by over-powering the moral incentive with the sensuous. Even allowing that an evil disposition, always subject to the moral feeling arising out of *Wille*, could feel the force of the obligation to undergo regeneration, the chief effect would presumably be feelings of futility, moral discouragement, and a sense of despair that I could ever marshall the resources of will to act on that sense of obligation. The danger thus emerging is that this sense of futility would "rob a man of his courage and reduce him to a state of sighing moral passivity in which nothing great or good is undertaken." (pp. 184–5; p. 172). An additional problem potentially vitiating my motivation is the fact that, were I actually to try to change my underlying moral structure, I could never really know if I had succeeded, leaving me in an utterly precarious posture.

Man cannot attain naturally to assurance concerning such a revolution... either by immediate consciousness or through the evidence furnished by the life which he has hitherto led, for the deeps of the heart (the subjective first ground of his maxims) are inscrutable to him. (p. 51; p. 46)

Kant's point is in keeping with at least the first part of his general principle that the moral agent "can form no certain and definite concept of his real disposition through an immediate consciousness thereof and can only abstract it from the way of life he has actually followed" (p. 77; p. 71). But this is simply to say that I can only have sure knowledge of the legality of my acts, not their morality.[6]

Given the initial difficulty of overcoming my feelings of futility and moral despair, then, the additional fact that I could never really know if I had succeeded in undergoing moral regeneration could have devastating effects. If the absolute assurance that I have been morally successful is impossible in principle, I can gain no motivational foothold in my own consciousness for overcoming my fear of moral failure.

The chief purpose of Kant's comments about divine aid or grace is to counteract this motivational problem. We can detect this, not only in the overall direction that his several discussions of divine aid in the *Religion* take, but in his most explicit attempt to define the notion of grace itself. As Kant puts it, "only a *capability of receiving*, which is all that we, for our part, can credit to ourselves; and a superior's decree conferring a good for which the subordinate possesses nothing but the (moral) receptivity is called *grace*" (p. 75n.; p. 70n.). The language of grace offsets the lack of assurance that we are either capable of, or have successfully undertaken, the moral revolution. This result manifests the general tendency of Kant's discussion to transform his commentary on moral regeneration into insights into moral psychology. His accompanying tendency subtly then to enlist the latter as a way of explaining the former accounts for no small part of the difficulty involved in understanding his overall position. In the end, I think it is fair to say that, for all his comments on the matter, Kant remains utterly agnostic on the question of the reality of grace. This view helps to mitigate the apparent tensions between his seeming hospitality to themes drawn from orthodox Christian theology in the *Religion* and the much more stringent and philo-sophically austere position he articulates in the first two *Critiques*, where the notion of ongoing divine action is marginalized, if not rejected altogether. What is interesting is the way Kant's characteristic expansion of the religious role played by subjective, autonomous moral consciousness is brought to an abrupt halt by radical evil. Positive commentary about God is reintroduced precisely because Kant has no other way to resolve the difficulties that radical evil has generated. This larger point remains valid whether we take Kant's appeals to divine aid to be actual comments about divine activity or simply motivational devices designed to offset a sense of moral futility. After all, in his rejection of devilishness, Kant had already established the possibility of moral regeneration apart from divine aid by showing it to be a duty. He does not really need to appeal to God to guarantee its possibility, but only to help us to act on this possibility. And however true it may be to say that his appeals to grace are best viewed in terms of their impact on the psychology of the moral agent, the appeals are sufficiently explicit as to call into question the self-sufficiency of human autonomy. At the very least, the moral agent has to undertake religious thought experiments in order to round out the religious life, thought experiments best thematized in terms of the surpris-ingly orthodox language of divine grace. Whether or not these thought experiments have a true content is less important than the fact that radical evil makes it necessary to undertake them. Or to make the same point in different terms: the fact that Kant ultimately takes a reductionistic view of grace does not cancel out the accompanying fact that he appeals to grace in a constructive way. He is not merely surveying the traditional topics of historical, revealed religion with a view to their moral meaning. In the case of the issue of grace, at least, the appeal is required, not optional, if Kant is to solve the problem of moral regeneration.

This interplay between the moral agent's motivation and the possibility of divine aid symbolizes the fine line Kant is walking throughout the *Religion*. Indeed, the way his appeal to a presumed object of hope may in fact, upon inspection, be an appeal to the agent's own moral consciousness is perhaps the most significant of the "wobbles" in Kant's overall position: the commingling of references to God and references to responsible human effort is precisely what makes the *Religion* such a telling and suggestive cultural marker. Kant's account thus puts a premium on accurately characterizing the proper object of hope and its effects on my motivation as a moral agent. We have seen that this object of hope is divine assistance in overcoming radical evil and restoring the predisposition to good to a position of preeminence. Less obvious is how I hope for this aid without allowing my trust in its delivery to undermine me morally. What is interesting about Kant's position is the way the theory of radical evil appears to force him in an Augustinian direction, while his conception of grace or divine aid reintroduces an obviously Pelagian element based on human effort and merit. The resulting position – in keeping with my characterization of his entire account of radical evil and moral regeneration – is not so much incoherent as it is unstable.

Thus, for example, when Kant allows that "some supernatural cooperation may be necessary" if we are to escape from radical evil, he immediately adds that "man must make himself worthy to receive it" (p. 44; p. 40). Likewise, upon saying that we find ourselves "impelled to believe in the cooperation or management of a moral Ruler of the world," he adds that what God may actually do is "the abyss of a mystery," while "man knows concerning each duty . . . what he must himself do in order to be worthy of that supplement" (p. 139; p. 130). Perhaps his clearest rendering of the matter occurs in his statement of what he calls "a basic principle," namely, the principle

that each must do as much as lies in his power to become a better man, and that only when he has not buried his inborn talent . . . but made use of his original predisposition to good in order to become a better man, can he hope that what is not within his power will be supplied through cooperation from above. (p. 52; p. 47)

For Kant, we "merit" God's grace when we do our imperfect best. As I have been suggesting, his intention is not really to endorse a full-fledged doctrine of justification and reconciliation but to defend against passivity and a sense of moral failure and futility. Although we can rationally expect that God will somehow offset our moral weakness, we are "not entitled on this account to be idle in this business and to let Providence rule."

Rather must man proceed as though everything depended upon him; only on this condition dare he hope that higher wisdom will grant the completion of his well-intentioned endeavors. (pp. 100–1; p. 92)

Again, we see how Kant's most direct comments about moral regeneration gradually metamorphose into insights into the moral psychology of an agent in the grip of radical evil.[7]

This tendency toward metamorphosis helps to ease – or at least to distract attention from – the conflict between divine aid and human freedom embedded in the very question of moral recovery. In addition, however, the metamorphosis considerably waters down the object of hope as an actual object, once again turning the strictly religious interest back to the subject, or the believing moral agent. Correctly interpreted, the object of hope that is presumably "outside" the believer – namely, divine aid – turns back reflexively onto the believer as a fresh moment in his or her moral consciousness: talk about divine aid becomes a new form of moral encouragement, which the believer is obligated to act upon. In correctly decoding the language of grace, the religious self learns something about itself rather than something about a state of affairs outside of itself. Kant's account of moral regeneration gains its distinctive pattern from this peculiar interweaving of substantive religious claims and a religious epistemology grounded in the idea of the self-sufficiency of the believing subject.

This tendency is capsulized in an important remark in the fourth and final book of the *Religion* where, in elaborating on what he calls the "genuine maxim of certainty, which alone is compatible with religion," Kant says:

Whatever, as the means or the condition of salvation, I can know not through my own reason but only through revelation, and can incorporate into my confession only through the agency of an historical faith, and which, in addition, does not contradict pure moral principles – *this I cannot, indeed, believe and profess as certain, but I can as little reject it as being surely false*; nevertheless, without determining anything on this score, I may expect that whatever therein is salutary will stand me in good stead so far as I do not render myself unworthy of it through defect of the moral disposition in good life-conduct. (p. 189; p. 177, emphasis added)

The "moral certainty" residing in this principle is not certainty regarding a state of affairs separate from my own consciousness; rather, it is "certainty in the eye of conscience (and more than this cannot be required of a man)" (p. 189; p. 177). What I can have a clear conscience about is not the reality of grace or of the content of a putative revelation, but the sincerity with which I believe and the honesty with which I strive to possess a moral disposition: I can know with certainty whether or not I am a hypocrite.

The fragile balance here between an appeal to something "outside" me that I seem to require for salvation, and the epistemological self-sufficiency of my own conscience, is symptomatic of Kant's more specialized approach to the specific issue of grace. Kant makes the appeal to what is "outside" the believer in order to draw attention in a fresh way to what is already immanent in the believer's consciousness. Here, as throughout the *Religion*, Kant is feeling his way toward a solution to the problem of "positivity" in religion – the problem, that is, of reconciling what is naturally present in human consciousness with what breaks in from the outside and is mediated by a tradition that puts in question the autonomy of the believer. Or perhaps it is more accurate to say that Kant is rather unexpectedly stumbling upon the problem of positivity, due to the newly discovered limitations placed on freedom by radical evil. A "positive" religion makes sense when the individual is discovered not to be fully self-sufficient. The "main point" of a positive faith, as Lukács puts it in his account of positivity in the young Hegel, is the independence of religious propositions from private opinion together with the demand that the believer should regard the propositions "as binding on himself even though he has not created them. Positivity, then, means primarily the suspension of the moral autonomy of the subject."[8] However much Kant might resist having his own religious views take him in the direction of a positive faith, his appeals to divine aid in the solution to the problem of moral regeneration suggest that he fully grasps the rationale behind the notion of positivity.[9] Having spent the bulk of the critical period working out a theory of a purely rational moral religion, Kant discovers late in his career that his own theory of radical evil brings back into view the question of whether or not the religious believer is truly self-sufficient.

It is thus a bit tricky to say with any precision exactly what it is that Kant thinks the believer ought to "believe": on the one hand, Kant does not want to place the emphasis on theoretically dubious beliefs about states of affairs outside the believer; but on the other hand, he is admitting that radical evil requires the believer to hope for outside aid in ways that seem to entail certain religious beliefs. There is of course the possibility that Kant is simply using the appeal to grace as a kind of heuristic device (reminiscent of his notion of the "regulative," as opposed to "constitutive," employment of principles of reason in the first *Critique*),[10] employed to produce a specific moral result and then to be dropped as, in itself, a matter of indifference and beyond all possible theoretical knowledge in any case. This strategy would be consistent with Kant's general tendency in the *Religion* to decode the historical side of religion – such as scripture, tradition, and church – in terms of the "inner" moral meaning. But what we are seeing in connection with the problems disclosed by radical evil and moral regeneration is the limit point beyond which such a reductionism cannot proceed without considerable qualification. We have already confronted this limit point in connection with Kant's appeal to scripture when describing moral regeneration in Johannine rather than conceptual terms. In such an instance, Kant is not merely confronting the limits of his reductionistic strategy, he is actually having to reverse the strategy. Yet they are limits that Kant is always trying to overcome and a reversal that he attempts to avoid, as in his constant warnings in this case not to allow the expectation of divine assistance to produce a slackening of moral effort. Unlike, say, Luther, Kant is not interested in our fallenness as a way of drawing our attention to grace; instead, he is interested in grace as a means of keeping us morally stimulated and encouraged, even once we have apprehended the depths of our depravity.

This lesson is particularly well illustrated by the way Kant first devises, and then dissolves, an antinomy bearing on the relation between freedom and grace. The issue before him is the relation between an ecclesiastical or historical faith, and a rational or pure moral faith (pp. 116–19; pp. 107–10). The antinomy resides in the question of whether good life conduct must precede belief in an atonement produced by grace, or if belief in atonement must precede good life conduct. On the one hand, "it is quite impossible to see how a reasonable man... can in all seriousness believe that he needs only to credit the news of an atonement rendered for him," as though nothing depends on him (p. 116; p. 107). Atonement cannot occur unless it has been earned through renewed virtue. On the other hand, however, if

men are corrupt by nature, how can a man believe that by himself, try as hard as he will, he can make himself a new man well-pleasing to God, when – conscious of the transgressions of which up to the present he has been guilty – he still stands in the power of the evil principle and finds in himself no capacity adequate for future improvement? (p. 117; p. 108)

The second side of the antinomy seems to lead one to the conclusion that "faith in a merit not his own, whereby he is reconciled with God, must precede every effort to good works" – a conclusion that, as Kant himself is quick to point out, "goes counter to the previous proposition" (p. 117; p. 108).

Several things are at work in Kant's depiction and resolution of this antinomy, for it is a densely compacted mixture of metaphysical issues, bearing on our moral state, and epistemological issues, bearing on what we need to "know" in order to improve our moral state. Its abrupt appearance midway through Book Three seems somewhat forced or artificial – as though Kant is having a sudden fit of architectonic nostalgia. Nonetheless, its appearance is useful, for insofar as Kant frames the antinomy in a way designed to expose the drawbacks of each side, his discussion effectively brings to a climax the pressures inherent in his overall account of the interplay among freedom, grace, and hope. His solution to the antinomy – which is not really a true solution so much as it is the gradual disclosure that the antinomy is "only apparent" (p. 110) – is a classic instance of the practical overriding the theoretical in Kant's depiction of the authentic religious life. For Kant effectively reframes the antinomy in the terms of both theoretical and practical reason and shows how it is utterly irresolvable and intractable from the theoretical point of view. By contrast, the practical point of view – though it may not lead to a genuine solution to the antinomy – at least produces a question we can answer and answer, as far as Kant is concerned, quite easily. By then claiming that the dead-end, theoretical approach is associated with the second part of the antinomy, and the more promising practical approach with the first, Kant subtly fuses together his judgment that the antinomy is "only apparent" with a clear strategic victory for the first part of the antinomy, which places moral effort before belief in divine assistance.

Thus, we find Kant claiming that the "contradiction" coming to expression in the antinomy "cannot be resolved theoretically," by which he means it cannot be resolved through "insight into the causal determination of the freedom of a human being, i.e., into the causes which bring it about that a man becomes good or bad" (p. 117; p. 108). In other words, we cannot have knowledge of an act of freedom. This is, by now, such an obvious principle of Kant's moral philosophy that it is difficult to stifle the suspicion that Kant's argumentation here is a bit of a set-up. Indeed, when he then poses the matter practically rather than theoretically, it is like walking into the clear light of day:

But practically, the question arises: What, in the use of our free will, comes first (not physically but morally)? Where shall we start, i.e., with a faith in what God has done on our behalf, or with what we are to do to become worthy of God's assistance (whatever this may be)? In answering this question we cannot hesitate in deciding for the second alternative. (p. 118; p. 108)

By then going on to show that the part of the antinomy requiring divine assistance first is needed only for the *theoretical* solution of the antinomy, Kant tilts decisively in favor of the practical perspective. The victory of the practical approach is then made complete when Kant claims that, in any case, belief in atonement really only amounts to a belief in our *own* rational capacity to become well-pleasing to God – a potential savior figure, in whom we would believe, merely embodies a moral capacity available to all (p. 119; pp. 109–10). Consequently, what Kant calls "the object of saving faith" informing the second part of the antinomy turns out to be a rational "archetype lying in our reason" (p. 119; p. 110). What seems at first to be "outside" of us is in fact "inside."

The antinomy thus dissolves. It arises "through a misunderstanding," because we have mistakenly regarded "the self-same practical idea, taken merely in different references, as two different principles" (p. 119; p. 110).

Whether or not this is really so is less important than the fact that the so-called antinomy epitomizes the way Kant broaches the subject of grace or divine aid as though he is going to make substantive use of it, only to translate the reference to grace into a fresh way of emphasizing self-reliance. Just as telling is the accompanying fact that Kant's solution illustrates the way this translation process leaves basically unaddressed the problem causing all the difficulty in the first place – the problem, that is, of how the fallen agent is to will its way upwards again. Bluntly stated: Kant's so-called solution to his so-called antinomy begs the question that he himself has formulated in the second part of his antinomy. He has concluded by emphasizing self-reliance above belief in outside aid, whereas the difficulty posed by the second part of the antinomy concerns the efficacy of self-reliance if the moral agent "still stands in the power of the evil principle and finds in himself no capacity adequate for future improvement" (p. 117; p. 108).

To suggest, then, that Kant's view of grace or divine assistance is effectively transformed into a moral imperative is not to claim that his position regains the stability and inner consistency of a purely moral theory of religion. Signs of instability are not so easily interpreted away, and not simply because of the uneasy mix of Augustine and Pelagius in Kant's account. The deeper problem throughout Kant's discussion is produced by the fact that, on the one hand, the moral drama concerning fall and regeneration is a drama of the self against *itself*, while, on the other hand, Kant has not entirely jettisoned the traditional language of divine grace in the telling of this drama. The fact that the language of grace may be given a moral meaning does not alter the accompanying fact that Kant is caught between two vocabularies, with his cramped posture the result of the governing irony: his own vocabulary of autonomy has not itself gained full autonomy, due to a fall that autonomy has suffered through its own willing. This is the basic situation produced by radical evil, a situation that, in turn, assures that, as Kant works his way out to the edges of his own position, he finds himself in paradox.

Moral conversion and the divine perspective

The idea that God supplements our best – though inadequate – efforts to overcome radical evil does not exhaust Kant's account of divine aid. For there is a second strand in Kant's account, one that is confusingly interwoven with his depiction of the difference between the gradual reform of one's public, phenomenal conduct and the non-temporal revolution in one's noumenal disposition. Both of these strands are further interwoven with Kant's accounts of christology and atonement, as his discussion of the sheer possibility of a "personified idea of the good principle" is tied to his solution to the problem of how to atone for the "surplus" of guilt that we carry up to the point of moral conversion. At stake here are not simply problems concerning the relationship between human autonomy and transcendent action, but difficult issues of personal and moral justice as well.

As we have seen, the first sense in which Kant appeals to the idea of divine assistance involves the notion of a supplement to our moral effort. The second sense, however, involves the notion of "perspective" rather than supplement: Kant squeezes a beneficial result out of his depiction of the way God "sees" or "views" moral regeneration. His point is a puzzling one, for – once again – he introduces it as though he were explaining how moral regeneration occurs but then elaborates on it in a way that simply presupposes that the conversion has already happened.

Thus, we find Kant posing the key question: "But if a man is corrupt in the very ground of his maxims, how can he possibly bring about this revolution by his own powers?" (p. 47; pp. 43). In responding to his own question, Kant invokes a twofold distinction. First, he distinguishes between the revolutionary nature of our dispositional change and the gradual, evolutionary nature of the accompanying "reform" in our phenomenal, "sensuous nature"; and second, he distinguishes between our experience of gradual, "continual *progress* from bad to better" and God's view of the change "as a revolution" (p. 48; p. 43). These distinctions are not simply spin-offs of Kant's phenomena–noumena dichotomy, they are also reminders of his distinction in the first *Critique* between a "sensible" and an "intellectual" intuition. As rational yet finite beings, we are limited by our possession of a mere "sensible intuition," which means that we cannot experience things-in-themselves but can only have experience that is thematized in terms of the pure intuitions of space and time.[11] Kant's enforcement of this point marks one of the decisive differences between his pre-critical and critical outlooks.

God, on the other hand, is distinguished in part by the possession of an *intellectual* intuition. God does experience things-in-themselves, noumenal as opposed to merely phenomenal reality – a divine attribute that is, as it were, an epistemological analogue to God's moral quality of a "holy will."[12] Applied to the distinction between gradual reform in our phenomenal behavior and revolutionary change in the underlying disposition, Kant's new distinction yields the claim that God views our gradual progress as a completed whole, turning this divine ability to "see" the completeness of our moral change at the intelligible level into a divine favor that offsets the discrepancy between revolutionary noumenal change and merely evolutionary change in phenomenal life conduct.

For Him who penetrates to the intelligible ground of the heart (the ground of all maxims of the will) and for whom this unending progress is a unity, i.e., for God, this [moral gradualism] amounts to his being actually a good man (pleasing to Him); and, thus viewed, this change can be regarded as a revolution. (p. 48; p. 43)

God does not experience our moral condition temporally, only noumenally. Our "unending progress" is for God a "unity," implying that divine aid in this second sense amounts to something like God's willingness to treat what we experience as merely progressive as in fact complete and already actual. It is quite literally a case of God's "overlooking" the fact that our moral progress at the level of daily life conduct occurs only incrementally.

This passage is as frustrating as it is important. It appears at the point where Kant has posed – as forcefully as he does anywhere in the *Religion* – the question of *how* a moral agent fallen into radical evil can possibly undergo conversion. As an answer to this question, however, his appeal to the divine perspective is a complete failure. In the first place, there is the obvious logical point that what Kant actually says here about the divine point of view requires as its antecedent condition the completion of the moral conversion: the reason "this change can be regarded as a revolution" by God is that it has already occurred. It is useless, then, to imply that the appeal to the divine perspective helps us to understand how the disposition can be renewed once it is in the grip of radical evil. In fact, the appeal to the divine perspective simply begs the question that Kant himself has proposed. He has not asked, "How does God view moral regeneration?," but "How can a being corrupt in the disposition bring about the morally obligatory change of heart?," and an answer to the first question cannot convincingly serve as an answer to the second.[13]

To be sure, the discovery that God's way of viewing the change does not account for the change itself effectively protects the autonomy of the moral agent. That is, nothing in what Kant says here about the divine point of view threatens our ability to impute responsibility to the agent thus changed. But this result also intensifies the question of just why Kant appeals to the divine perspective at all when attempting to clarify the process of moral regeneration. Individual autonomy may be saved, but we are not closer to understanding how the autonomous agent escapes the grip of radical evil.

The puzzlement deepens if we ponder the implications of Kant's contrast between the sensuous, human intuition and its intellectual, divine counterpart. Because we necessarily possess a sensuous intuition, we experience – at most – a gradual improvement in our behavior following a moral conversion, from which we might cautiously infer the conversion itself. The same epistemological point holds here as in Kant's general policy of denying absolute certainty regarding the status of anyone's moral disposition, even one's own (p. 63; pp. 56–7). Alternatively, as we have just seen, for "Him who penetrates to the intelligible ground of the heart," what is merely gradual and progressive for us amounts to our "actually" being good. God "sees" the totality of the moral conversion, intuits our "unending progress" as "a unity," and counts our moral change "as a revolution" at any given moment of our worldly pilgrimage. Since we are limited, sensuous beings, we cannot share this insight into the noumenal ground of our phenomenal acts, but can only hope the change has occurred.

But the converse applies as well: God can "see" things in no other way. That is, God is not exercising a free and gracious option in viewing our moral change as complete; instead, God is viewing things in the only way God can. This is the whole point of Kant's attributing to God an intellectual rather than a sensuous intuition. Just as God's possession of a holy will means that God cannot break the moral law – which is not, for Kant, a divine limitation only because God would not *want* to break it – God's possession of an intellectual intuition means that God does not experience our moral state in temporal terms. It is hardly an act of grace or supernatural "cooperation," then, for God to view our moral change as a completed whole if that is the only way in which God can view it. This is not divine assistance in a cooperative venture so much as it is a divine *limitation* in a universe filled with Kantian constraints.

Consequently, the appeal to the divine perspective does not clarify the process of moral conversion so much as it intensifies the question of how we achieve it. Once again, we see here the general tendency of Kant's account of moral regeneration to circle back on itself to an emphasis on human autonomy and the psychology of moral agency. The manifestation of this general tendency in this particular case is especially telling because of the way our discovery of a fresh sense in which we can pose to ourselves a moral obligation is triggered by the disclosure of a limit on God: upon inspection, an appeal to transcendence turns into a thinly disguised way of posing to ourselves the question of how we are to do what is demanded of us. Yet, paradoxically, Kant's justification for appealing to transcendence in the first place was the disclosure of a limitation on *ourselves* produced by radical evil. Consequently, his position oscillates between the depiction of a debility and the expression of a demand, with traditional biblical imagery helping him to give tangible expression to the oscillation, even as Kant attempts to express a philosophical content incompatible with much of that imagery. That is, he goes "outside" this world in order finally to underscore an obligation that can only be met *in* the world. Kant's problem thus seems to be that reason alone cannot give full expression to the desired philosophical content – Kant cannot tell a complete story about our salvation in terms that keep both reason and autonomy unambiguously intact. The will that cripples itself in its own act of willing thereby discovers itself mirrored in severe cognitive limitations.

6

Autonomy and atonement

But godliness is not a surrogate for virtue.

Kant

The relation of history to reason remains constitutive for the discourse of modernity – for better or worse.

Jürgen Habermas

The surplus of moral debt

To this point, we have seen a series of difficulties emerge as Kant attempts to show how a fallen freedom can, through its own powers, overcome the effects of its fallenness. These various difficulties fuse into a complex maze as Kant tries to supplement appeals to human effort with appeals to divine activity, but without jeopardizing the element of autonomy required to keep his view recognizably Kantian. Upon inspection, Kant's notion of a mysterious divine supplement to our imperfect efforts at renewal translates into a strategy for motivating a potentially discouraged moral agent; and his appeal to the divine perspective on moral regeneration turns out to beg the very question the appeal seems designed to answer.

But the most severe difficulty facing Kant remains to be addressed. This difficulty arises out of an unavoidable implication of Kant's rigorous emphasis on duty in his depiction of the moral life, and Kant's way of handling the problem produces the most dramatic – and unstable – intermingling of rational and biblical idioms in his entire account of moral regeneration. It is just here that topics such as christology, atonement, and justification make their appearance in Kant's discussion, "like strange visitors from another world," as Karl Barth once put it.[1] The problem pressuring him in such a direction is what we might call the problem of the "surplus." Kant puts the matter this way:

Whatever a man may have done in the way of adopting a good disposition, and, indeed, however steadfastly he may have persevered in conduct conformable to such a disposition, *he nevertheless started from evil*, and this debt he can by no possibility wipe out. For he cannot regard the fact that he incurs no new debts subsequent to his change of heart as equivalent to having discharged his old ones. Neither can he, through future good conduct, produce a surplus over and above what he is under obligation to perform at every instant, for it is always his duty to do all the good that lies in his power. (p. 72; p. 66)

If the state antecedent to moral regeneration is the condition of radical evil – which, after all, is what produces the obligation to undergo regeneration – then the moral agent has acquired a tremendous moral "debt" produced by the prior adoption of an evil disposition. But the revolution in disposition constituting moral regeneration cannot be invoked to pay off this debt, for any morally good act (including *that* one) is always obligatory in its own moment. Because of Kant's stringent conception of duty, no given moral act can count for or serve as a proxy for another: in Kant's world, a missed moral opportunity is lost forever. Far from leaving us simply wondering how a vicarious atonement might be reconciled with his theory of autonomy, Kant leaves us wondering how even an individual self can atone for *itself*. The problem of the surplus thus becomes the problem of atoning for, or otherwise offsetting, the effects of an evil past. One might say that this is Kant's version of Ivan's anguished concern about the evident injustice involved in God's simply forgiving the evil-doer, a forgiveness that, for Ivan, only the victim is entitled to give.[2]

Kant is evidently influenced in his depiction of this problem by traditional juridical conceptions of atonement, where the idea of making appropriate reparation (as opposed to the cultic idea of sacrificing blood) predominates. It is in this context that he not only once again cites St. Paul, but also makes two references to St. Anselm, the only such references in the book.[3] But what is finally in control here is not a rehabilitated theological doctrine, but Kant's own deep concern for symmetry and proportionality. The notion of proper reparation for a past debt does not appear because Kant has suddenly had a fit of orthodoxy; it appears because it is well-suited to expressing in recognizable form Kant's overriding concern for the moral economy of the universe. At stake is not a theological idea, but Kant's insistence that the moral law is *always* binding, making it impossible to squeeze multiple results out of any single moral act. His views on moral regeneration have to be shaped in a way that protects this basic insight.

Kant thus finds himself in yet another dilemma. On the one hand, he has to argue the possibility of moral regeneration so as to demonstrate the grounds for rationally hoping that radical evil can be overcome. If he cannot do this, then not only is the moral agent left in a potentially discouraged and futile posture, but the comprehensive Kantian drive toward moral perfection in the universe is jeopardized. The *impossibility* of moral regeneration would imply an irrational universe. On the other hand, however, he has to argue the possibility of renewal in a way that does not entail an unpaid moral debt. For if Kant fails here, then he has succeeded in demonstrating the possibility of moral regeneration only at the cost of sacrificing the very principle of rationality his demonstration was meant to vindicate. A rational universe entails both the possibility of moral regeneration *and* the idea that moral debts are paid off by the one who acquired them.

Working his way out of this dilemma is perhaps the most severe challenge facing Kant as he charts out the process of moral regeneration.

Rational atonement: the role of christology

It is noteworthy that Kant effects his solution to this dilemma in the context of his christology. Strictly speaking, there is no reason whatsoever why a christology should appear in the *Religion*, since the book is represented as an inquiry into the moral content of historical religions in general, rather than as a moral interpretation of Christianity alone. What is interesting is the way an explicitly Christian frame of reference keeps coming into view and takes considerable control at the decisive moments in Kant's account of moral regeneration. We saw this previously in connection with Kant's employment of Johannine and Pauline motifs as he addressed the moment of moral rebirth.

Now we find him making substantive use of a rational christology in order to effect a rational theory of atonement and thereby escape from the dilemma I have just described. What is crucial to recognize is that, although Kant is surely not slipping into a truly orthodox position, he is not simply appealing to Christ as an illustrative figure who is easily interchangeable with other religious or moral figures. There is an important, intrinsic connection for Kant between the figure of Christ and what he at one point calls the "breaking" of the "power" of radical evil to hold rational beings under its spell (pp. 82–3; p. 77). Apparently, apart from the existence of Jesus, the power of evil to hold us remains unbroken. The issue is not one of certain beliefs we are to hold about this historical figure, but concerns the occurrence of a past event that is evidently the necessary condition of the possibility of overcoming radical evil. It is Jesus of Nazareth, rather than anybody else, who is the personified version of the rational principle, residing in all rational beings, that turns out to be the basis of our own hope for moral regeneration. Perhaps inadvertently, Kant has raised the question of whether the delivery from radical evil is dependent in principle on the life of one historical figure. He has thus once again stumbled upon the problem of positivity, involving an apparent need to appeal to a truth that is "outside" the believer – and potentially incommensurate with the believer's natural consciousness – for the sake of a complete theory of salvation. For evidently it is Jesus, and not we ourselves, who breaks the power of the evil principle to hold us in its grip. Obviously, what Kant has to achieve is a depiction of this christological function that somehow translates the appeal to the figure of Christ into an appeal to our own autonomy, for otherwise he has simply produced a heteronomous solution to the problem of moral regeneration.

Kant attempts just such a translation in Book Two of the *Religion*. In Section One of this Book, Kant effects what is either a gross equivocation or an underappreciated and genuinely profound theological maneuver. He depicts Christ as the "personified idea of the good principle," which is to say, a man possessing a disposition always well-pleasing to God (pp. 60ff.; pp. 54ff.). What makes Jesus the Christ is his "unqualified obedience" to the moral law and his consciousness of all duties as divine commands (p. 62; p. 56). The business of Section One of Book Two is twofold. It is to demonstrate the "objective reality" of the personified idea of the good principle, doing so in a way that shows it to be an "archetype" present in all rational beings rather than something logically dependent on the historical figure of Jesus (or any other historical figure); and to confront and overcome the "difficulties which oppose the reality of this idea" (p. 66; p. 60).

It is in connection with this second task that Kant makes his interesting move. His background assumption structuring his account is not the ready-made existence of a disposition totally well-pleasing to God, but the existence of radical evil; only the latter could produce "difficulties" opposing the reality of the personified idea of the good principle. Accordingly, when Kant lays out these difficulties, they include both the problem of how a defective disposition can, through its own resources, regenerate itself (pp. 66–7; pp. 60–1) and the problem of the "surplus," concerning the offsetting of the debt accrued since the fall into radical evil (pp. 71ff.; pp. 65ff.). In other words – and here is his move – Kant shows the possibility of his own christology by solving the problem of moral regeneration. By thus yoking together the question of the sheer possibility of a totally good disposition with the question of how the obstacles to moral conversion are overcome, Kant effectively deploys his christology in a way that yields a doctrine of justification. But because his christology pivots on the idea of an archetype present in all rational beings, his account theoretically protects his principle of autonomy.

When addressing the question of how a corrupt disposition can produce the act that makes the disposition good, Kant falls back on the two-perspectives strategy he had earlier employed when initially discussing the change of heart. Once again we find Kant generating a constructive result out of philosophical caution, the caution here represented by the inability of rational beings to apprehend the underlying moral disposition. Although, in this instance, Kant is attempting to demonstrate the possibility of his christology, his use of the twofold, human–divine perspective on the change in disposition is virtually identical with the first instance of its use. It is also just as unsatisfactory in actually answering the question prompting the dualistic reply.

"Now the difficulty lies here," Kant reminds us. "How can a disposition count for [*gelten*] the act itself, when the act is *always* (not eternally, but at each instant of time) defective?" (p. 67; p. 60). This appears to be a fresh way of asking how the defective disposition gets out of its self-made problem; if the disposition is truly corrupt, any act arising out of it will be evil. This includes that primordial, grounding or foundational "act" by which the disposition chooses its own incentive structure. As in the case of his earlier use of the twofold perspective, however, Kant's answer to this problem presupposes that the moral revolution has already occurred. We have to regard our conduct "as it appears" to us phenomenally as being "*always* inadequate to a holy law."

But we may also think of this endless progress of our goodness toward conformity to the law, even if this progress is conceived in terms of actual deeds, or life-conduct, as being judged by Him who knows the heart, through a purely intellectual intuition, as a completed whole, because of the *disposition*, supersensible in its nature, from which this progress itself is derived. Thus may man, notwithstanding his permanent deficiency, yet expect to be *essentially* well-pleasing to God, at whatever instant his existence be terminated. (p. 6; pp. 60–1)

Again, this is not to answer the question of how a disposition overrides its own defect; rather, it is to describe the epistemological results of the overriding. Likewise – as in the case in Book One that I examined in the previous chapter – Kant not only seems to be generating a positive result from a dualism originally introduced to denote an epistemological limitation, he seems to imply that there is something gracious or merciful about God's viewing the matter in the only way God can possibly view it. Finally, Kant once again appears to be substituting his doctrine of moral regeneration for the postulate of immortality. His theory of salvation moves more and more into "this" world. If the converted moral agent is essentially "well-pleasing to God, at whatever instant his existence be terminated," the duration adequate to the moral perfection spoken of in the second *Critique* is no longer necessary. Moral regeneration in the *Religion* may be difficult or impossible to explain, but it seems to make for a neater universe. A note of otherworldliness certainly remains in Kant's account, but not in the odd form of a Kantian heaven; instead, it remains in the form of an appeal to a transcendent agency. If Kant could figure out a way to do so, he would drop even this appeal and render the theory of moral regeneration in terms that would turn exclusively on the appeal to our own autonomy. But the constraints generated by his own theory of radical evil and its spin-off problems keep him from being able to do this.

What is significant for our purposes at this point is that the dual perspective strategy here is linked, not simply to the question of moral conversion, but to the christological issue as well. The christological issue, in turn, is the context within which Kant faces the problem of the surplus of moral debt. To repeat the key point, Kant's account of the possibility of the personified idea of the good principle triggers his solution to the problem of the surplus: Kant's christology actually yields atonement and justification. As I have already suggested, however, Kant has a real solution to the problem of surplus – and not merely a new difficulty – only if his principle of the autonomy of the moral agent is not compromised in the production of these doctrines. The question is whether he can have both autonomy and atonement.

Kant begins his attempt at a solution by reminding us that the debt produced by radical evil "is no *transmissable* liability which can be made over to another like a financial indebtedness."

[Rather] is it *the most personal of all debts*, namely, a debt of sins, which only the culprit can bear and which no innocent person can assume even though he be magnanimous enough to wish to take it upon himself for the sake of another. Now this moral evil... brings with it endless violations of the law and so *infinite* guilt. The extent of this guilt is due... to the fact that this moral evil lies in the *disposition* and the maxims in general, in *universal basic principles* rather than in particular transgressions... It would seem to follow, then, that because of this infinite guilt all mankind must look forward to *endless punishment* and exclusion from the kingdom of God. (p. 72; p. 66)

It is more than a little ironic that Kant seems here, in connection with wicked acts, to be coming far closer to endorsing a principle of linkage, over time, among the moral agent's acts than he ever does in connection with the relation between virtuous acts. His comment draws its life from the insight that there is something *cumulative* about our wickedness, and the comment itself is pervaded with the motif of duration, in the form of the idea of something that is continuing to the point of being "endless." Beyond this unintended irony, however, Kant's point seems clear. An evil that is radical entails a radical punishment, one that is, moreover, immune to any vicarious solution. This is the Kantian doctrine of the highest good stood on its head: instead of proposing the rational demand that happiness be conceived in proportion to virtue, Kant is here proposing the equally rational demand that a fitting punishment be linked or somehow associated with radical evil.

By itself, this assessment of the matter would appear to rule out any constructive relation between christology and moral regeneration, since, in contrast to orthodox Protestant theology, Kant can hardly rely on the suffering of the crucified Christ to count as the needed punishment. But Kant is developing his account against the background of what he has just said about the rationality of the personified idea of the good principle. In the section preceding his response to the difficulties opposed to this idea – including the problem of the surplus – Kant has linked together three expressions: the personified idea of the good principle; the Son of God; and the "archetype" of moral perfection that resides universally in reason (pp. 60–1; pp. 54–5). "We need... no empirical example to make the idea of a person morally well-pleasing to God our archetype; this idea as an archetype is already present in our reason" (p. 62; p. 56). It is already present (though not necessarily thematized), because it is the latent product of reason's drive toward totality as it reflects on moral action. This product is the idea of moral perfection, rendered in this context as a disposition totally well-pleasing to God. The Son of God merits this designation precisely by having such a disposition. Jesus is the Christ because he always acts from duty while simultaneously viewing all of his duties as divine commands (pp. 63–6; pp. 57–9). Perhaps the decisive clue to Jesus' identity as the Christ resides in the fact that his answer to the question regarding the most important commandment is, in Kant's view, simply a variation on the categorical imperative. For Jesus

combines all duties (1) in one *universal* rule (which includes within itself both the inner and the outer moral relations of men), namely: Perform your duty for no motive other than unconditioned esteem for duty itself, i.e., love God (the Legislator of all duties) above all else; and (2) in a *particular* rule, that, namely, which concerns man's external relation to other men as universal duty: Love everyone as yourself, i.e., further his welfare from good-will that is immediate and not derived from motives of self-advantage. (pp. 160–1; p. 148)

The archetypal quality of Christ's disposition is disclosed in that fact that, for him, "precepts of holiness" are at the same time "laws of virtue" (p. 161; p. 178).

The key element in Kant's solution to the problem of surplus is the universal, rational, archetypal character of this quality that makes Christ the Christ. Kant clearly wants to put the emphasis here, rather than on the philosophically subversive possibility that the historical Jesus is somehow unique or necessary for the breaking of the power of radical evil. Although Kant nowhere reconciles these two discrete features of his christology, he unmistakably places the accent on the aspect that he is able to integrate with his principle of autonomy. Christ *does* atone for the sin of radical evil, but his atoning function turns out to reside in a rational feature that we can make our own: to appropriate Christ as the one who atones is in fact to make manifest and gain access to a feature of our own moral structure. Indeed, Kant goes so far as to appeal to the archetypal character of the personified idea of the good principle to show its reality: *our* having it supports its real presence in Christ. "From the practical point of view this idea is completely real in its own right, for it resides in our morally legislative reason" (p. 62; p. 55). The archetype possesses its reality prior to any historical manifestations, but it so happens to have been made manifest in Christ. Kant's account amounts to a kind of logos christology, ethically conceived. As Vincent McCarthy has aptly phrased it, in light of Kant's theory of practical reason, "we can now retranslate the prologue of the Gospel of John to read, 'In the beginning was the idea of mankind in its complete moral perfection.' "[4] In his resolution of the problem of the surplus, Kant will graft this rationalist christological insight onto a rather awkward theory of punishment for the sin of an evil disposition. His specific aim is to offset the third and last difficulty facing the objective reality of the personified idea of the good principle. In doing so, he simultaneously produces his autonomous atonement.

Rational atonement: the role of punishment

Having established that the debt of radical evil is "the most personal of all debts," and working with the assumption that the debt must be paid through some form of (as yet unspecified) punishment, Kant poses the following question:

Can the moral consequence of his former disposition, the punishment (or in other words the effect upon the subject of God's displeasure), be visited upon his present state, with its bettered disposition, in which he is already an object of divine pleasure? (p. 73; p. 67)

Kant's reliance on judicial metaphors as he attempts to depict the conse-

114

quences of previous wickedness constrains him considerably as he seeks a solution to his difficulty. For he wants both to satisfy the judicial requirement that a fitting punishment occur and to avoid the unjust asymmetry that would follow if the punishment were visited upon a regenerated moral agent. His own competing requirements intersect, producing the following attempt at a solution:

Since the question is not being raised as to whether, *before* his change of heart, the punishment ordained for him would have harmonized with the divine justice (on this score no one has any doubts), this punishment *must not* be thought of (in the present inquiry) as consummated prior to his reformation. *After* his change of heart, however, the penalty cannot be considered appropriate to his new quality (of a man well-pleasing to God), for he is now leading a new life and is morally another person; and yet satisfaction must be rendered to Supreme Justice, in whose sight no one who is blameworthy can ever be guiltless. Since, therefore, the infliction of punishment can, consistently with the divine wisdom, take place *neither before nor after* the change of heart, and is yet necessary, we must think of it as carried out *during* the change of heart itself, and adapted thereto. (p. 73; p. 67)

We face here not only the problem of making sense of this passage, but the additional problem of fitting its apparent meaning into Kant's wider philosophical scheme. For on the surface, Kant's theory about when the required punishment occurs would appear to rest on the appeal to something he has previously taken pains to rule out – namely, the idea that the change of heart involved in moral regeneration occurs in time and enjoys temporal duration. Certainly it appeared that Kant's earlier invocation of the Johannine language of rebirth and new creation was designed to enforce the separation between the moral and the temporal, a dichotomizing that, to be sure, has its problems, but they are problems that are compounded rather than alleviated by the move Kant seems to be making here.

Moreover, Kant's further description of what he means by the punishment occurring "during" the change of heart appears to compromise his ethical rigorism. That is, his way of giving sense to the aspect of "duration" here seems to rely on the idea that, for an unspecified period, the moral agent is neither fully good nor fully wicked – in stark contrast to his more typical admonition that it is "of great consequence to ethics in general to avoid admitting, so long as it is possible, of anything morally intermediate..." (p. 22; p. 18). It may be that, in confronting the problem of a just punishment to offset the surplus of debt, Kant has reached the limit point within his own analysis implied by the phrase, "so long as it is possible."

The problem, then, is that Kant has boxed himself in: the solution to the problem of the surplus of debt requires a punishment, but the punishment itself entails a linkage between the moral and the temporal that strains against other features of Kant's philosophy. He is in effect "schematizing" the rational idea of moral regeneration with his appeal to temporal duration in the account of punishment. In other words, he is giving temporal form to what otherwise remains purely rational and abstract, just as he schematizes the categories of the understanding in terms of time in the first *Critique*.[5] There can be no application of the categories except in terms of time, Kant tells us in that earlier context; time is even superior to space with respect to its capacity to instantiate what otherwise might remain purely ideal.[6] Insofar as his theory of the enduring, temporal locus of punishment hints at a schematizing of the purely rational idea of moral conversion, Kant is edging toward the one thing his moral philosophy perhaps needs more than anything else – namely, a systematic account of how to relate the noumenal moral realm to our real-life, phenomenal experience of moral agency. For if everyday moral experience teaches us anything, it is that the basic forms of moral experience – such as reflection and deliberation, decision-making, and the experiences of duty or guilt – occur temporally. The moral life takes narrative form. As we saw in chapter 4, however, Kant's theory of ethics is notorious for the way it systematically seals off moral considerations from temporal influence. Yet a curious – and probably significant – feature of his doctrine of moral conversion concerns the way the needed element of punishment expresses a moral requirement quite explicitly in terms of time.

Kant's actual explanation of the punishment during the change of heart makes use yet again of the strategy of dual perspectives on the process of moral regeneration. From the divine perspective, which apprehends the intelligible act of a renewed disposition, the "departure from evil" and the "entrance into goodness" are virtually analytic. There may be a logical distinction to make between "the laying off of the old man and the putting on of the new," but there are here

not two moral acts separated by an interval of time but only a single act, for the departure from evil is possible only through the agency of the good disposition which effects the individual's entrance into goodness, and *vice versa*. (p. 74; p. 68)

Kant seems to be making an implicit point here about the motivation of the agent undergoing moral regeneration, related to our earlier puzzlement concerning how it could ever occur to someone with an evil disposition to attempt to change. Insofar as there is the beginning of a Kantian answer here, it would appear to be one that begs the question: in order for it to occur to the moral agent to depart from evil, the good disposition must already be present. The "good principle is present quite as much in the desertion of the evil as in the adoption of the good disposition..." (p. 74; p. 68).

Obviously, this distinction does not really explain anything so much as it provides Kant with the sort of maneuvering room he needs for locating the required punishment of the "old man." At the same time, however, the apparent absence of a truly significant, full-blooded distinction between the departure from evil and the entrance into good would appear to thwart Kant's stated intention to locate the punishment in the change of heart itself. One of his framing premises, after all, is that the punishment cannot be justly visited upon the agent possessing a regenerated disposition; but if the regenerated disposition is the necessary precondition for the departure from evil, it is not clear where Kant can locate the punishment without overriding his own premise. Kant presses ahead nonetheless, ultimately specifying the locus of the punishment of the "old man" in the following formula: the "coming forth from the corrupted into the good disposition is, in itself (as 'the death of the old man,' 'the crucifying of the flesh'), a sacrifice and an entrance upon a long train of life's ills."[7]

Evidently, Kant's point is that, following moral conversion, the struggles, trials, and temptations that the "new man" faces – faces precisely by virtue of having become good again – are viewed as punishments for the earlier self. The regenerated moral agent accepts this sacrifice

in the disposition of the Son of God, that is, merely for the sake of the good, though really they are due as *punishments* to another, namely to the old man (for the old man is indeed morally another). (p. 74; p. 68)

Kant clearly recognizes that he is walking a narrow path here, as evidenced especially by a lengthy footnote in which he works out in detail the relation of the punishment to both the "old" and "new" selves. One might say that Kant is employing a theological idiom in order to express his own philosophical insight that the renewed moral agent remains finite and sensuous, just as the earlier, fallen agent remained rational and capable of recovery. The agent's continuing finitude – its capacity to be affected by sensuous inclinations – is the condition of the possibility of the punishment; the punishment, in turn, must attend moral regeneration if Kant's rational standards are to be observed. Only such a cluster of insights as these can enable Kant to construe the required punishment as fair.

In what amounts to a Kantian adaptation of the Lutheran *simul justus et peccator*, Kant thus asks whether one " 'in whom there is no condemnation' " can "believe himself justified and at the same time count as *punishment* the miseries which befall him on his way to an ever greater goodness..." (p. 75n.;

p. 69n.). The moral agent's "newness" resides in the changed disposition: "So far as he is a new man... these sufferings are not ascribed to him as punishments at all" (p. 75n.; p. 69n.). In light of this changed disposition, the "old" self really is left behind; the change in disposition is the fundamental change. If this were the end of the matter, no just punishment could be visited upon the moral agent and no resolution of the problem of the "surplus" could occur.

Yet Kant achieves his argumentative goal by drawing once again on his metaphysical distinction between a change of disposition and a change in phenomenal life conduct. For whereas the former is complete, once-for-all, and produces a new moral agent undeserving of punishment, the latter is always "a continual becoming," a process of "continual progress" that, "as revealed in conduct," always "remains deficient and infinitely removed" from complete holiness (p. 75n.; p. 69n.). The ever-imperfect gradualism of actual life conduct serves, as it were, as a kind of trace of the old fallen self. Consequently, in reply to his own question of whether the renewed moral agent can rationally view "the miseries which befall him on his way to an ever greater goodness" as punishment, Kant replies: "Yes, but only in his quality of the man whom he is continually putting off."

Everything (and this comprises all the miseries and ills of life in general) that would be due him as punishment in that quality (of the old man) he gladly takes upon himself in his quality of new man simply for the sake of the good. So far as he is a new man, consequently, these sufferings are not ascribed to him as punishments at all. The use of the term "punishment" signifies merely that, in his quality of new man, he now willingly takes upon himself, as so many opportunities for the testing and exercising of his disposition to goodness, all the ills and miseries that assail him, which the old man would have had to regard as punishments and which he too, so far as he is still in the process of becoming dead to the old man, accepts as such. (p. 75n.; p. 69n.)

This is a rather remarkable comment even by the standards of a book filled with remarkable comments. Kant seems here to want to have it both ways, or at least to have the term "punishment" convey two entirely separate meanings. For in the course of this comment, "punishment" goes from being something external to the moral agent that is visited upon the agent in the form of the "miseries and ills of life in general," to being an opportunity for moral growth. Kant sets the issue up as though it were a simple matter of the "old man" facing life's ills with the former perspective, while the "new man" assumes the latter: the "old man" experiences the world as a kind of penalty box, and the "new man" experiences it as what William James called a "moral gymnasium," filled with opportunities for moral discipline in the form of tests and moral challenges. But then Kant sabotages his own point with his concluding reminder that the "new man" is "still in the process of becoming dead to the old man," creating a troubling note of ambiguity. It is troubling because of the way Kant himself has ruled out as unfair the visitation of the punishment upon the renewed moral agent who, precisely in his or her condition of renewal, is not deserving of the punishment, since the agent "is now leading a new life and is morally another person..." (p. 73; p. 67). His inability to work out a convincing theory of the enduring personal identity of the moral agent *as* moral agent (rather than as a merely empirical self) is coming back to haunt him.

Kant's language here thus reinforces my earlier suggestion that his theory of punishment depends upon the diluting of his own ethical rigorism. Justice requires that some punishment be exacted, if the debt accumulated by a radically evil disposition is not to be unpaid at the moment of moral regeneration. But justice also requires that this punishment not be visited on the morally renewed agent, who – as a genuinely different person, "as it were a new creation" (p. 47; p. 43) – does not deserve it. Kant's solution is to appeal to the ongoing, temporal duration within which the effects of the renewed disposition gradually appear phenomenally. In keeping with the by-now familiar pattern that is evident throughout the *Religion*, Kant is drawing on a principle that originates as an epistemological limit (in this case, our inability fully to apprehend the renewed moral disposition through "actions which are met with in the world of sense" [p. 75n.; p. 69n.]) in order to make a positive, constructive point regarding the moral life. He exploits what he says we cannot know in order to make some of his most fundamental constructive claims regarding moral regeneration.

Autonomy and atonement

Despite the array of conceptual difficulties we might locate and ponder in connection with Kant's account of the surplus of guilt, it seems only fair to say that there is something quite ingenious about what Kant has done here. For by thus distinguishing between the old and new selves, and by locating the punishment in the ongoing process of moral struggle when the new self is viewed phenomenally, Kant effectively fuses atonement and autonomy, thereby getting what he wants. A true atoning sacrifice occurs, mandated by the moral economy of Kant's universe, a universe requiring symmetry and correct proportion – "just desserts," as it were – in all moral matters. Moreover, it is a sacrifice that can be made comprehensible through appeal to the disposition of the Son of God, for this disposition, as we have seen, is constituted by a rational archetype universally available. Kant never appeals to anything in Christ that is not potentially accessible to all.

The upshot is that the morally regenerated agent really becomes Christ-like, in the sense of taking on the punishment of another. What makes the resulting atonement Kantian is the fact that the "other," here, who has earned the punishment, is the moral agent's own earlier self. In this setting, the absence of a Kantian principle integrating the intelligible, moral self across time is a help, not a hindrance, since this absence enables Kant really to depict "otherness" in connection with a moral agent who, as an empirical self, is one and the same. The self substitutes for itself and can render this substitution symbolically through appeal to Christ's own sacrifice. In this carefully delimited context, Kant actually employs the expression, *"vicarious substitute"* (p. 74; p. 69). The "long train of life's ills" that the regenerated self bears as punishment for the old self is thus analogous to Christ's death on the cross.

Only it must be remembered that (in this mode of representation) the suffering which the new man, in becoming dead to the *old*, must accept throughout life is pictured as a death endured once for all by the representative of mankind. (pp. 74–5; p. 69)

What occurs in this "vicarious" atonement, then, is not the moral agent's recovery through the efficacious power of Christ, but rather a recovery based on a moral pattern made manifest in Christ. The recovery itself is no more explained by Kant in this context than in the earlier ones; his concern here is mainly to exhibit the reality of the personified idea of the good principle by solving the problem of the surplus of debt produced by an evil disposition. Christology and moral regeneration converge, not because the moral agent is dependent upon Christ, but because the Christ principle is continuous with the agent's ever-present capacity for regeneration.

This continuity between the agent's moral capacity and the Christ principle is really the only thing keeping Kant's position from culminating in reliance on the historical figure of Jesus, a result that would of course be a catastrophe for his rational religion. The reason he comes tantalizingly close to subverting his own rationalist posture is the material link between the sheer possibility that we can recover from radical evil and Kant's claim that Jesus, precisely in his historical appearance, broke the power of the evil principle to hold rational beings against their will (pp. 82–3; p. 77). A surprising mixture of christological traditions mingles in Kant's depiction of an almost Manichean battle between the forces of good and evil serving as the framework for grasping the christological point. "The good principle," Kant tells us, "has descended in mysterious fashion from heaven into humanity not at one particular time alone but from the first beginnings of the human race" (p. 82; p. 77). But this rationalist christological tendency is blended together with a complementary idea that takes Kant on to odd ground. For the good principle "made its appearance in an actual human being" and became "an example to all others"; by this example, "he opens the portals of freedom to all who, like him, choose to become dead to everything that holds them fettered to life on earth to the detriment of morality."

So the moral outcome of the combat, as regards the hero of this story (up to the time of his death), is really not the *conquering* of the evil principle – for its kingdom still endures, and certainly a new epoch must arrive before it is overthrown – but merely the breaking of its power to hold, against their will, those who have so long been its subject, because another dominion (for man must be subject to some rule or other), a moral dominion, is now offered them as an asylum where they can find protection for their morality if they wish to forsake the former sovereignty. (pp. 82–3; p. 77)

The good principle may be present in all rational beings, but the possibility of its sovereignty may be dependent upon its appearance in the specific figure of Jesus. As Kant's comments make perfectly clear, he is not watering down his rationalist commitment to the view that the predisposition to good inherent in rational beings is independent of the appearance of Jesus. What is in question here is not the potential for good, but the actuality of becoming good in the face of the power of the evil principle.

Kant's account is thus animated by the distinction between the morally good and the power of the morally good. The role played by this distinction simply confirms what I have been suggesting all along: Kant's christology is integral to his overall theory of radical evil, for it is the debility produced by radical evil that requires the christological account. As we have already seen, there is no problem reconciling Kant's view of Jesus with his overriding rationalist principle, since the thing that makes Jesus the Christ is an archetype residing in all rational beings. But the second part of the distinction – the capacity of Jesus to break the power of the evil principle to hold rational beings against their will – is not so easily absorbed by the rationalist religious insight. In this respect, there seems to be something distinctive about Jesus, for without his historical appearance, we would not be any less rational, nor would we be any less moral in potential, but we might be less able to act morally in fact. His historical appearance does not make us what we essentially are, nor does his suffering take the place of the punishment we must each undergo to offset the surplus of guilt. But his appearance may be required to free us so that we might make good on our essential moral capability.[8]

Given Kant's rather cryptic gestures in this direction, it is impossible, finally, to resolve this question with any degree of certainty. Moreover, it is perfectly obvious that Kant both intends his overall religious outlook to remain independent of the merely empirical realm of historical events, and that his account of the punishment for the accumulated moral debt depends, not on the suffering of Jesus, but on the punishment of the moral agent undergoing regeneration.

But although the issue of a potential pivot point in history that frees us from the power of evil cannot finally be resolved on the basis of what Kant tells us in the *Religion*, it is fair to say, I think, that the truly telling point is that the issue even arises. The sheer fact that it is at least plausible to argue that, in one limited sense, the completion of Kant's rational religion requires an appeal to a specific historical figure, indicates the depth of the problem into which his theory of radical evil has led him. We can perhaps best think of the issue as symptomatic of Kant's general ambivalence toward the topic of grace. Indeed, even in the conclusion to his effort to resolve the problem of the surplus, Kant introduces yet another note of this ambivalence. Again, the problem all along has been that the inexplicable act producing a moral conversion cannot offset or pay off the moral debt acquired ever since the original fall into radical evil. Whatever else we can or cannot say about the act leading to conversion, we can at least say that it was obligatory in its own moment and cannot also serve to offset the accrued debt. Kant's search for the "surplus" that *will* offset the debt culminates in the conception of ongoing, temporal punishment I described earlier.

But rather than let the matter rest there, Kant goes on to say that this surplus, over and above the act producing moral regeneration, "is itself a profit which is reckoned to us *by grace*" (p. 75; p. 70). His explanation of this comment is once again ambiguous, increasing the instability running throughout his entire discussion of moral regeneration, since the ambiguity concerns the relative balance of human and divine effort constituting the regeneration process. For it has become clear by now that the payment of this punishment to produce the needed surplus is fundamental to Kant's overall theory of this process. This is because of the provocative way his theory of the possibility of christology – the possibility, that is, of a person- ified idea of the good principle – quite literally becomes a theory of the possibility of moral regeneration. Thus, when explaining what it means to say that the surplus "is reckoned to us *by grace*," Kant repeats his by now well-worn point about God's capacity to apprehend as a completed whole what we can only grasp as gradual progress.

That what in our earthly life... is ever only a *becoming* (namely, becoming a man well-pleasing to God) should be credited to us exactly as if we were already in full possession of it – to this we really have no legal claim, that is, so far as we know ourselves (through that empirical self-knowledge which yields no immediate insight into the disposition but merely permits of an estimate based upon our actions)... Thus the decree is always one of grace alone, although fully in accord with eternal justice, when we come to be cleared of all liability by dint of our faith in such goodness; for the decree is based upon a giving of satisfaction (a satisfaction which consists for us only in the idea of an improved disposition, known only to God). (pp. 75–6; p. 70)

Kant seems here to be confusing his point about how the punishment occurs and serves to offset our debt with his point (also made earlier in the *Religion*) about God's capacity to apprehend the renewed disposition. Moreover, he comes dangerously close here to suggesting that moral regeneration is effected providentially rather than autonomously – that God's knowledge of it somehow helps it to occur. This would indeed be grace, but grace of a sort that would utterly undermine Kant's efforts throughout Book Two to preserve the element of autonomy.[9] His eagerness to protect autonomy is once again evident in his follow-up warning that this entire account of what he suddenly calls "the idea of *justification*" (p. 76; p. 70) merely answers a "speculative question" and possesses no practical importance. Evidently, Kant does not want his fairly expansive gesture toward grace to induce moral passivity or to encourage excessive reliance on God.

But in a final comment that appears to give back with the one hand what he had just taken away with the other, Kant says that this "deduction of the idea" of justification "should not be passed over in silence just because it is speculative."

Otherwise, reason could be accused of being wholly unable to reconcile with divine justice man's hope of absolution from his guilt – a reproach which might be damaging to reason in many ways, but most of all morally. (p. 76; p. 70)

In other words, there *is* a practical interest in the account of justification. As was the case with Kant's other references to grace, the reference here serves as a ground of rational hope, offsetting the potential despair attending our attempt to conceive the possibility of the personified idea of the good principle. The appeal to grace in the solution to the problem of the surplus of debt gets Kant past a conceptual logjam. Once again, however, his attempt to harmonize appeals to divine help and appeals to autonomous action signals the theological and cultural halfway house in which Kant is dwelling. It is not that he is unable to decide where to live. Rather, he cannot inhabit the dwelling of his choice full-time, because the free will as Kant himself conceives it fails in its efforts at total self-reliance.

7

Autonomy and transcendence

What mainly occurred in the process that is interpreted as secularization . . . should be described not as the *transposition* of authentically theological contents into secularized alienation from their origin but rather as the *reoccupation* of answer positions that had become vacant and whose corresponding questions could not be eliminated.

Hans Blumenberg

Apart from some earlier attempts, it has been reserved in the main for our epoch to vindicate, at least in theory, the human ownership of treasures formerly squandered on heaven; but what age will have the strength to validate this right in practice and make itself their possessor?

Hegel

The irony of Kant's philosophy of religion

Kant's ultimate inability to show conclusively how an autonomous will gets out of its self-made problem can perhaps be thought of as the final moment in a philosophical vision that begins and ends in irony. The originating irony resides in the fact that, though it is we who impose order on the world and give it form, we do so in a way that leaves the world devoid of any intrinsic value or purpose: we spontaneously fashion a world that has no room for our freedom. Transcendental method discloses that in the course of constituting the world in terms of space, time, and causality, we render the world a spiritual wasteland: at the purely theoretical level, we produce a world with no metaphysical comforts, a world we cannot really live in. Complete theoretical understanding does not produce the good life.

We should thus view Kant's reference to "the primacy of the practical," as he develops it especially in the *Critique of Practical Reason*, as an offer of escape from the wasteland produced by theoretical reason. Something about human freedom overrides or eludes the theoretical prison that reason has spontaneously constructed for itself, though escape occurs only with the aid of a

125

dubious distinction between appearance and reality. Kant is himself ultimately so confident of the metaphysical weight implicit in our presumed sense of moral obligation that no note of desperation enters into this offer of escape. Yet once Kant's own theory of freedom leads him to the doctrine of radical evil, we find him speaking, if not in desperation, at least with a peculiar oscillation of idioms as he tries to reconcile the reality of evil with his metaphysical trust. It is this oscillation that is the chief sign of the concluding irony: Kant must appeal to transcendence to salvage autonomy. Moreover, as Kant works his way to the outer edges of his own theory of freedom, he has to rely more and more on appeals to divine action in order to guarantee the symmetry of his universe and thus avoid the series of surds that Ivan perversely relishes. Yet this same symmetry had previously served as the premise that, in the second *Critique*, had assured Kant of the existence of God. Consequently, Kant's position not only moves from an originating irony to a concluding one, but it depends for its full articulation upon a deep and complex circularity. No doubt Ivan would finally find no comfort here.

This latent circularity is probably connected in complicated ways with a deep ambivalence on Kant's part toward the very idea of God and God's relation to our earthly situation. In the controversial – and probably indecipherable – language of his *Opus Postumum*, Kant remarks at one point that "God is the morally practical self-legislating Reason," and that the "concept of God is not that of a . . . thing which exists independently of my thinking."[1] Language such as this represents that strand in Kant's thought designed to marginalize talk about God as a separate being and to divinize reason. For some, the question even arises as to whether the aging Kant is influenced by the resurgent Spinozism enjoying a revival of interest in Germany at the turn of the century.[2] Kant's account of moral regeneration, on the other hand, exposes a second strand in the fabric of his religious thought, according to which the gap between ourselves and God is radicalized, with God playing the role of an actor, due to our fallen state. One peculiarity of Kant's position is that his mature philosophy should retain enough maneuvering room for him to incorporate this second strand into his outlook.

It is perhaps worth reminding ourselves at this point that the source of Kant's maneuvering room is his peculiar notion of the *parerga*, or non-rational elements of the religious life. It is easy to underestimate the *parerga* – to write the idea off as something of an embarrassment – but this would be a mistake. For not only does Kant get tremendous mileage out of his use of the *parerga*, but the very topic signals just the sort of thing our postmodernist, anti-essentialist, and fundamentally nominalist era should find interesting in Kant (as at least Derrida, for one, has pointed out).[3] The *parerga* consist of those topics that Kant can neither fit neatly under the rubric of a religion "within the limits of reason alone" nor entirely do without: they "do not belong within" the limits of pure reason "but border upon it." They come into view, because reason is "conscious of her inability to satisfy her moral need" and thus "extends herself to high–flown [*überschwenglichen*] ideas capable of supplying this lack, without, however, appropriating these ideas as an extension of her domain" (p. 52; pp. 47–8). One lesson of this study is that far more license is conveyed by these words than Kant would like us to suppose; they are perhaps the ultimate example of Kant's by-now familiar tendency to produce a meaty religious result from a cautionary epistemological remark. Seemingly tacked on as excuses to treat certain traditional theological topics in a reductionistic way, the *parerga* turn out instead to betray the fact that Kant's philosophy of religion cannot fully succeed in its reductionistic aspirations. Their sheer presence in the *Religion* is not a polite concession to the pious nor to the suspicious eyes of the Prussian censor; instead, their presence is testimony to the limits of a "religion within the limits of reason alone."

Kant of course takes great pains to deny any theoretical, cognitive value to the *parerga* – but this epistemological caution is really no different from the safeguards he erects around the postulates of practical reason, including the existence of God. That is, by itself Kant's cautionary language about how to take the *parerga* diminishes their importance no more than it diminishes the importance of the postulates. And insofar as the specific *parergon* of grace assumes the role of a "necessary hypothesis" needed to display all the entailments of the idea of moral regeneration, the idea of grace wavers between being a heuristic device needed to keep us morally encouraged, and becoming what virtually amounts to a new postulate without which Kant's account of moral regeneration would be in complete shambles.[4] At the very least, we can view grace as the refinement of insights already latent in the postulation process in the second *Critique*, where there is an explicit appeal to divine action in relation to the achievement of the highest good.[5] In the *Religion*, the *parergon* of grace effectively smuggles in an appeal to divine action that is more robust and fully thematized due to the specific situation produced by radical evil. The more dire his account of the human situation becomes, the more articulated become Kant's hints about divine action, however inscrutable such action is admitted to be.

In taking this view, I am suggesting that Kant does not abide by his own warning against adopting a work of grace into our maxims for a practical use (p. 53; p. 49), for I think this is exactly what he does. For another lesson of this entire study is that, apart from our ability at least to hope that a gracious initiative may aid our moral recovery, moral regeneration appears to be impossible. In light of such a constructive, substantive role played by the appeal to divine action, then, we see more clearly the deeper cause of the fissure that leaves Kant's religious philosophy rippling with instability. It is not simply that the appeal to transcendent action coexists awkwardly with the more characteristic appeal to human autonomy; more than this, the appeal to transcendent action seriously compromises Kant's Newtonianism. Kant himself would of course shrink from such a suggestion, but the point is made inescapable by his own language. In entertaining the *parerga*, reason contemplates "the inscrutable realm of the supernatural," Kant tells us, where "there is something more than she can explain to herself . . ." (p. 52; p. 48). Likewise, when reason confronts the awesome task of moral regeneration, it must grant, not that God will work upon the will in a natural way, but "that some supernatural cooperation may be necessary" for our moral recovery (p. 44; p. 40). The fact that Kant continuously stresses that we must do all we can to merit divine aid does not offset the accompanying fact that his position is couched in terms of an appeal to supernatural action. By not entirely jettisoning the notion of supernatural grace from his account of the religious life, Kant reveals that his position cannot afford strict adherence to its own Newtonianism in the solution of its own deepest problems. As we saw in chapter 5, Kant tries valiantly to translate these appeals to divine action into commentary on the psychology of the moral agent. Nonetheless, it is probably fair to couch the overall issue in terms of yet another irony: this most Newtonian of eighteenth-century thinkers completes his philosophy of religion by detecting and exploiting the moral value in vague appeals to supernatural action. If he eliminates the vagueness and becomes more blunt in these appeals, Kant unduly compromises both the rationalism of his basic position and the integrity of his fundamentally mechanistic outlook. But without these appeals, he runs the even greater risk of leaving the moral agent in defeat and despair. Kant's notorious inability to integrate physics and freedom in a single coherent outlook culminates in this odd situation, just as his exploitation of the notion of the *parerga* helps to mask his dilemma.

The divide in the road: after Kant

Kant's impact on the philosophical and religious thought of the nineteenth and twentieth centuries is unquestionable, but it is sometimes difficult to state precisely. In large part, this is because of the subtle and divergent ways his influence can be felt, even by a single thinker. A Protestant theologian such as Rudolf Bultmann, for example, can be thoroughly Kantian in one way – as in the adoption of a radically dualistic distinction between two kinds of thinking, or two approaches to reality – while explicitly non-Kantian in another way – as in the rejection of the moral emphasis in the description of faith.[6] The question of where the Kantianism in modern culture begins and ends, and why its impact should assume the forms it does, touches on some of the most difficult issues in the historiography of modern Western thought.

The current study adds to the complexity because of the two perspectives from which we can view Kant's doctrines of radical evil and moral regeneration. We can view them as a cluster of problems intrinsic to the critical philosophy, threatening the achievement of the highest good and, thus, the symmetry of the universe, and threatening as well each rational being with a tragic, personal inner contradiction. Or Kant's doctrines can be taken as symptomatic of a larger problem within modern religious thought as a whole, displaying the increasing competition between human autonomy and divine sovereignty – between the immanent, historical arena and providence – in the culture's depiction of its proper ends and objects of hope. It is within this wider context that Kant's set of concerns can be viewed as his equivocal vote in the referendum over otherworldliness to which I alluded at the very outset of this study.

I also briefly alluded at the outset to the path linking Kant to the divergent options marked out by the middle of the next century by Kierkegaard and Marx – two seminal thinkers born on the same day in May, five years apart. This link is worth emphasizing, given the way Kierkegaard and Marx are usually depicted as post-Hegelian thinkers reacting to the ambitious program of dialectical idealism. But it hardly requires a denial of the Hegelian connection to suggest that the options they represent signal extreme versions of one-sided reactions to the mixture of human and divine effort with which Kant's account of moral regeneration leaves us: Kierkegaard and Marx represent what happens when just one of the two aspects of Kant's account of moral regeneration is taken up and emphasized in isolation from the other aspect. As such, their positions shed light on Kant's own effort to have it both ways.

In Kierkegaard's hands, the muted Kantian appeal to grace is transformed into a full-blown "project of thought" in which a transcendent act alone is the only antidote to our willed "error," or sin.[7] Contrary to our usual view of these matters, it is in fact Kierkegaard and not Kant who has the more "rational" position here. For where Kant attempts to offset a willed error with another act of will and ends up on the borders of incoherence, Kierkegaard openly shows that the only way to offset a willed error is through a reconciling act coming from the "outside," producing the "new creature" that even Kant admits each of us must become.[8] Kierkegaard's ultimate appeal to "paradox" in his depiction of this position is as much a display of the internal consistency of the non-Socratic or Augustinian outlook as it is an acknowledgment of the incommensurability between faith and reason.[9] For the appeal to paradox here is not a concession to irrationality; rather, it is an orderly and deliberate display of where we are taken by the originating hypothesis that faith does not naturally cohabit with the given forms of human nature, such as reason. Faith has only unnatural relations with reason, which is why the term paradox comes into play. Kierkegaard calls Kant's bluff: if you really want to avoid dependence upon God for delivery from the human predicament, then cast the originating predicament in purely Socratic rather than Augustinian terms.

It is no doubt Kant's unwillingness to be Socratic in his depiction of radical evil – his unwillingness, that is, to attribute evil to ignorance – that gives his position its profundity and complexity. Moral evil is for him no mere epistemological infection, awaiting the cure of the more complete encyclo-pedia, the more progressive schools, and the more rational civic arrange-ments. But it is this same unwillingness to be Socratic that gets him into trouble, in light of his subsequent inability to appeal cleanly and economically to the free will as the source of its own salvation. For his own very different reasons and in his own very different way, Kierkegaard sees that a reconciling faith "is not an act of will,"[10] but the disclosure of a hiatus between ourselves and eternity. There is no more straightforward modern vote for "otherworld-liness" in the account of salvation than Kierkegaard's accent on the "God-man" who breaks into time bringing "eternal blessedness" to a humanity that, on its own, can only will its way deeper into error, like a worm burrow-ing its way further from the light. History by itself – the temporal realm untouched by the eternal – delivers no salvation.

Alternatively, Kant's more characteristic tendency to locate our moral recovery in our own efforts – however impossible he has made it for himself fully to do this – leads at least in some sense to Marx. Moreover, Kant's own tentative remarks about what he calls an ethical commonwealth suggest the hint of a link between his largely privatized theory of autonomy and a more historicized, social conception of purposeful human activity, as we find in Marx.[11] Marxism might be crudely characterized as the culmination of the German philosophical tradition's effort to overcome Kant's second postulate of practical reason – the culmination, that is, of the tradition's effort to expel the last remnants of otherworldliness remaining in the position of the philos-opher who had put the notion of "praxis" on the philosophical map. Not incidentally, without the second postulate, there is simply no rational need to entertain the third; once the otherworldliness of the idea of the immortality of the soul is dissolved into action in *this* world, there is no place for God to be, let alone anything left for God to do.

In his own account of moral regeneration in the *Religion*, Kant himself, as we have seen, has gone some distance in superseding his own postulate, but only at the cost of then increasing the need for an act of divine grace that seems just as arbitrary as anything we might discover in the original postulation process. Kant never quite finished the task of absorbing heaven into earth that his entire program – and particularly his emphasis on autonomy – continually hints at. This is precisely the task that Marx completes. He is concerned not only to unmask Kantianism as the philosophical legitimation and rationalization of a society gone middle class;[12] he is concerned to disclose and overcome Kantianism's very real half-heartedness about the material world, as exemplified not only by the lingering references to God, but by the whole Kantian doctrine of the noumenal realm. In his own way and for his own purposes, Marx would grasp the importance of the fact that Kant never fully threw off his pietist background, however sophisticated his philosophical expression of it may have become. There always remained something vaguely "unworldly" about the Königsberg bachelor, in a deeper and more philosophical sense of the word, as well as in a more ordinary and personal sense.

In Marx's case even more than in Kierkegaard's, the mediation of Hegel – and of Feuerbach as well – must be kept in view for my trajectory to make sense. Marx was hardly the first German thinker who wanted to overcome the phenomena–noumena dichotomy.[13] I am not concerned here to deny Hegel's importance to either Marx or Kierkegaard, but only to trace some of the relevant routing back to Kant. Like the Kierkegaardian project of thought and turn toward eternity, Marxism's accent on the social dimensions of human action and its insistence on a purely immanent and materialist – though still progressive – conception of history represent the flowering of one side of Kant's view of moral regeneration. Perhaps most telling here is the fact that in the cases of Kierkegaard and Marx alike, what undergoes the greatest transformation as it passes through the hands of the later thinker is Kant's theory of personal, individual autonomy. Kierkegaard transforms what he takes to be our illusion of autonomy "backwards," as it were, by calling on a fundamentally Lutheran conception of a naked sinner in bondage, standing alone before an angry yet gracious judge. Retrieving the Reformation sense of the otherness of God, Kierkegaard deflates the aspirations codified in the modern conception of autonomy by revealing it to be a disguised, largely unconscious form of despair, producing neither happiness nor fulfillment, but only estrangement.[14] For his part, Marx decodes the latent ideological implications of our sense of autonomy in terms of an underlying bourgeois hegemony and attempts to displace the false consciousness implicit in the illusion of personal autonomy with a call to historically generated social praxis. As Kierkegaard's transfiguration of Kantianism radicalizes the split between history and eternity, placing our hopes solely in the latter, Marx's strategy overcomes the split altogether and makes the purely immanent possibilities of history the only possibilities there are.

In these two broad options, we have the full realization of the starkly divergent possibilities latent in Kant's account of moral regeneration, making his account a kind of pivot point for the culture at large. We also have, in both instances, more consistency than we find in the halfway house in which Kant himself leaves us.

By contrast, the oddity of the liberal tradition of post-Kantian religious thought resides in the fact that it is the intentional perpetuation of life in the halfway house and of wobbling as a life style. Here, Kant's straddling of idioms, his effort to blend vocabularies – however unsuccessful – is particularly telling, for he is previewing the fundamental dilemma facing his liberal successors. That is, with his accounts of radical evil and, especially, moral regeneration, Kant is neither engaging in mere reductionism nor backsliding half-heartedly into a discredited orthodoxy. Instead, he is attempting to chart out something like the Christian doctrines of original sin, justification, and sanctification without the benefit of a supernatural apparatus – the same act, but no net. His basically Pelagian instincts guarantee in advance that Kant will run together the last two doctrines in troublesome ways; and his commitment to something very much like the first doctrine assures that his own ethical rationalism will not be adequate to the task of finding a way out of the problem as Kant depicts it. Moreover, as we have seen, his attempt to jettison the supernatural apparatus is not as successful as he would like or as we would initially suppose. But what is revealing here is not the failure so much as the attempt.

If Kierkegaard and Marx represent the two divergent extreme possibilities latent in Kant's account of salvation, liberal mediating theologies right up to the present day represent the continuation of Kant's own effort to muddle through. Indeed, the difficulties Kant confronts in the *Religion* are ample reminders that muddling is itself perhaps what distinguishes the liberal thinker. However diverse the actual occasions may be, the core theological debates since Kant suggest that the instability in his own account of autonomy and transcendence – human effort and outside aid – has not disappeared. The nineteenth century's preoccupation with the "faith and culture" issue, the Barth–Brunner debate over a "point of contact," Bultmannian debates about demythologizing and "act of God" language, and liberation theology's translation of piety into praxis all exemplify the point without by any means exhausting the examples. The issues at stake in these and similar debates were much easier to address when everyone could take for granted a supernaturalist framework. Like Kant himself, later thinkers not as single-minded as either Kierkegaard or Marx are still trying to figure out how to vote in the referendum over otherworldliness – or else they are distracting attention from the fact that they are as equivocal and confused on this point as Kant seems to be.[15]

In light of these subsequent developments, the wobbling in Kant's position becomes instructive in fresh ways. The liberal Protestant tradition, in particular, can perhaps be characterized as the sustained effort to display areas of overlap or congruence between insights into ourselves and language about God, the persuasiveness of the latter being underwritten by the presumed self-evidence of the former.[16] Kant's own postulation of the existence of God – beginning with an incorrigible experience of moral obligation, moving through the transcendental disclosure of freedom, and culminating in moral certainty of God's reality – exemplifies this liberal characteristic. Indeed, part of the lesson of this study is that Kant evidently presupposes a latent commensurability between the idioms of Protestant Christianity and of his own ethical rationalism. It is this presupposition that helps to breathe life into *Religion within the Limits of Reason Alone.*

But a more important lesson of this study is that the presumed commensurability does not run as deeply as Kant suspects, and the breakoff point manifests itself in the uneasy competition between human autonomy and transcendent action: the cumbersomeness of Kant's account is produced by the fact that the latter cannot be translated into the former without remainder. No trick of translation or exercise in reductionism, however sophisticated, can offset this deeper incommensurability.

Kant's ultimate inability to reconcile or intelligibly integrate his appeals to human autonomy and divine action, then, does not betray a failing in the critical philosophy so much as it perhaps heralds a crucial moment in modern theological history. It is the moment when the appeal of translating Christian orthodoxy into something more intellectually palatable becomes so strong that it masks the reasons why such a translation may be self-defeating or simply impossible. Alternatively, it is the moment when the starkness of choice concerning the very idea of "salvation" gains precision, a starkness exemplified by the fork in the road leading to Kierkegaard in one direction and Marx in the other.

The temptations of the metanarrative

The middle, liberal path that Kant represents proves bumpy because he is trying to tell a story using vocabularies that ultimately turn out to be incompatible with one another. If we distinguish between the competing vocabularies, on the one hand, and Kant's desire to tell a story, on the other, we can glimpse a final and perhaps especially telling way of interpreting his account of radical evil and moral regeneration. Kierkegaard and Marx suggest what happens when just one of the vocabularies is adopted and vigorously expanded, and liberal mediation suggests the continuation of Kant's own effort to juggle both the language of immanent human effort and of hidden transcendent action. Despite the diversity of these options, however, they share in common the underlying urge to tell the "story" of human "salvation" – the story, that is, of what is problematic or fallen about the human condition, how this fallenness or alienation keep our present existence from being all that it might be, and how the actual mechanisms of our salvation work, whether "in" history or not. However different even Kierkegaard and Marx themselves may be, they share this common grounding in a metanarrative, an implicit trust that their accounts make sense against the background of a totalizing depiction of our proper destiny, be it eternal blessedness or a socialist workers' paradise free of alienation. It never occurs to either thinker that there simply may be no story to tell, any more than it occurs to Kant that certain needs of reason may go unmet. They are all telling the Western story of human history after life in the garden.[17]

What comes into view here is the possibility that an explicit vote for immanence in the referendum over otherworldliness – as cast by Marx – is not the most radical option generated by Kant's mixture of possibilities. At some point, it may occur to someone to give up the temptation to tell the totalizing narrative, regardless of its content – which is more or less what we have in a thinker like Nietzsche, who wants to do for teleological thinking what Newtonianism did for supernaturalism.[18] From this standpoint, it is not that there is necessarily a totalizing story about human fulfillment to be told, the content and specific features of which may shift and vary on a scale of Kierkegaard to Marx. Rather, the very tendency to tell a story, to deploy a grounding metanarrative, turns out itself to be one of the shifting and contingent features of history, just as optional as any of the old-styled content. Not even Marx, let alone Kierkegaard and Kant, could ever grasp the deeply subversive possibility that such notions as "fulfillment," "meaning in history," and "salvation" – however secularized they become – are purely optional features of the culture, and perhaps just as lifeless as beliefs about virgins having babies and dead men emerging from tombs. The difficulty for this deeper sort of critic – a difficulty faced by Nietzsche in his day as by thinkers like Foucault and Rorty in our own – is to unmask and interpret the tendencies of the story-tellers without thereby becoming dependent on a totalizing narrative of one's own that informs and generates the unmasking.[19]

This is extremely rough interpretive ground, made more uneven by current debates over modernity and postmodernity, the cogency of secularization theses, and a new agnosticism about the possibility of ever understanding or appropriating texts of the past. But just as Kant has always factored unavoidably and significantly into our accounts of philosophy becoming "modern," he factors into these more recent conversations as well. From this more radical vantage point, Kant is not the fork in the road marking divergent options so much as he is simply symptomatic of the crippling effects produced by the temptations of the metanarrative. All that we have canvassed in this study – freedom's fall, the subsequent bind in which freedom finds itself, the oscillation and wobbling of Kant's proposed solution, the sudden trumping of a rational idiom by a biblical one – is thus perhaps best viewed as the effort of a great thinker to express a new content for humanity's self-understanding while still saddled with a form of expression antithetical to most of that content. Kant's juggling of rational and biblical idioms, in particular, hints at this deeper issue, one that is very much bound to the border period in which Kant is living and, for that reason, something of which he himself could not possibly be aware. The issue concerns the modern West's efforts to wean itself away from the sensibility produced by a profoundly Christian culture as it seeks to give an account of itself, and its tendency to retain the older sensibility as a framing device even as the weaning period is presumably over. Kant's problem is that he cannot be content simply to speak of autonomy: he wants to tell a story about it, too. He wants human autonomy to displace God and to assume the traditional divine prerogatives, but then he neglects to throw off the ingrained habits of thought produced by a culture eager to tell what God is up to in history. Such a result virtually guarantees the kind of instability evident in the *Religion*.

In his effort to show the ways in which the modern world is genuinely different from a medieval Christian past – and thus "legitimate" in its own right, rather than "belated" – Hans Blumenberg has offered some suggestive clues as to how to interpret Kant's awkward situation.[20] A large part of our modern difficulty in understanding our world and ourselves arises from the way in which a Christian theological heritage continues to force "questions" on us which should no longer in fact *be* questions for us. "The modern age's readiness to inherit . . . a mortgage of prescribed questions and to accept as its own the obligation to pay it off goes a long way towards explaining its intellectual history."[21] In the course of its rise to a position of cultural hegemony, Christian theology expanded the range of issues that had to be considered and debated *as* issues, thus creating what Blumenberg calls "new 'positions' in the framework of statements about the world and man that are possible and expected."[22] That is, Christianity both showed certain things to be questions for humankind that had not previously been thought to be questions, and it gave answers to these questions in terms of its own belief structure. Foremost among these was the question of the direction and meaning of history as a whole, a question taken over from Judaism but one that assumed a systematic new form following the delay of the Parousia and, especially, following the career of Augustine. The "answer" to the question of the point of history as a whole not only depends heavily on the idea of a hidden and purposeful intelligence behind the visible world, but it covertly privileges teleological forms of causality and causal explanation in other domains of life as well. The Christian idea of providence thus subtly paves the way for the persistence of a teleological trust, even after the intellectual and social backing for belief in divine providence begins to crumble, subsequent to a newly emergent mechanistic view of nature in the seventeenth century. At one level, then, Blumenberg is concerned to play out Nietzsche's insight that "every form of teleology is only a derivative of theology."[23]

But Blumenberg's account is not merely a warmed-over secularization thesis, aimed at showing, for example, that modern theories of progress – including Marxist views of history – are simply secularized eschatologies. Indeed, part of the occasion of his book is his effort to criticize just this view – associated especially with Karl Löwith – because of the way such a view puts in question the healthy distinctiveness (the "legitimacy") of the modern age.[24] In the effort to distance himself from Löwith, Blumenberg makes two points that are particularly relevant to our attempt to understand Kant's awkward straddling of vocabularies and his use of both vocabularies for the sake of a grounding metanarrative.

First, Blumenberg argues that there is nothing inevitable or necessary about certain questions that arise as humans confront the world and try to make sense of it. The unspoken belief that there are such perennial questions is itself one of the most powerful features of the West's Christian legacy. The "meaning of history as a whole" is for Blumenberg the chief example of a question that has the look of something intrinsic and mandatory, the look of a question that *must be answered* by each succeeding age if it is to make sense of itself. But for Blumenberg, the question of the meaning of history is purely contingent, the accidental if understandable product of the imprinting on

Western culture of the biblical heritage produced by the intimate connection between Christianity and the very idea of the West. There is no intrinsic need or obligation to answer this question, as evidenced, thinks Blumenberg, by the fact that the Greeks did not experience this issue as a question.[25]

Second and more importantly, Blumenberg argues that much of the deep cultural and conceptual confusion characteristic of modernity has been generated by our continuing to feel the force of questions that should no longer be questions for us, and which in fact *are* no longer questions for us. In producing, over time, its (purely contingent) questions, Christianity has created "positions" in the framework of our accounts of the world and ourselves; these positions "cannot simply be 'set aside' again or left unoccupied in the interest of theoretical economy."[26] But neither are the questions that originally produced the "positions" still questions for us, any more than anyone is still seriously wondering how many angels can balance on the head of a pin. The problem is that we do not see this situation clearly – we do not see that we have inherited question-and-answer positions but not the original questions themselves. We feel the force of the original questions in the form of an inarticulate need, we feel obligated to provide answers in response to that felt need, but we have outgrown the questions.[27] We thus find ourselves compromising a potentially new content for thought about ourselves and the world by trying to reconcile that content with questions largely incommensurate with the new content, which is a little like trying to run a jet aircraft on coal. The fact that we are not even too clear sometimes about what the question is in the first place – that "we *imply* what we now understand the question to be, rather than consciously and critically stating it"[28] – only muddies the water further. Good philosophy is diagnostic and therapeutic, rather than metaphysically ambitious: it attempts to diagnose the levels of confusion produced by our forms of forgetfulness, thereby putting certain ideas in a new and positive light, while simultaneously helping us to get out from under the hangover effects of other ideas. In an approving nod again in the direction of Nietzsche, Blumenberg says "philosophy is among the approaches to a kind of thinking that removes problems by specifying the conditions under which they no longer arise."[29]

Blumenberg is by no means attempting to deny the historical continuity between the pre-modern and modern worlds, or between medieval Christian ideas and modern secular substitutes. He is evidently opposed to the idea of radical breaks or ruptures in the historical record characteristic of a thinker like Foucault. Instead, he is simply trying to argue for continuity based on the identity of the *functions* performed by ideas about ourselves and the world, rather than an identity of a *content* that gradually finds secular form.[30]

The perpetuation of a form of language – such as the language of Christian theology – can obscure the fact that the belief content packed into the language has changed drastically. In such a case, the "constancy of language is an index of a constant function for consciousness but not of an identity of content."[31] Moreover, Blumenberg's disclosure of the historical contingency of certain question positions is not aimed at the elimination of those positions – as though by fiat – for the simple reason that it is no use pretending or wishing that a certain position did not assume a place in our framework of accounts of the world if in fact it did. This last point is nicely brought out by Blumenberg's reference to

> the reproach that Leibniz advanced against Descartes, that through the radicalness of his doubt and the questionable perspicuity of its elimination he had introduced into the world a demand for certainty, which on account of the rigor of its requirements could not be fulfilled by him or by anyone else, but which could not be revoked and rejected merely on account of the impossibility of satisfying it.[32]

Like real cats, conceptual cats cannot be put back in the bag once they are out. Cadres of anti-Cartesian philosophers may, in our own day, debunk the Cartesian "demand for certainty," but debunking is not the same as ignoring. Blumenberg would presumably want to say that Descartes' "quest for certainty" is not a secularized substitute for the Christian "quest for salvation " – a "transposition" of a theological content into a secularized variant – but the "reoccupation" of an answer position that had become vacant but whose originating question still had spill-over effects in the form of the needs to which Descartes was responding with the *cogito*. By switching our attention from an identity of content to an identity of function, Blumenberg preserves the integrity of historical continuity without belittling or underestimating the ways in which the modern world is genuinely different from the medieval.

Blumenberg's point, then, is that the modern West shares little or none of the context surrounding the origin of the questions that some moderns still feel a need to answer, questions that typically find their real originating context in the thought forms and interpretive structures of medieval theology. Modern answers – though "totally heterogeneous" in content in comparison with earlier answers – "take on identical functions in specific positions" in systems of interpretation of the world and of ourselves.[33] But this "reoccupation" by a new answer of a "position" once held by an old one conceals the fact that the question producing all the intellectual effort no longer applies to the new historical situation – any more than, say, questions about demons apply to modern discussions of epilepsy and its etiology, despite the historical continuity between belief in demons and the discovery of epilepsy.

In a manner somewhat reminiscent of Wittgenstein, then, Blumenberg offers a view of our modern intellectual landscape based on the insight that we are held captive by a certain picture, and cannot hope to achieve cultural clarity until we gain release. The picture holding us captive blinds us to the possibility that much of our intellectual effort is generated by questions that should no longer be questions for us, but which perpetuate themselves in the form of felt needs or obligations. Proper philosophy helps us to grasp our situation accurately, by forcing us to be more articulate and explicit about just what questions we are trying to answer with our own intellectual efforts. Should this clarification occur, we may discover in a fresh way the value – the "legitimacy" – of the content of modern thought, because we are no longer saddled with the self-defeating task of trying to relate the new content to questions that originally arose in a historical setting wholly different from our own. We may discover that, though we inherit question "positions" that need filling with new answers, we do not necessarily inherit the original questions themselves. In fact, it is far more likely that we have outgrown them.

I think Kant's philosophy of religion exemplifies the situation that Blumenberg is describing. This is true regarding both Kant's urge to tell a totalizing narrative – to give reason and autonomy a "career," as it were – and his effort to have human autonomy displace divine action. Indeed, the latter is no doubt the source of the need for the former; in taking over the prerogatives of God, autonomy becomes providential, and thereby deserves a narrative. Blumenberg's distinction between an identity of content and an identity of function – the difference, that is, between merely secularizing a given idea and having a truly new idea meant to fill or reoccupy an inherited position – suggests why Kant's account of moral regeneration is bound to wobble. His inherited theological framework makes it virtually impossible to state his own position coherently, leaving him in a position similar to that of someone who thinks we should stop telling racist jokes and tell only non-racist jokes, when the real point turns out to be that the age of joke-telling is behind us.

Kant's urge to give autonomy a career is thus linked in complex ways with his appeals to transcendence. The crippling effects of this linkage become manifest through comparison with a more purely theological account of human life, for which the appeal to transcendence – though perhaps unbelievable – is natural and fitting rather than conceptually awkward. The difficulty of Kant's situation is implicitly illuminated by Blumenberg's remark that for Christian theology there was no need for questions about the totality of the world and history, about the origin of man and the purpose of his existence, to be unanswerable. This explains the readiness with which it introduced titles into the budget of man's needs in the area of knowledge, to honor which was bound to be difficult or even impossible for any knowledge that did not appeal, as it did, to transcendent sources. Its strength could only be the weakness of its heirs.[34]

In his effort to have human autonomy succeed God and assume the major role in a salvation story, Kant steps right into the dilemma described here by Blumenberg. With the overriding emphasis on autonomy rather than transcendence, but with autonomy depicted in terms of a narrative requiring an appeal to transcendence for the narrative to achieve closure, Kant's position "is essentially modern in its content . . . but heavily affected by Christianity in the function that the content is forced to perform."[35] His theory of autonomy marks a potentially decisive break away from an outlook we can readily identify as pre-modern, yet his succumbing then to the temptation to give autonomy a journey – about which to tell a story – leaves Kant drawing on the superseded outlook in fumbling ways. Perhaps the most telling feature of Kant's effort to work out a theory of moral regeneration is the fact that he cannot quite figure out how to complete his story in autonomy's own terms, but has to recall the biblical idiom in order to avoid the disastrous prospect of leaving the story incomplete and fragmentary. In its drive for satisfaction, reason rounds itself out through appeal to the very resource it was meant to supplant. In thus having the Bible save rationality and transcendence rescue autonomy, Kant makes his predicament altogether clear.

Conclusion

Viewing Kant's position in this way serves to remind us that his moral and religious philosophy is not so much a collection of "arguments" as it is an effort to articulate a deeply felt sensibility. Just as the initial comparison with the desperate vision of Ivan Karamazov helps us to grasp this point, so does Blumenberg's suggestion that someone like Kant is attempting the impossible feat of performing on two playing fields at once. Kant's problem is that the emergent new sensibility is seriously compromised by a received tradition largely antithetical to it: he is not dealing with philosophical argumentation so much as he is juggling centuries. This is why it is simply not adequate to try to rehabilitate the doctrines of the *Religion* along purely conceptual and argumentative lines, as contemporary analytic philosophers sometimes try to do with the doctrines of the first *Critique*.[36] Such a shallow approach hardly does justice to the latent historical pressures and cultural tensions that make Kant's works – perhaps the *Religion* above all – so provocative and enduring. The problems affecting the *Religion* are not something Kant could ever have "corrected," but only lived through.

The problems affecting the *Religion* also go a long way toward illustrating Richard Rorty's suggestion that "interesting philosophy is rarely an examination of the pros and cons of a thesis. Usually it is, implicitly or explicitly, a contest between an entrenched vocabulary which has become a nuisance and a half-formed new vocabulary which vaguely promises great things."[37] Kant's "half-formed vocabulary" of human autonomy is struggling to make itself articulate, like a newborn taking its first breaths. In retrospect, we can appreciate that the promised emancipation of the vocabulary of autonomy would never be fully realized, for the subsequent, highly dubious career of the notion of autonomy in modern Western thought has done as much to disclose subtle new forms of coercion as to free us from an outmoded world view. Such a career trajectory insinuates that Kant's problems are not merely the result of the protracted effects of an earlier tradition that viewed "freedom" as submission to the divine will, but the result as well of problems intrinsic to the very idea of autonomy. Kant's idealist successors would be quick to grasp the point, appreciating that reason itself is a social reality, subject to social and historical influences in ways that compromise a purely Kantian view of freedom. It would be only a small step to the additional possibility that reason is subject to unconscious and deeply subterranean influences as well, a possibility already broached in primitive form in Kant's own time by Herder. Such possibilities as these emerge with increasing momentum as soon as the philosophers begin to achieve what Kant could never fully do, which is to think historically.[38]

With respect to the issue of autonomy, then, Kant's tradition of discourse does not culminate with Kierkegaard and Marx – or even with Nietzsche – but reaches up to and through the Freudian project.[39] Kant's own agnosticism regarding our moral tidal patterns hints at a source of character formation that reason cannot reach and to which it perhaps cannot fully respond, even though this source must be a feature of reason itself. The characteristic Kantian appeal to the "inscrutability" of the fall suggests one way in which we forfeit self-mastery, while Kant's inability fully to ground moral recovery in our own efforts implies another. In some profound and awful sense, I am opaque to myself, considered as a moral agent. The lesson is clear: the problem of evil brings Kant closer and closer to the insight that reason is not fully self-governing, but is subject to forces too murky to specify. For Kant, the glory of the idea of autonomy resides in the claim that the free will can legislate laws to itself. But when even he puts in question the independence of the will from influences beyond its control, the very idea of self-governance is severely compromised.

I said at the beginning of this chapter that Kant's religious philosophy begins and ends in irony. I might just as easily have said that it begins and ends in the experience of contingency, for in some fundamental sense the moral and religious life itself is for Kant profoundly and utterly contingent. Because of the familiar Kantian emphasis on the particular form our moral activity ought to take, this note of contingency can be obscured from view – Kant's ethical formalism has the capacity to leave in the shadows whatever is unique and idiosyncratic, just as Newtonian regularity makes disreputable serious scientific interest in what is unrepeatable. But the fact that there is a proper, universalizable form for the free will to assume neither supersedes nor offsets the accompanying fact that, in its successive acts, the will assumes no predictable rational pattern, not even retrospectively. Kant cannot "explain" virtue or evil; most of all, he can neither explain nor demarcate with any precision the hidden combination of will and grace producing moral regeneration. Their inscrutability is simply the epistemological expression of their contingency. Perhaps this should come as no surprise, for Kant's famous comment about his sense of awe and wonder before the "starry heavens above" and the "moral law within"[40] is nothing if not an expression of his sense of the sheer contingency of things.

Still, the note of contingency is genuinely subversive. For although autonomy both saves us from the moral desert in which theoretical reason leaves us and raises our self-worth in the face of a cold and impersonal universe, the utter mystery of autonomy's actual exercise keeps it from being an unambiguous source of metaphysical comfort. In unhooking freedom from Newton, Kant leaves us in the most intractable puzzlement about ourselves and our deepest motivations. Ivan may have worried about a world filled with torturers – but Kant leaves us with the deeper worry that you or I might become one of them.

Notes

Introduction

1 Charles Taylor, *Hegel* (Cambridge: Cambridge University Press, 1975), pp 8–9.

2 Richard Rorty, *Contingency, Irony, and Solidarity* (Cambridge: Cambridge University Press, 1989), p. 30.

3 Karl Marx, *The German Ideology*, ed. C. J. Arthur (New York: International Publishers, 1970), p. 97.

4 Karl Barth, *Protestant Thought from Rousseau to Ritschl*, trans. Brian Cozens (New York: Simon and Schuster, 1969), p. 176.

5 Kant, *Die Religion innerhalb der Grenzen der blossen Vernunft*, vol. VI of The Prussian Academy Edition of *Gesammelte Schriften* (Berlin: Georg Reimer, 1907–1983), p. 37; English trans., *Religion within the Limits of Reason Alone*, trans. Theodore M. Greene and Hoyt H. Hudson (New York: Harper Torchbooks, 1960), p. 32, emphasis Kant's. Hereafter, all references to this work will appear within parentheses in the text, with the page number in the Prussian Academy edition followed by the page number in the Greene and Hudson translation.

6 Despite his remark that the theory of radical evil is "the last thing one would expect" to find in Kant's writings, Barth appreciated that the Kantian insight that "in the same incomprehensible freedom of reason in which the good, lawful will can be made actual, its great opposite, a will for evil, can be made manifest too" was implicit in Kant's writings before 1793 and deserved explicit treatment; Barth, *Protestant Thought*, p. 178. More recent commentators have approached the theory of radical evil precisely with a view to its systematic – and therefore unsurprising – place in Kant's moral philosophy. See, e.g., Allen W. Wood, *Kant's Moral Religion* (Ithaca and London: Cornell University Press, 1970), chapters 4, 6; Bernard Carnois, *The Coherence of Kant's Doctrine of Freedom*, trans. David Booth (Chicago and London: The University of Chicago Press, 1987), chapter 5.

7 Richard Kroner once said that, for Kant, "morality makes the world incomprehensible," which is best understood as a comment about freedom rather than about morality: *Kant's Weltanschauung*, trans. John E. Smith (Chicago and London: University of Chicago Press, 1956), p. 29.

8 Emil Fackenheim, "Immanuel Kant," in Ninian Smart, John Clayton, Patrick Sherry, and Steven T. Katz (eds.), *Nineteenth Century Religious Thought in the West*, vol. I (Cambridge: Cambridge University Press, 1985), p. 28. Fackenheim's way of

putting the issue helpfully underscores something that is easily missed in treatments of Kant's religious thought that place a one-sided emphasis on the purely moral dimension – namely, the fact that much of Kant's later religious thought (especially the *Religion*) can be fruitfully viewed as a vaguely secularized continuation of the traditional problem of nature and grace.

9 I would not want to make too much out of the common tendency to speak of Kant as the "philosopher of Protestantism." Still, it is well worth drawing attention to the obvious, but easily underestimated, fact that, even during the Enlightenment, the heritage of the Reformation was unavoidable for a thinker dwelling on such issues as moral evil and human salvation, let alone for a thinker raised and schooled on Prussian pietism. But the heritage works on Kant in subtle ways rather than in terms of conscious indebtedness. As Michel Despland has pointed out, Kant nowhere quotes either Luther or Calvin in *Religion within the Limits of Reason Alone*, nor does Kant even represent the Reformation as a key turning point in the history of religious "progress." "As a matter of fact, it is completely ignored. The next important turning point in the history of religious progress after Jesus is the Enlightenment": *Kant on History and Religion* (Montreal and London: McGill-Queens University Press, 1973), p. 181. Concerning the specifically theological sources behind the *Religion*, see the standard study of Josef Bohatec, *Die Religionsphilosophie Kants in der 'Religion innerhalb der Grenzen der blossen Vernunft'* (Hildesheim: Georg Olms, 1966), pp. 19–32. Bernard Reardon's recent assessment seems apt: "Although it is far wide of the mark to describe Kant as the philosopher of Protestantism in its classical forms, the designation could well hold as regards its modern liberal manifestations, which to a considerable extent stem from Ritschl": *Kant as Philosophical Theologian* (London: The Macmillan Press, 1988), p. 183. I make my own connections between Kant and modern liberal theology in chapter 7.

10 My interpretive motifs of "straddling" and "wobbling" indicate my point of disagreement with Roger J. Sullivan's otherwise admirable and extremely useful recent volume, *Immanuel Kant's Moral Theory* (Cambridge: Cambridge University Press, 1989). Sullivan and I agree on the powerful role played in Kant's thinking by the Protestant Christian tradition as well as by the rationalist–Enlightenment tradition, just as we agree that the importance of the religious life for Kant is often underestimated by interpreters who focus too narrowly on certain of his ethical writings. But it seems to me that Sullivan moves too easily to a reconciliation of these competing traditions in his account of Kant's later works. Sullivan states, for example, that Kant's philosophy of religion "represents his *resolution* of the enormously difficult challenge of fidelity both to the faith of the Enlightenment in the power of human reason and to the faith of the ordinary person in God and the importance of religion, particularly the Christian faith" (p. 273, emphasis mine). By contrast, I think the instability in Kant's thinking not only remains, but is intensified. To a great extent, the point of my book is to show that this instability is not the result of an argumentative failure on Kant's part, but is symptomatic of

a change in historical epochs, with the aging Kant caught in the middle, just as the *Religion* appears to be caught between idioms.

11 Stanley Cavell, "Emerson, Coleridge, Kant," in John Rajchman and Cornell West (eds.), *Post-Analytic Philosophy* (New York: Columbia University Press, 1985), p. 106.

12 Mary Midgley, *Wickedness: A Philosophical Essay* (London: Routledge and Kegan Paul, 1984), p 208n.7.

13 Ernest Gellner, *Legitimation of Belief* (Cambridge: Cambridge University Press, 1974), p. 185, emphasis Gellner's.

14 Bernard Yack, *The Longing for Total Revolution* (Princeton: Princeton University Press, 1986), p. 20.

1 Ivan and Kant

1 Fyodor Dostoyevsky, *The Brothers Karamazov*, trans. David Magarshack (New York: Viking Penguin, 1982), pp. 282–3.

2 John le Carré, *A Murder of Quality* (New York: Bantam Books, 1980), p. 130.

3 Dostoyevsky, *Brothers Karamazov*, p. 287.

4 This is the lead question that Ernest Becker frames for himself in his sometimes chaotic but always interesting book, *The Denial of Death* (New York: Free Press, 1973). For a helpful account of the connection between narrative and explanations, see Alasdair MacIntyre, "Epistemological Crises, Dramatic Narrative and Philosophy of Science," *The Monist* 60 (1977), p. 453–72.

5 Kant, "Beantwortung der Frage: Was ist Aufklärung," Prussian Academy Edition, vol. VIII (Berlin: Georg Reimer, 1912), p. 35; English trans. "What is Enlightenment?," in *On History*, trans. Lewis White Beck (New York: Bobbs-Merrill, 1963), p. 3.

6 Ann Loades nicely summarizes the matter when she says, "Rousseau's achievement was comparable to that of Newton, and his effect on Kant was to help him secure a basis for his theology in his analysis of morality rather than in the realms of natural philosophy or theoretical metaphysics": *Kant and Job's Comforters* (Newcastle upon Tyne: Avero Publications, 1985), p. 15.

7 Olivier Reboul, *Kant et le Problème de Mal* (Montréal: Presses de l'université du Montréal, 1971), p. 187.

8 There is detailed account of the historical background to pietist education in Königsberg in Ann Loades, *Kant and Job's Comforters*, part I.

9 Ernst Cassirer, *Kant's Life and Thought*, trans. James Haden (New Haven and London: Yale University Press, 1981), pp. 15–18.

10 Kant, "On the Failure of All Attempted Philosophical Theodicies," trans. Michel Despland in Despland, *Kant on History and Religion* (Montreal and London: McGill-Queen's University Press, 1973), p. 292.

11 Ernst Cassirer, *Rousseau, Kant, Goethe: Two Essays*, trans. James Gutman, P.O. Kristeller, and J. H. Randall, Jr. (New York: Harper Torchbook, 1963), p. 7.

.12 Ernst Cassirer, *The Philosophy of the Enlightenment*, trans. Fritz C. A. Koelln and James P. Pettegrove (Princeton: Princeton University Press, 1951), p. 141.

13 Quoted in Karl Barth, *Protestant Thought from Rousseau to Ritschl*, trans. Brian Cozens (New York: Simon and Schuster, 1969), p. 178.

14 For surveys of the background of Kant's thinking on the general problem of evil, see Reboul, *Kant et le Problème du Mal*, chapter 2; Loades, *Kant and Job's Comforters*, pp. 29–45.

15 This question arises especially in connection with Kant's so-called *Opus Postumum*, the complete text of which was not available until 1938. Kant's rather rambling comments in this piece of writing (almost certainly written after 1800) can be taken to imply a repudiation of his moral argument for the existence of God. But see George Schrader, "Kant's Presumed Repudiation of the 'Moral Argument' in the *Opus Postumum*: An Examination of Adickes' Interpretation," *Philosophy* 26 (1951), pp. 228–41. There is a good summary of the issues raised by this text in Bernard Reardon, *Kant as Philosophical Theologian* (London: The Macmillan Press, 1988), chapter 10. Other efforts to show changes in Kant's religious views that take into account the entire trajectory of his career include what Michel Despland calls the "new departures" in Kant's writings on religion after about 1791, in *Kant on History and Religion*, part II; and Yirmiahu Yovel's interesting effort to historicize Kant's thinking on such fundamental matters as the doctrine of the highest good, in *Kant and the Philosophy of History* (Princeton: Princeton University Press, 1980). See also my own earlier effort to strike the right balance between emphasizing the reductionistic and the constructive aspects of Kant's approach to the historical and ecclesiastical side of religious tradition: *The Historical Dimensions of a Rational Faith: The Role of History in Kant's Religious Thought* (Washington D.C.: University Press of America, 1977).

16 We might say that the transformation from logic to metaphysics also characterizes Kant's deduction of the categories in the first *Critique*, where he moves from the logical forms of judgment to the naming of the categories. *Kritik der reinen Vernunft*, second ed., Prussian Academy Edition, vol. III (Berlin: Georg Reimer, 1911), pp. 84–99; English trans. *Critique of Pure Reason*, trans. Norman Kemp Smith (New York: St. Martin's Press, 1965), pp. 104–19. Hereafter referred to as *Pure*, followed by page numbers in the Prussian Academy edition and, in parentheses, the English translation.

17 A helpful account of the historical background of the idea of "critique" is offered by Paul Connerton, *The Tragedy of Enlightenment: An Essay on the Frankfurt School* (Cambridge: Cambridge University Press, 1980), pp. 16–26.

18 Allen Wood, *Kant's Moral Religion* (Ithaca and London: Cornell University Press, 1970), p. 208. See also Wood's entire chapter 4.

19 Bernard Williams, *Moral Luck* (Cambridge: Cambridge University Press, 1981), p. 21.

20 In a section of the *Critique of Practical Reason* called "On Assent Arising from a Need of Pure Reason," Kant stipulates that a "need of pure reason in its speculative use

leads only to hypotheses; that of pure practical reason, to postulates." In a way, the entire constructive side of the second *Critique* can be read as an extended commentary on this remark. See *Kritik der praktischen Vernunft*, Prussian Academy Edition, Vol.V (Berlin: Georg Reimer, 1913), p. 142; English trans., *Critique of Practical Reason*, trans. Lewis White Beck (New York: Bobbs-Merrill, 1956), p. 147. Hereafter referred to as *Practical* followed by page numbers in the Prussian Academy edition and, in parentheses, the English translation. In his commentary on the second *Critique*, Lewis White Beck employs a contrast between a purely rational need and (with one eye on William James's notion of the "will to believe") a pragmatic need. Beck suggests that if his interpretation is correct, "there can be no need of *pure* reason for the postulates, not because pure reason may not have some needs but because its need is exhausted in issuing the moral command. If reason is taken in the broader sense of concern with the promotion of the good under human limitations, the difference between [Kant's] view and that of the pragmatists becomes chiefly verbal..." Beck, *A Commentary on Kant's Critique of Practical Reason* (Chicago and London: The University of Chicago Press, 1960), p. 254.

21 See Kant's summary of his dispute with Wizenmann, who had challenged the legitimacy of moving from a need of reason to the reality of the object of that need, *Practical*, pp. 143–4n. (p. 149n.).

22 *Practical*, p. 143 (p. 148).

23 *Ibid.*, p. 143 (p. 148).

24 *Ibid.*, pp. 110–11 (pp. 114–15).

25 *Ibid.*, p. 124 (p. 129).

26 *Ibid.*, p. 122 (p. 126).

27 *Ibid.*, pp. 122–3 (pp. 126–7).

28 *Ibid.*, p. 122 (p. 127).

29 *Ibid.*, p. 132 (p. 137).

30 *Ibid.*, p. 124 (p. 129).

31 *Ibid.*, pp. 124–5 (pp. 128–30).

32 *Ibid.*, p. 110 (p. 114).

33 *Ibid.*, p. 110 (p. 114).

34 *Ibid.*, p. 110 (p. 114).

35 Kant, *Grundlegung zur Metaphysik der Sitten*, Prussian Academy Edition, vol. IV (Berlin: Georg Reimer, 1911), pp. 392–9. English trans., *Foundations of the Metaphysics of Morals*, trans. Lewis White Beck (New York: Bobbs-Merrill, 1959), pp. 9–16.

36 *Practical*, p. 110 (p. 114).

37 Wood, *Kant's Moral Religion*, p. 38.

38 Kant, *Grundlegung*, pp. 395–6 (English trans. pp. 11–12).

39 *Practical*, p. 110 (pp. 114–15).

40 *Ibid.*, p. 110 (p. 115).

41 In his *Vorlesungen über die philosophische Religionslehre* (Prussian Academy Edition, Vol. 28), the published version of which probably dates from 1783–4, Kant says at

one point that "all morality, that is, all good conduct which is done merely because our reason commands it, would come to nothing if our true worth were determined by the course of things and the fate we meet with in it." English trans., *Lectures on Philosophical Theology*, trans. Allen W. Wood and Gertrude M. Clark (Ithaca and London: Cornell University Press, 1978), p. 121.

42 Dostoyevsky, *Brothers Karamazov*, p. 287. For an insightful discussion of the role played by Ivan's standpoint in current theological accounts of the problem of theodicy, see Kenneth Surin, *Theology and the Problem of Evil* (Oxford: Basil Blackwell, 1986), pp. 96ff.

43 Loades, *Kant and Job's Comforters*, parts III and IV; Reboul, *Kant et le Problème du Mal*, chapter II.

44 For example in his "Idea for a Universal History from a Cosmopolitan Point of View" of 1784, in *On History*, pp. 11–26.

45 *Lectures on Philosophical Theology*, p. 118. Kant also remarks in these lectures, "if we ask where the evil in individual men comes from, the answer is that it exists on account of the limits necessary to every creature"(*ibid*). The account of radical evil in the *Religion* utterly repudiates the connection of evil with a mere "limitation" in human nature. See Wood, *Kant's Moral Religion*, pp. 108ff.

46 Despland, *Kant on History and Religion*, p. 171.

47 Kant, "Idea for a Universal History from a Cosmopolitan Point of View," p. 15.

48 *Ibid.*, pp. 15–16.

49 For a further account of Kant's connection to Leibniz, see Reboul, *Kant et le Problème du Mal*, pp. 43–8.

50 Despland, *Kant on History and Religion*, p. 171.

2 Kant's definition of moral evil

1 Sharon Anderson-Gold, "Kant's Rejection of Devilishness: The Limits of Human Volition," *Idealistic Studies* 14 (1984), p. 35.

2 In his early article on Kant's theory of radical evil, Emil Fackenheim took the view that the main point of the theory was to allow Kant to correct a problem latent in his earlier writings, namely, the fact that he had evidently left it impossible to attribute moral evil to the free will. If the will was truly acting freely, it was acting virtuously; if it was not acting virtuously, it was acting heteronomously and not freely. As I shall suggest further on in this chapter, Fackenheim's approach does not adequately take into account Kant's ability to distinguish between *Wille* and *Willkür*: Fackenheim, "Kant and Radical Evil," *University of Toronto Quarterly* 23 (1954), pp. 339–53. While not concentrating on the problem of radical evil, Fackenheim's more recent essay on Kant's religious thought in the Cambridge *Nineteenth Century Religious Thought in the West* is a far more nuanced account, very valuable for the way it brings out some of Kant's deeper concerns. See note 11 above to the Introduction. Sharon Anderson-Gold offers some helpful comments

regarding the idea of transcendentally deducing moral evil, "Kant's Rejection of Devilishness," p. 37.

3 In contrast to the view that Kant's account of the propensity toward evil might be taken this way, Daniel O'Connor has argued that Kant's account "mixes up the Critical and historical modes; there is a shift from the reflective analysis of the capacity for evil to claims about the actual evil uniformly found in all men." O'Connor concludes that it is preferable "to regard the notion of radical evil as part of a speculative idea about human history which Kant was developing during the same period (1784–1797) in which he produced his major systematic works in moral philosophy." O'Connor, "Good and Evil Disposition," *Kant-Studien* 76 (1985), p. 298. I am myself not convinced that Kant's works during this most important period of hìs career can be so neatly divided into "Critical" and "speculative." It is clear, however, that – as O'Connor points out – Kant persistently mixes claims presented as known a priori and appeals to human experience – most notoriously, no doubt, in his explicit claim that it is "through experience" that we know that man is evil "by nature"; *Religion*, p. 32 (p. 27).

4 The phrase is H. J. Paton's, quoted by Mary J. Gregor, "Translator's Introduction" to Kant, *Anthropology From a Pragmatic Point of View* (The Hague: Martinus Nijhoff, 1974), p. xvi.

5 Kant, *Grundlegung zur Metaphysik der Sitten*, Prussian Academy Edition, Vol. IV (Berlin: Georg Reimer, 1911), p. 421. English trans., *Foundations of the Metaphysics of Morals*, trans. Lewis White Beck (New York: Bobbs-Merrill, 1959), p. 39.

6 *Ibid.*, pp. 440n., 421n. (English trans. pp. 17n., 38n.).

7 Kant, *The Doctrine of Virtue* (part II of *The Metaphysics of Morals*), trans. Mary J. Gregor (Philadelphia: University of Pennsylvania Press, 1964), p. 56. For a helpful clarification of the relation between maxims and ends, see Allen W. Wood, *Kant's Moral Religion* (Ithaca and London: Cornell University Press, 1970), pp. 40ff.

8 Lewis White Beck, *A Commentary on Kant's Critique of Practical Reason* (Chicago and London: University of Chicago Press, 1960), p. 38.

9 *Practical*, pp. 26–7 (p. 26). (See note 22 above to chapter 1.)

10 At one point in his recent study of Kant's theory of freedom, Bernard Carnois misleadingly refers to radical evil as a "privation": *The Coherence of Kant's Doctrine of Freedom*, trans. David Booth (Chicago and London: University of Chicago Press, 1987), p. 123.

11 Kant, *Lectures on Philosophical Theology*, trans. Allen W. Wood and Gertrude M. Clark (Ithaca and London: Cornell University Press, 1978), p. 117.

12 In the Introduction to *The Metaphysics of Morals* (published in 1797), Kant says: "The faculty of desiring in accordance with concepts is called the faculty of doing or forbearing as one likes insofar as the ground determining it to action is found in the faculty of desire itself and not in the object. Insofar as it is combined with the consciousness of the capacity of its action to produce its object, it is called *Will* or *Choice [Willkür]*; if not so combined, its act is called a *wish*. The faculty of desire whose internal ground of determination and, consequently, even whose likings

are found in the reason of the subject is called the *Will* [*der Wille*]. Accordingly, the Will is the faculty of desire regarded not, as is will, in its relation to action, but rather in its relation to the ground determining will to action. The Will itself has no determining ground; but, insofar as it can determine will, it is practical reason itself." *Metaphysik der Sitten*, Prussian Academy Edition, Vol. VI (Berlin: Georg Reimer, 1914), p. 214; English trans., *The Metaphysical Elements of Justice* (part I of *The Metaphysics of Morals*), trans. John Ladd (New York: Bobbs-Merrill, 1965), p. 12.

13 *Ibid.*

14 For a good account of the wider historical context of the terms *Wille* and *Willkür*, see Ralf Meerbote, "*Wille* and *Willkür* in Kant's Theory of Action," in Moltke Gram (ed.), *Interpreting Kant* (Iowa City: University of Iowa Press, 1982), pp. 69–84. See also Meerbote's essay, "Kant on the Nondeterminate Character of Human Actions," in William L. Harper and Meerbote (eds.), *Kant on Causality, Freedom, and Objectivity* (Minneapolis: University of Minnesota Press, 1984), pp. 143–51.

15 Carnois, *Kant's Doctrine of Freedom*, p. 84.

16 *Ibid.*, p. 150n.3.

17 It is this distinction that seems to be missing in Fackenheim's essay, "Kant and Radical Evil."

18 Regarding this latter sort of reading of the *Religion*, see G. E. Michalson, Jr., *The Historical Dimensions of a Rational Faith: The Role of History in Kant's Religious Thought* (Washington, D.C.: 1977), chapters 2 and 3.

19 In his earlier *Lectures on Philosophical Theology*, Kant says "we must note that of all the many creatures there are, man is the only one who has to work for his perfections and for the goodness of his character, producing them from within himself. God therefore gave him talents and capabilities, but left it up to man himself how he would employ them. He created man free, but gave him also animal instincts; he gave man senses to be moderated and overcome through the development of his understanding. Thus created, man was certainly perfect both in his nature and as regards his predispositions. But regarding the development of these predispositions, he was still crude and uncultivated. Man himself had to be responsible for this development, through the cultivation of his talents and the goodness of his will"; *Lectures on Philosophical Theology*, p. 116.

20 *Practical*, pp. 73–6 (pp. 76–9).

21 "Respect for the moral law . . . is a feeling produced by an intellectual cause . . . This feeling, under the name of moral feeling, is therefore produced solely by reason." *Practical*, pp. 73, 76 (pp. 76, 79).

22 Beck, *A Commentary on Kant's Critique of Practical Reason*, p. 221.

23 *Practical*, p. 73 (p. 76).

24 *Ibid.*, pp. 72ff. (pp. 75ff.).

25 *Ibid.*, p. 73 (p. 76).

26 Reboul, *Kant et le Problème du Mal* (Montréal: Presses de l'université de Montréal, 1971), p. 66, translation mine.

27 I shall suggest at the end of chapter 3, however, that the sheer, inescapable fact of our bodiliness is perhaps the reason that radical evil turns out to be *universal*.

28 On the limits of "moral rebellion" within Kant's scheme, see the interesting account in Allen W. Wood, *Kant's Moral Religion* (Ithaca and London: Cornell University Press, 1970), pp. 212–13. Wood disputes the interpretation given by John Silber, "The Ethical Significance of Kant's *Religion*," Editor's Introduction to English translation of the *Religion*, p. cxxix. See also Anderson-Gold, "Kant's Rejection of Devilishness."

29 On the confusion concerning Kant's meaning, see especially Wood, *Kant's Moral Religion*, pp. 215–17.

30 *Ibid.*, p. 216.

31 O'Connor, "Good and Evil Disposition," p. 297.

32 *Ibid.*

33 Carnois tries to solve this problem by suggesting that the three degrees indicate three "levels of consciousness" of the propensity to evil "as it appears to consciousness without claiming to reveal what (the propensity) is in itself or what its root is." Carnois, *Kant's Doctrine of Freedom*, p. 105.

34 Kant immediately qualifies – and vastly complicates – this point by distinguishing between two senses of "act": one sense bears on the free choice of one's subjective "disposition," and the other sense bears on the specific acts undertaken in accordance with the underlying disposition. I elaborate on these two senses of "act" in chapter 3.

35 I shall examine this issue more thoroughly in chapter 3.

36 For a summary of Kant's views on existing approaches to the problem of evil, see James Collins, *The Emergence of Philosophy of Religion* (New Haven and London: Yale University Press, 1967), pp. 168ff.

37 E.g., Wood, *Kant's Moral Religion*; Fackenheim, *Nineteenth Century Religious Thought*.

38 Michel Despland suggests that the change occurs with Kant's essay, "On the Failure of All Attempted Philosophical Theodicies" of 1791. "With this essay," says Despland, "Kant passed through his turning point in the problem of evil, and finally consciously confronted a problem which was intrinsically present in the process that had begun in the sixties of limiting the validity and the scope of theological judgements applied to the world as a whole." Despland, *Kant on History and Religion* (Montreal and London: McGill-Queen's University Press, 1973), pp. 171–2. Even this approach, however, seems to place the emphasis on certain conceptual difficulties within the critical philosophy as the source of the change, rather than on a fundamental alteration of perspective brought about by life experience.

39 Norman Hampson, *The Enlightenment* (Baltimore: Penguin Books, 1968), p. 100. I hasten to add that I fully endorse Laurence Dickey's salutary warning against using a select group of prominent French *philosophes* as our sole model of the Enlightenment. In contrast to the French situation, Dickey points out, "by all

accounts there is little evidence to suggest that the *Aufklärer* engaged in anything like a 'war on Christianity' in the eighteenth century," a comment that of course finds significant backing in the career of Kant. See Dickey, *Hegel: Religion, Economics, and the Politics of Spirit, 1770–1807* (Cambridge: Cambridge University Press, 1987), p. 18.

40 It should be said, however, that the opening pages of Book Three of the *Religion* could be read in a Rousseauvian way if lifted out of the context of the total account of radical evil: *Religion*, pp. 93–4 (pp. 85–6).

41 Vincent A. McCarthy, *Quest for a Philosophical Jesus; Christianity and Philosophy in Rousseau, Kant, Hegel, and Schelling* (Macon, Georgia: Mercer University Press, 1986), p. 47. See my review of McCarthy's richly detailed book in the *Journal of the American Academy of Religion* 56 (1988), pp. 596–7.

42 Josef Bohatec, *Die Religionsphilosophie Kants in der "Religion innerhalb der Grenzen der Blossen Vernunft"* (Hildesheim: Georg Olms, 1966), p. 636; F. Paulsen, *Immanuel Kant: His Life and Doctrine*, trans. J. E. Creighton and A. Lefevre (New York: Ungar, 1963), p. xiii.

43 Theodore M. Greene, "The Historical Context and Religious Significance of Kant's *Religion*," in English trans. of the *Religion*, pp. xxv–xvii; Lewis White Beck, *Early German Philosophy: Kant and his Predecessors* (Cambridge and London: Harvard University Press, 1969), pp. 446ff.

44 Reboul, *Le Problème du Mal*, p. 37.

45 Peter Gay, *The Enlightenment: An Interpretation*, vol. II (New York: Alfred Knopf, 1969), p. 171.

46 Perhaps the ultimate interpretive expression of this hybrid status is Reboul's suggestion that there are "three men in Kant": the rationalist metaphysician, the Lutheran theologian, and the philosopher of the Enlightenment. Reboul, *Le Problème du Mal*, pp. 37–41.

47 Not surprisingly, given the implications of his theory of autonomy, Kant explicitly rejects the motif of the "inheritance" of Adam's sin. In a very peculiar note in which he ponders the possibility of inheriting the propensity to evil, Kant seems to anticipate the thinking that lies behind the doctrine of the immaculate conception: *Religion*, p. 80n. (p. 75n.).

48 Keith Ward, *The Development of Kant's View of Ethics* (Oxford: Basil Blackwell, 1972), pp. 172–4.

49 For accounts of this part of the *Religion*, see Michalson, *Historical Dimensions*; Despland, *Kant on History and Religion*; Carl A. Raschke, *Moral Action, God, and History in The Thought of Immanuel Kant* (Missoula: University of Montana Press, 1975); and Yirmiahu Yovel, *Kant and the Philosophy of History* (Princeton: Princeton University Press, 1980).

50 E.g., See Jean-Louis Bruch, *La Philosophie Religieuse de Kant* (Paris: Aubier, 1968), ch. 6.

3 "This evil is radical . . ."

1 Emil Fackenheim, "Kant and Radical Evil," *University of Toronto Quarterly* 23 (1954), pp. 339–53.

2 Some further parallels are drawn out by Philip L. Quinn, "Original Sin, Radical Evil and Moral Identity," *Faith and Philosophy* 1 (1984), pp. 188–202. See also Quinn's related article, "Christian Atonement and Kantian Justification," *Faith and Philosophy* 3 (1986), pp. 440–62.

3 Alternatively, Daniel O'Connor has dubbed the disposition the "maxim of maxims," while Yirmiahu Yovel uses the expression "ultimate disposition." See O'Connor, "Good and Evil Disposition," *Kant-Studien* 76 (1985), p. 290; Yovel, *Kant and the Philosophy of History* (Princeton: Princeton University Press, 1980), p. 52. O'Connor draws attention to the connection between Kant's theory of the disposition and his solution to the Third Antinomy in the *Critique of Pure Reason*: O'Connor, pp. 290–1.

4 *Pure*, B579, p. 373n. (p. 475n.) (See note 17 above to chapter 1.)

5 It seems not merely incidental that it is in the context of his distinction between the two sorts of "acts" that Kant himself draws the parallel between his emerging position and the doctrine of original sin: *Religion*, p. 31 (p. 26). See O'Connor, "Good and Evil Disposition," p. 292.

6 As we shall see in chapter 4, Kant will have enough problems on his hands in this regard in connection with the issue of temporality, or moral change over time.

7 Allen W. Wood, *Kant's Moral Religion* (Ithaca and London: Cornell University Press, 1970), p. 220.

8 John Silber, "The Ethical Significance of Kant's *Religion within the Limits of Reason Alone*," in English trans. of *Religion*, pp. cxiv–cxv.

9 Lewis White Beck, *A Commentary on Kant's Critique of Practical Reason* (Chicago and London: University of Chicago Press, 1960), p. 122.

10 A complete Kantian theory of personal identity would, of course, also have to integrate the empirical self and the transcendental ego of the *Critique of Pure Reason* – suggesting the impossibility of such a task.

11 For a helpful account of the difficulty of relating the disposition to our individual acts of maxim-making – discussed in the context of the multiple Kantian "selves" – see Lee Carlton Barrett, "Sin and Self-Identity: Two Responses to Kant," unpublished Yale University Ph.D. dissertation (1984), chapters 1–2.

12 An interesting attempt to chart out this further "self" has been made by Leslie Mulholland, "Freedom and Providence in Kant's Account of Religion: The Problem of Expiation," unpublished paper read at Marquette University, November, 1987, p. 17.

13 At the same time, as Sharon Anderson-Gold has pointed out, "Kant repeatedly insists that freedom is not incompatible with determination, only with predetermination"; "Kant's Rejection of Devilishness: The Limits of Human Volition," *Idealistic Studies* 14 (1984), p. 39.

14 Silber, "Ethical Significance," p. cxvi.

15 Bernard Carnois, *The Coherence of Kant's Doctrine of Freedom*, trans. David Booth (Chicago and London: University of Chicago Press, 1987), pp. 95–6.

16 Peter Laska, "The Problem of an Ultimate Determining Ground in Kant's Theory of the Will," in Lewis White Beck (ed.), *Proceedings of the Third International Kant Congress* (Dordecht: D. Reidel, 1972), p. 390.

17 Some provocative fresh lines of interpretation of Kant's theory of sensuous existence have been opened up by Robin May Schott, *Cognition and Eros: A Critique of the Kantian Paradigm* (Boston: Beacon Press, 1988). Schott explains (p. vii) that her "project began as an investigation into the relation between cognition and eros in Kant's theory of objectivity, which has become paradigmatic for modern views about knowledge. Kant posits a split between cognition, on the one hand, and feelings and desires, on the other hand. The question arose whether this splitting off of feeling and sensuality from cognition captures the essence of knowledge, as Kant claims, or whether it requires the knower to perform distorting operations on him- or herself in order to conform to the conditions of objective knowledge." Schott helpfully traces the traditions informing Kant's attitudes back to their Greek and Christian roots and goes on to offer very interesting insights into the relation between Kant's moral theory and what she calls the "fetishistic qualities of Kant's theory of knowledge": pp. 137ff.

18 Friedrich Nietzsche, *The Gay Science*, Section 256, quoted in Sabina Lovibond, *Realism and Imagination in Ethics* (Minneapolis: University of Minnesota Press, 1983), p. 143.

19 *Practical*, p. 162 (p. 166). (See note 22 above to chapter 1.)

20 Lovibond, *Realism and Imagination in Ethics*, p. 143.

4 A "change of heart"

1 For Kant's rejection of "devilishness," see the *Religion*, p. 35 (p. 30). For references to the ever-present "seed of goodness," see the *Religion*, pp. 38, 45, 66 (pp. 34, 41, 60). (See note 5 to the Introduction.)

2 Sharon Anderson-Gold, "Kant's Rejection of Devilishness: The Limits of Human Volition," *Idealistic Studies* 14 (1984), p. 40.

3 See note 12 above to chapter 2.

4 The relevant passages are excerpted in *Erasmus-Luther: Discourse on Free Will*, trans. Ernest F. Winter (New York: Frederick Ungar, 1961), pp. 97–138.

5 *Ibid.*, p. 77.

6 See also the discussion of "moral feeling" in *Practical*, pp. 73–6 (pp. 76–9). (See note 20 of chapter 1.)

7 The references to biblical passages are Kant's own.

8 I shall be returning to a closer look at this Pauline image in my discussion of the "punishment" for the sin of radical evil in chapter 6.

9 Jean–Louis Bruch, *La Philosophie religieuse de Kant* (Paris: Aubier, 1968), p. 80.

10 It is also worth noting that extreme emphasis was placed on the explicit experience of conversion at the Collegium Fridericianum, where Kant was schooled. Kant detested the faking of religious experiences that this emphasis evidently encouraged. See Olivier Reboul, *Kant et le Problème du Mal* (Montréal: Presses de l'Université de Montréal, 1971), pp. 187ff.

11 For further discussion of Kant's use of the Genesis account, see Michel Despland, *Kant on History and Religion* (Montreal and London: McGill-Queen's University Press, 1973), pp. 190–1.

12 See Kant's rather improbable use of Psalms 59 (which he calls a "prayer for revenge") to illustrate his approach, *Religion*, p. 110n. (p. 101n.).

13 See G. E. Michalson, Jr., *The Historical Dimensions of a Rational Faith: The Role of History in Kant's Religious Thought* (Washington, D. C.: University Press of America, 1977), pp. 78–91.

14 It is worth noting that Kant also employed the book of Genesis to help him deal with the conceptual difficulty of accounting for the rise of freedom in history in "Mutmasslicher Anfang der Menschengeschichte," Prussian Academy Edition, vol. VIII (Berlin: Georg Reimer, 1912), pp. 109–23; English trans., "Conjectural Beginning of Human History," trans. Emil Fackenheim in *On History*, ed. Lewis White Beck (New York: Bobbs-Merrill, 1963), pp. 53–68.

15 Bruch, *La Philosophie religieuse de Kant*, pp. 83–4.

16 *Pure*, B581, pp. 374–5 (p. 476). (See note 16 above to chapter 1.)

17 *Ibid.*, B232–56, pp. 166—80 (pp. 218–33).

18 "The situation, then, is this: there is an order in our representations in which the present, so far as it has come to be, refers us to some preceding state as a correlate of the event which is given; and though this correlate is, indeed, indeterminate, it none the less stands in a determining relation to the event as its consequence, connecting the event in necessary relation with itself in the time-series": *Pure*, B244, p. 173 (p. 225).

19 *Pure*, B294–315, pp. 202–14 (pp. 257–75).

20 *Ibid.*, B566–86, pp. 366–77 (pp. 467–79). There is a vast secondary literature on this issue. For helpful recent discussions, see Allen Wood, "Kant's Compatibilism," in Wood (ed.), *Self and Nature in Kant's Philosophy* (Ithaca and London: Cornell University Press, 1984), pp. 73–101; and Ralf Meerbote, "Kant on Freedom and the Rational and Morally Good Will," in *Ibid.*, pp. 57–72.

21 *Pure*, B579, p. 373 (p. 475).

22 *Ibid.*, B580, p. 374 (p. 475).

23 *Ibid.*, B578, p. 372 (p. 474).

24 *Ibid.*, B578, p. 372 (p. 474). However, John Silber has pointed out that Kant's "early confidence that in principle science can predict all human activity is absent in the third *Critique*": Silber, "The Ethical Significance of Kant's *Religion*," in English trans. of *Religion*, p. xcix.

25 *Pure*, B586, p. 377 (p. 479).

26 For further discussion of this issue, see G. E. Michalson, Jr., "The Impossibility of

Religious Progress in Kant," chapter 3 of Peter Slater (ed.), *Philosophy of Religion and Theology: 1976* (Missoula: Scholars Press, 1976), pp. 17–29.

27 Leslie Mulholland, "Freedom and Providence in Kant's Account of Religion: The Problem of Expiation," unpublished paper read at Marquette University, November, 1987, pp. 26ff.

28 Kant, *The Doctrine of Virtue* (part II of *The Metaphysics of Morals*), trans. Mary J. Gregor (New York: Harper and Row, 1964), p. 71.

29 Paul Stern, "The Problem of History and Temporality in Kantian Ethics," *Review of Metaphysics* 39 (1982), pp. 528–9.

30 Mulholland, "Freedom and Providence," p. 21.

31 *Ibid.*, p. 10.

5 Moral regeneration

1 Michel Despland, *Kant on History and Religion* (Montreal and London: McGill-Queen's University Press, 1973), p. 183.

2 Against the background of his own substantial work on Kant, Allen Wood has recently reexamined the issue of Kant's relation to deism, in "Kant's Deism," unpublished paper read at Marquette University, November, 1987.

3 David Hume, *Dialogues Concerning Natural Religion*, ed. Norman Kemp Smith (New York: Social Sciences Publishers, 1948), p. 227,

4 *Pure*, B833, p. 522 (p. 635). (See note 16 above to chapter 1.)

5 Alister McGrath, *Iustitia Dei: A History of the Christian Doctrine of Justification*, vol. I (Cambridge: Cambridge University Press, 1986), p. 2.

6 Karl Jaspers, "Das Radikal Böse bei Kant," in *Rechenschaft und Ausblick* (Munich: R. Piper, 1951), pp. 100–3.

7 Interesting efforts have been made to reconcile grace, or providence, with the needed element of freedom in Kant's position. See Allen W. Wood, *Kant's Moral Religion* (Ithaca and London: Cornell University Press, 1970), pp. 238ff.; and Leslie Mulholland, "Freedom and Providence in Kant's Account of Religion: The Problem of Expiation," unpublished paper read at Marquette University, November, 1987. Mulholland argues that there are "two respects in which providence can be a condition of moral improvement without being determining: first, providence can provide the condition that enables the individual to recover the original stance from which a new choice of supreme maxim can be made; secondly, providence can, through the practical experience of the consequences of evil, provide the means to teach the individual that it is necessary to change. Both conditions would be necessary for the change of heart . . . The problem in Kant is that he does not see that there can be an external condition of moral improvement even though it is not determining of the action produced": Mulholland, p. 35. John Silber vigorously argues against any such reconciliation of divine and human action, saying that Kant's view of freedom "shatters on the problem of forgiveness" and that "even God cannot help the guilty individual without violating the

moral law." Silber adds: "If Kant had consistently held to his theory of unqualified freedom, he would have followed the line of argument taken by Ivan Karamazov": Silber, "The Ethical Significance of Kant's *Religion*," in English trans. of *Religion*, pp. cxxxi, cxxxiii.

8 Georg Lukács, *The Young Hegel: Studies in the Relations between Dialectics and Economics*, trans. Rodney Livingstone (Cambridge, Massachusetts: Massachusetts Institute of Technology Press, 1976), p. 18.

9 Viewing the problems posed by moral regeneration in terms of the issue of positivity helps to explain much of what Hegel was up to in the early years of his writing career. He was trying to finish off what Kant had only half-heartedly started. In addition to Lukács' classic – if perhaps somewhat skewed – treatment of the early Hegel, see Laurence Dickey, *Hegel: Religion, Economics, and the Politics of Spirit 1770–1807* (Cambridge: Cambridge University Press, 1987), chapter 4; and Charles Taylor, *Hegel* (Cambridge: Cambridge University Press, 1975), chapter 2.

10 *Pure*, B222–23, pp. 160–1 (p. 211).

11 *Ibid.*, B33–58, pp. 49–64 (pp. 65–82).

12 Kant even makes the peculiar point that God "cannot be an object of sensible intuition even to himself": *Pure*, B71, p. 72 (p. 90). There is a good account of what Kant means by God's "holiness" in Despland, *Kant on History and Religion*, pp. 267ff.

13 When Kant works out much the same point in a different context within the *Religion*, he seems to be aware of this problem of logical order. See *Religion*, pp. 74ff., esp. p. 76 (pp. 68ff., esp. p. 70).

6 Autonomy and atonement

1 Karl Barth, *Protestant Thought from Rousseau to Ritschl*, trans. Brian Cozens (New York: Simon and Schuster, 1969), p. 297.

2 "I do not want a mother to embrace the torturer who had her child torn to pieces by his dogs! She has no right to forgive him! If she likes, she can forgive him for herself, she can forgive the torturer for the immeasurable suffering he has inflicted upon her as a mother; but she has no right to forgive him for the sufferings of her tortured child": Fyodor Dostoyevsky, *The Brothers Karamazov*, trans. David Magarshack (New York: Viking Penguin, 1982), p. 287.

3 Added to the Berlin edition. See English translation of the *Religion*, pp. 66n., 67n.

4 Vincent McCarthy, *Quest for a Philosophical Jesus: Christianity and Philosophy in Rousseau, Kant, Hegel, and Schelling* (Macon, Georgia: Mercer University Press, 1986), p. 78.

5 *Pure*, B176ff., pp. 133ff. (pp. 180ff.) (See note 17 above to chapter 1.) For an account of the relevance of Kant's theory of schematism to his moral and religious philosophy – including a discussion of what he calls the "schematism of analogy" in the *Religion* – see G. E. Michalson, Jr., *The Historical Dimensions of a Rational Faith: The*

Role of History in Kant's Religious Thought (Washington, D.C.: University Press of America, 1977), pp. 91–114.

6 *Pure*, B178, pp. 134–5, (p. 181); B184, p. 138 (p. 185).

7 Richard Swinburne argues that, in his account of punishment, Kant unfairly sets up conditions that no one could ever satisfy: Swinburne, *Responsibility and Atonement* (Oxford: Oxford University Press, 1989), pp. 89–90n.

8 My views on this matter have changed since I originally criticized Michel Despland's effort to read Kant's christology in this way. See Despland, *Kant on History and Religion* (Montreal and London: McGill-Queen's University Press, 1973), pp. 198–9; and Michalson, *The Historical Dimensions*, pp. 126ff. Ironically, in his review of my earlier book, Despland seemed to indicate a softening of the position with which I am now essentially agreeing. His review is in the *Journal of the American Academy of Religion* 49 (1981), pp. 332–3.

9 Allen Wood makes an interesting, if somewhat strained, attempt to reconcile divine forgiveness with moral freedom in *Kant's Moral Religion* (Ithaca and London: Cornell University Press, 1970), pp. 237ff.

7 Autonomy and transcendence

1 Quoted in Bernard M. G. Reardon, *Kant as Philosophical Theologian* (London: The Macmillan Press, 1988), pp. 159–60.

2 *Ibid.*, p. 159.

3 See the use to which Jacques Derrida has put the *parerga* of Kant's *Critique of Judgment* in *The Truth in Painting*, trans. Geoffrey Bennington and Ian McLeod (Chicago and London: University of Chicago Press, 1987).

4 It is worth remembering that one of Kant's definitions of a "postulate" in the second *Critique* is that of a "necessary hypothesis": *Practical*, p. 11n. (p. 12n.). (See note 20 above to chapter 1.)

5 This point stands whether or not one agrees with Yovel that the *Religion* supersedes the second postulate. See Yirmiahu Yovel, *Kant and the Philosophy of History* (Princeton: Princeton University Press, 1980), pp. 112–13.

6 Of course, some may argue that Bultmann's existentialist emphasis in the account of faith is simply a thinly disguised moral view. This, for example, is the view of Bultmann held by Wolfhart Pannenberg. I have tried to explain the stakes involved in this cluster of issues in *Lessing's "Ugly Ditch": A Study of Theology and History* (University Park and London: The Pennsylvania State University Press, 1985), chapter 7.

7 Soren Kierkegaard, *Philosophical Fragments*, trans. David Swenson and Howard V. Hong (Princeton: Princeton University Press, 1967), chapter 1, "A Project of Thought." For an account of the inner logic of this "project of thought," see my discussion in Michalson, *Lessing's "Ugly Ditch"*, chapters 4 and 5.

8 Kierkegaard, *Philosophical Fragments*, pp. 22–4.

9 I have previously tried to make this point clear in *Lessing's "Ugly Ditch"*, pp. 82–6.

10 Kierkegaard, *Philosophical Fragments*, p. 77.
11 See especially Book Three of the *Religion*. Two recent helpful discussions of the connection between Kant and Marx are Seyla Benhabib, *Critique, Norm, and Utopia: A Study of the Foundations of Critical Theory* (New York; Columbia University Press, 1986), chapter 3; and Dick Howard, *From Marx to Kant* (Albany: State University of New York Press, 1985). See also Lucio Colletti, "Kant, Hegel and Marx," in Colletti, *Marxism and Hegel* (London: New Left Books, 1973).
12 Martin Baker, "Kant as a Problem for Marxism," in Roy Edgley and Richard Osborne (eds.), *Radical Philosophy Reader* (London: Verso, 1985), pp. 3–17. See also the helpful summary of Lukács' analysis of Kant's philosophy as the impotent philosophical correlate to the antinomies of bourgeois life and thought offered by J. M. Bernstein, *The Philosophy of the Novel: Lukács, Marxism and the Dialectics of Form* (Minneapolis: University of Minnesota Press, 1984), esp. pp. xvi–xix, 16–22. Lukács's interpretive approach is self-consciously pursued by Lucien Goldmann in his *Immanuel Kant*, trans. Robert Black (London: NLB, 1971).
13 A very helpful recent addition to the vast literature on post-Kantian developments is Frederick C. Beiser, *The Fate of Reason: German Philosophy from Kant to Fichte* (Cambridge and London: Harvard University Press, 1987).
14 See Kierkegaard, *The Sickness unto Death*, trans. Howard V. Hong and Edna H. Hong (Princeton: Princeton University Press, 1980). See also Ronald M. Green, "The Limits of the Ethical in Kierkegaard's *The Concept of Anxiety* and Kant's *Religion within the Limits of Reason Alone*," in Robert L. Perkins (ed.), *International Kierkegaard Commentary: The Concept of Anxiety* (Macon, Georgia: Mercer University Press, 1985), pp. 63–87.
15 Langdon Gilkey's essay, "Cosmology, Ontology, and the Travail of Biblical Language," *Journal of Religion* 41 (1961), pp. 194–205, remains a shrewd and still timely pinpointing of the equivocalness of the liberal tradition. Gilkey states: "My own confusion results from what I feel to be the basic posture, and problem, of contemporary theology: it is half liberal and modern, on the one hand, and half biblical and orthodox, on the other, i.e., its world view or cosmology is modern, while its theological language is biblical and orthodox," p. 194. In other words, not much has changed since Kant's *Religion within the Limits of Reason Alone*.
16 Obviously, this definition would cover certain leading contemporary Roman Catholic theologians as well, such as Karl Rahner and David Tracy.
17 The notion of the "metanarrative" has of course been given fresh currency by the work of Jean-Francois Lyotard. See especially *The Postmodern Condition: A Report on Knowledge*, trans. Geoff Bennington and Brian Massumi (Minneapolis: University of Minnesota Press, 1984): "Simplifying to the extreme, I define *postmodern* as incredulity toward metanarratives," p. xxiv.
18 Fredric Jameson speaks of the "Nietzschean position" as the "final option" in his own canvassing of the interpretive possibilities evoked by the theme of "Marxism and historicism" – the other options being what Jameson calls "antiquarianism," "existential historicism," and "structural typology." See Jameson, "Marxism and

Historicism," in *The Ideologies of Theory, Essays, 1971–86, Vol. II: The Syntax of History* (London: Routledge, 1988), p. 169.

19 A good example of this dilemma is conveyed by some remarks by Richard Rorty: "The suggestion that truth, as well as the world, is out there is a legacy of an age in which the world was seen as the creation of a being who had a language of his own. If we cease to attempt to make sense of the idea of such a nonhuman language, we shall not be tempted to confuse the platitude that the world may cause us to be justified in believing a sentence true with the claim that the world splits itself up, on its own initiative, into sentence-shaped chunks called 'facts' . . . The difficulty faced by a philosopher . . . like myself . . . is to avoid hinting that . . . my sort of philosophy corresponds to the way things really are. For this talk of correspondence brings back just the idea my sort of philosopher wants to get rid of, the idea that the world or the self has an intrinsic nature." Richard Rorty, *Contingency, Irony, and Solidarity* (Cambridge: Cambridge University Press, 1989), pp. 5, 7–8.

20 Hans Blumenberg, *The Legitimacy of the Modern Age*, trans. Robert M. Wallace (Cambridge and London: The Massachusetts Institute of Technology Press, 1983).

21 *Ibid.*, p. 65.

22 *Ibid.*, p. 64.

23 *Ibid.*, p. 139.

24 Robert M. Wallace, "Translators Introduction," in *Ibid.*, xi–xxv.

25 Wallace, *Ibid.*, p. xix.

26 Blumenberg, *Ibid.*, p. 64.

27 *Ibid.*, pp. 48–9.

28 Wallace, *Ibid.*, p. xxvi.

29 Blumenberg, *Ibid.*, p. 143.

30 *Ibid.*, p. 64.

31 *Ibid.*, p. 87.

32 *Ibid.*, p. 65.

33 *Ibid.*, p. 64.

34 *Ibid.*, pp. 64–5.

35 Wallace, *Ibid.*, p. xxvi.

36 For example, Jonathan Bennett, *Kant's Analytic* (Cambridge: Cambridge University Press, 1966) and *Kant's Dialectic* (Cambridge: Cambridge University Press, 1974); and P. F. Strawson, *The Bounds of Sense* (London: Methuen and Company, 1966). In the Preface to his *Kant's Dialectic* (p. viii), Bennett acknowledges that "I continue to be, in the words of an unhappy reviewer of my earlier work, 'one of those commentators who are more interested in what Kant ought to have thought than in what he actually did think.' "

37 Rorty, *Contingency, Irony, and Solidarity*, p. 9.

38 "The Enlightenment faith in the universality and impartiality of reason ultimately rested upon another of its even more fundamental beliefs – the autonomy of reason. Reason was thought to be an autonomous faculty in the sense that it was

self-governing, establishing and following its own rules, independent of political interests, cultural traditions, or subconscious desires. If, on the contrary, reason were subject to political, cultural, or subconscious influences, then it would have no guarantee that its conclusions were universal and necessary; they might then turn out to be disguised expressions of political, cultural, or subconscious interests. Perhaps the clearest example of this belief in the autonomy of reason was Kant's noumenal–phenomenal dualism as it was laid down in the first *Kritik* and *Grundlegung*. It is important to see that the purpose of Kant's dualism was to save not only the possibility of freedom, but also the universality and impartiality of reason": Beiser, *The Fate of Reason*, p. 8.

39 There are of course several ways in which to link Kant and Freud, all of them problematic. My main point is simply to suggest that the seeds of a view of human nature that posits us as less than fully self-governing are already present in Kant. Blumenberg offers his own view of the connection (with Feuerbach as mediating figure) in terms of the category of "theoretical curiosity": *Legitimacy*, Part III, ch. 11. Questions have been raised about Blumenberg's way of handling the Kant–Freud connection by Robert Pippin, "Blumenberg and the Modernity Problem," *Review of Metaphysics* 40 (1987), pp. 552—3. For a different perspective on the relation between Kant and Freud, see Rorty, *Contingency, Irony, and Solidarity*, chapter 2, esp. pp. 30ff.: "It has often seemed necessary to choose between Kant and Nietzsche, to make up one's mind – at least to *that* extent – about the point of being human. But Freud gives us a way of looking at human beings which helps us to evade the choice . . . For Freud himself eschewed the very idea of a paradigm human being." p. 35.

40 *Practical*, p. 161 (p. 166).

Select bibliography

Works by Kant

Where I have used original sources, I have cited the relevant volumes of Kant's *Gesammelte Schriften* edited by the *Königliche Preussische Akademie der Wissenschaften* (Berlin: Georg Reimer, 1907–83). English translations have been taken from the editions listed below.

Anthropology from a Pragmatic Point of View, trans. Mary J. Gregor (The Hague: Martinus Nijhoff, 1974).

"Conjectural Beginning of Human History," trans. Emil Fackenheim, in Lewis White Beck (ed.), *On History* (New York: Bobbs-Merrill, 1963).

Critique of Practical Reason, trans. Lewis White Beck (New York: Bobbs-Merrill, 1956).

Critique of Pure Reason, trans. Norman Kemp Smith (New York: St. Martin's Press, 1965).

The Doctrine of Virtue (part II of *The Metaphysics of Morals*), trans. Mary J. Gregor (New York: Harper and Row, 1964).

Foundations of the Metaphysics of Morals, trans. Lewis White Beck (New York: Bobbs-Merrill, 1959).

"Idea for a Universal History from a Cosmopolitan Point of View," trans. Lewis White Beck, in Lewis White Beck (ed.), *On History* (New York: Bobbs-Merrill, 1963).

Lectures on Philosophical Theology, trans. Allen W. Wood and Gertrude M. Clark (Ithaca and London: Cornell University Press, 1978).

The Metaphysical Elements of Justice (part I of *The Metaphysics of Morals*), trans. John Ladd (New York: Bobbs-Merrill, 1965).

"On the Failure of All Attempted Philosophical Theodicies," trans. Michel Despland, in Michel Despland, *Kant on History and Religion* (Montreal and London: McGill-Queen's University Press, 1973).

Philosophical Correspondence 1759–99, trans., Arnulf Zweig (Chicago and London: University of Chicago Press, 1967).

Religion within the Limits of Reason Alone, trans. Theodore M. Greene and Hoyt H. Hudson (New York: Harper Torchbooks, 1960).

"What is Enlightenment?," trans. Lewis White Beck, in Lewis White Beck (ed.), *On History* (New York: Bobbs-Merrill, 1963).

Select bibliography

Secondary works

Acton, H. B., *Kant's Moral Philosophy* (London: Macmillan, 1970).

Allison, Henry E., *Kant's Transcendental Idealism: An Interpretation and Defense* (New Haven and London: Yale University Press, 1983).

"Morality and Freedom: Kant's Reciprocity Thesis." *Philosophical Review* 95 (1986): 393–425.

"Practical and Transcendental Freedom in the *Critique of Pure Reason.*" *Kant-Studien* 73 (1982): 271–90.

Anderson-Gold, Sharon, "Kant's Ethical Commonwealth: The Highest Good as a Social Goal." *International Philosophical Quarterly* 26 (1986): 23–32.

"Kant's Rejection of Devilishness: The Limits of Human Volition." *Idealistic Studies* 14 (1984): 35–48.

Auxter, Thomas, "The Unimportance of Kant's Highest Good." *Journal of the History of Philosophy* 17 (1979): 121–34.

Axinn, Sidney, "Ambivalence: Kant's View of Human Nature." *Kant-Studien* 72 (1981): 169–74.

Baker, Martin, "Kant as a Problem for Marxism." Roy Edgely and Richard Osborne (eds.), *Radical Philosophy Reader* (London: Verso, 1985): 3–17.

Barth, Karl, *Protestant Thought from Rousseau to Ritschl,* trans. Brian Cozens (New York: Simon and Schuster, 1969).

Beck, Lewis White, *A Commentary on Kant's Critique of Practical Reason* (Chicago and London: University of Chicago Press, 1960).

Early German Philosophy: Kant and his Predecessors (Cambridge and London: Harvard University Press, 1969).

Beiser, Frederick C., *The Fate of Reason: German Philosophy from Kant to Fichte* (Cambridge and London: Harvard University Press, 1987).

Benhabib, Seyla, *Critique, Norm, and Utopia: A Study of the Foundations of Critical Theory* (New York: Columbia University Press, 1986).

Bennett, Jonathan, *Kant's Dialectic* (Cambridge: Cambridge University Press, 1974).

Bernstein, J. M., *The Philosophy of the Novel: Lukács, Marxism and the Dialectics of Form* (Minneapolis: University of Minnesota Press, 1984).

Blumenberg, Hans, *The Legitimacy of the Modern Age,* trans. Robert W. Wallace (Cambridge, Massachusetts: Massachusetts Institute of Technology Press, 1983).

Bohatec, Josef, *Die Religionsphilosophie Kants in der "Religion innerhalb der Grenzen der blossen Vernunft"* (Hildesheim: Georg Olms, 1966).

Brown, Robert F., "The Transcendental Fall in Kant and Schelling." *Idealistic Studies* 14 (1984): 49–66.

Bruch, Jean-Louis, *La Philosophie religieuse de Kant* (Paris: Aubier, 1968).

Callinicos, Alex, *Making History: Agency, Structure and Change in Social Theory* (Ithaca and London: Cornell University Press, 1988).

Carnois, Bernard, *The Coherence of Kant's Doctrine of Freedom,* trans. David Booth (Chicago and London: University of Chicago Press, 1987).

Cassirer, Ernst, *Kant's Life and Thought*, trans. James Haden (New Haven and London: Yale University Press, 1981).

The Philosophy of the Enlightenment, trans. Fritz C. A. Koelln and James P. Pettegrove (Princeton: Princeton University Press, 1951).

Rousseau, Kant, Goethe: Two Essays, trans. James Gutman, P. O. Kristeller, and J. H. Randall, Jr. (New York: Harper Torchbook, 1963).

Cavell, Stanley, "Emerson, Coleridge, Kant." John Rajchman and Cornell West (eds.), *Post-Analytic Philosophy* (New York: Columbia University Press, 1985): 84–107.

Colletti, Lucio, *Marxism and Hegel*, trans. Lawrence Garner (London: NLB, 1973).

Collins, James, *The Emergence of Philosophy of Religion* (New Haven and London: Yale University Press, 1986).

Connerton, Paul, *The Tragedy of Enlightenment: An Essay on the Frankfurt School* (Cambridge: Cambridge University Press, 1980).

Derrida, Jacques, *The Truth in Painting*, trans. Geoffrey Bennington and Ian McLeod (Chicago and London: University of Chicago Press, 1987).

Despland, Michel, *Kant on History and Religion* (Montreal and London: McGill-Queen's University Press, 1973).

Dickey, Laurence, *Hegel: Religion, Economics, and the Politics of Spirit, 1770–1807* (Cambridge: Cambridge University Press, 1987).

Fackenheim, Emil, "Immanuel Kant." Ninian Smart, John Clayton, Patrick Sherry, and Steven T. Katz (eds.), *Nineteenth Century Religious Thought in the West, Vol: I* (Cambridge: Cambridge University Press, 1985): 17–40.

"Kant and Radical Evil." *University of Toronto Quarterly* 23 (1954): 339–53.

Förster, Eckhart (ed.), *Kant's Transcendental Deductions* (Stanford: Stanford University Press, 1989).

Galston, William A., *Kant and the Problem of History* (Chicago and London: University of Chicago Press, 1975).

Gellner, Ernest, *The Legitimation of Belief* (Cambridge: Cambridge University Press, 1974).

Gilkey, Langdon, "Cosmology, Ontology, and the Travail of Biblical Language." *Journal of Religion* 41 (1961): 194–205.

Goldmann, Lucien, *Immanuel Kant*, trans. Robert Black (London: NLB, 1971).

The Philosophy of the Enlightenment: The Christian Burgess and the Enlightenment, trans. Henry Maas (Cambridge, Massachusetts: Massachusetts Institute of Technology Press, 1973).

Green, Ronald M., "The Limits of the Ethical in Kierkegaard's *The Concept of Anxiety* and Kant's *Religion within the Limits of Reason Alone*." Robert L. Perkins (ed.), *International Kierkegaard Commentary: The Concept of Anxiety* (Macon, Georgia: Mercer University Press, 1985): 63–87.

Greene, Theodore M., "The Historical Context and Religious Significance of Kant's *Religion*." Introduction to Kant, *Religion within the Limits of Reason Alone*, trans. Greene and Hoyt H. Hudson (New York: Harper Torchbook, 1960): ix–lxxviii.

Gregor, Mary J., *Laws of Freedom* (New York: Barnes and Noble, 1963).

Select bibliography

Habermas, Jürgen, *The Philosophical Discourse of Modernity*, trans. Frederick Lawrence (Cambridge, Massachusetts: Massachusetts Institute of Technology Press, 1987).

Harper, William L. and Meerbote, Ralf (eds.), *Kant on Causality, Freedom, and Objectivity* (Minneapolis: University of Minnesota Press, 1984).

Herman, Barbara, "On the Value of Acting from the Motive of Duty." *Philosophical Review* 90 (1981): 359–82.

"The Practice of Moral Judgment." *Journal of Philosophy* 82 (1985): 414–36.

Hill, Thomas E., Jr., "Kant on Imperfect Duty and Supererogation." *Kant-Studien* 62 (1971): 55–76.

"Moral Purity and the Lesser Evil." *Monist* 66 (1983): 213–32.

Howard, Dick, *From Marx to Kant* (Albany: State University of New York Press, 1985).

Jameson, Fredric, *The Ideologies of Theory, Essays 1971–86, Vol. II: The Syntax of History* (London: Routledge, 1988).

Jaspers, Karl, "Das Radikal Böse bei Kant." Karl Jaspers, *Rechenschaft und Ausblick* (Munich: R. Piper, 1951): 90–113.

Kroner, Richard, *Kant's Weltanschauung*, trans. John E. Smith (Chicago and London: University of Chicago Press, 1956).

Speculation and Revelation in Modern Philosophy (Philadelphia: Westminster Press, 1961).

Laska, Peter, "The Problem of an Ultimate Determining Ground in Kant's Theory of the Will." Lewis White Beck (ed.), *Proceedings of the Third International Kant Congress* (Dordecht: D. Reidel, 1972): 387–92.

Loades, Ann, *Kant and Job's Comforters* (Newcastle upon Tyne: Avero Publications: 1985).

Lovibond, Sabina, *Realism and Imagination in Ethics* (Minneapolis: University of Minnesota Press, 1983).

Lukács, Georg, *The Young Hegel: Studies in the Relations between Dialectics and Economics*, trans. Rodney Livingstone (Cambridge, Massachusetts: Massachusetts Institute of Technology Press, 1976).

Lyotard, Jean-Francois, *The Postmodern Condition: A Report on Knowledge*, trans. Geoff Bennington and Brian Massumi (Minneapolis: University of Minnesota Press, 1984).

McCarthy, Vincent A., *Quest for a Philosophical Jesus: Christianity and Philosophy in Rousseau, Kant, Hegel, and Schelling* (Macon, Georgia: Mercer University Press, 1986).

McFarland, J. D., *Kant's Concept of Teleology* (Edinburgh: University of Edinburgh Press, 1970).

MacIntyre, Alasdair, *After Virtue* (Notre Dame: University of Notre Dame Press, 1981).

"Epistemological Crises, Dramatic Narrative and Philosophy of Science." *The Monist* 60 (1977): 453–72.

Marx, Karl, *The German Ideology*, ed. C. J. Arthur (New York: International Publishers, 1970).

Meerbote, Ralf, "Kant on Freedom and the Rational and Morally Good Will." Allen

W. Wood (ed.), *Self and Nature in Kant's Philosophy* (Ithaca and London: Cornell University Press, 1984): 57–72.

"Kant on the Nondeterminate Character of Human Actions." William L. Harper and Meerbote (eds.), *Kant on Causality, Freedom, and Objectivity* (Minneapolis: University of Minnesota Press, 1984): 138–63.

"*Wille* and *Willkür* in Kant's Theory of Action." Moltke Gram (ed.), *Interpreting Kant* (Iowa City: University of Iowa Press, 1982): 69–84.

Michalson, Gordon E., Jr., *The Historical Dimensions of a Rational Faith: The Role of History in Kant's Religious Thought* (Washington, D.C.: University Press of America, 1977).

"The Impossibility of Religious Progress in Kant." Peter Slater (ed.), *Philosophy of Religion and Theology: 1976* (Missoula: Scholars Press, 1976): 17–29.

"The Inscrutability of Moral Evil in Kant." *The Thomist* 51 (1987): 246–69.

Lessing's "Ugly Ditch": A Study of Theology and History (University Park and London: The Pennsylvania State University Press, 1985).

"Moral Regeneration and Divine Aid in Kant." *Religious Studies* 25 (1989).

"The Non-Moral Element in Kant's Moral Proof of the Existence of God." *Scottish Journal of Theology* 39 (1986): 501–15.

Midgley, Mary, *Wickedness: A Philosophical Essay* (London: Routledge and Kegan Paul, 1984).

Mulholland, Leslie, "Freedom and Providence in Kant's Account of Religion: The Problem of Expiation." Unpublished paper read at Marquette University, November, 1987.

O'Connor, Daniel, "Good and Evil Disposition." *Kant-Studien* 76 (1985): 288–302.

O'Neill, Onora, *Acting on Principle: An Essay on Kantian Ethics* (New York: Columbia University Press, 1975).

Paton, H. J., *The Categorical Imperative: A Study in Kant's Moral Philosophy*, fifth edition (London: Hutchinson, 1965).

Pippin, Robert, "Blumenberg and the Modernity Problem." *Review of Metaphysics* 40 (1987): 535–57.

Priest, Stephen (ed.), *Hegel's Critique of Kant* (Oxford: Oxford University Press, 1987).

Quinn, Philip L., "Christian Atonement and Kantian Justification." *Faith and Philosophy* 3 (1986): 440–62.

"Original Sin, Radical Evil and Moral Identity." *Faith and Philosophy* 1 (1984): 188–202.

Raschke, Carl, *Moral Action, God, and History in the Thought of Immanuel Kant* (Missoula: University of Montana Press, 1975).

Reardon, Bernard, *Kant as Philosophical Theologian* (London: The Macmillan Press, 1988).

Reboul, Olivier, *Kant et le Problème du Mal* (Montréal: Presses de l'université de Montréal, 1971).

Riley, Patrick, *The General Will before Rousseau: The Transformation of the Divine into the Civic* (Princeton: Princeton University Press, 1986).

Rorty, Richard, *Contingency, Irony, and Solidarity* (Cambridge: Cambridge University Press, 1989).

Schneewind, J. B., "The Divine Corporation and the History of Ethics." Richard Rorty, J. B. Schneewind, and Quentin Skinner (eds.), *Philosophy in History: Essays in the Historiography of Philosophy* (Cambridge: Cambridge University Press, 1984): 173–91.

Schott, Robin May, *Cognition and Eros: A Critique of the Kantian Paradigm* (Boston, Massachusetts: Beacon Press, 1988).

Schrader, George, "Autonomy, Heteronomy, and Moral Imperatives." *Journal of Philosophy* 60 (1963): 65–77.

"Kant's Presumed Repudiation of the 'Moral Argument' in the *Opus Postumum*: An Examination of Adickes' Interpretation." *Philosophy* 26 (1951): 228–41.

Shell, Susan, *The Rights of Reason: A Study of Kant's Philosophy and Politics* (Toronto: University of Toronto Press, 1980).

Silber, John, "The Ethical Significance of Kant's *Religion*." Introduction to Kant, *Religion within the Limits of Reason Alone*, trans. Theodore M. Greene and Hoyt H. Hudson (New York: Harper Torchbook, 1960): lxxix–cxxxiv.

"The Moral Good and the Natural Good in Kant's Ethics." *Review of Metaphysics* 36 (1982): 397–437.

Sloterdijk, Peter, *Critique of Cynical Reason*, trans. Michael Eldred (Minneapolis: University of Minnesota Press, 1987).

Stern, Paul, "The Problem of History and Temporality in Kantian Ethics." *Review of Metaphysics* 39 (1986): 505–45.

Sullivan, Roger J., *Immanuel Kant's Moral Theory* (Cambridge: Cambridge University Press, 1989).

Surin, Kenneth, *Theology and the Problem of Evil* (Oxford: Basil Blackwell, 1986).

Swinburne, Richard, *Responsibility and Atonement* (Oxford: Oxford University Press, 1989).

Taylor, Charles, *Hegel* (Cambridge: Cambridge University Press, 1975).

Walsh, W. H., "Kant's Moral Theology." *Proceedings of the British Academy* 49 (1964): 263–89.

Ward, Keith, *The Development of Kant's View of Ethics* (Oxford: Basil Blackwell, 1972).

Williams, Bernard, *Ethics and the Limits of Philosophy* (London: Fontana Press, 1985).

Moral Luck (Cambridge: Cambridge University Press, 1981).

Williams, Howard, *Kant's Political Philosophy* (Oxford: Basil Blackwell, 1983).

Wood, Allen W., "Kant's Compatibilism." Allen W. Wood (ed.), *Self and Nature in Kant's Philosophy* (Ithaca and London: Cornell University Press, 1984): 73–101.

"Kant's Deism." Unpublished paper read at Marquette University, November, 1987.

Kant's Moral Religion (Ithaca and London: Cornell University Press, 1970).

Kant's Rational Theology (Ithaca and London: Cornell University Press, 1978).

Yack, Bernard, *The Longing for Total Revolution* (Princeton: Princeton University Press, 1986).

Yovel, Yirmiahu, *Kant and the Philosophy of History* (Princeton: Princeton University Press, 1980).

Zeldin, Mary-Barbara, "The Summum Bonum, the Moral Law, and the Existence of God." *Kant-Studien* 62 (1971): 43–54.

Index